P9-DMC-342

PIONEERS IN WORLD ORDER

PIONEERS IN WORLD ORDER

AN AMERICAN APPRAISAL OF THE LEAGUE OF NATIONS

Edited by *HARRIET EAGER DAVIS*

COLUMBIA UNIVERSITY PRESS
New York

The League of Nations Association, under whose auspices these papers were prepared, expresses its appreciation to the Woodrow Wilson Foundation, the Milbank Memorial Fund, and the Carnegie Endowment for International Peace, whose contributions have helped to make possible the preparation and publication of this volume.

First Printing 1944
Second Printing 1945

Foreign agent: Oxford University Press, Humphrey Milford, Amen House, London, E.C. 4, England, and B. I. Building, Nicol Road, Bombay, India

MANUFACTURED IN THE UNITED STATES OF AMERICA

FOREWORD

BY RAYMOND B. FOSDICK

THIS BOOK has been written by Americans, all of whom were associated with an institution that was itself the result of American initiative and leadership—the League of Nations. What they have written here is the record of a gallant beginning in a new kind of world order—the pioneering attempts to establish a definitized system of international relationships in a century when such a system has suddenly become imperative.

Twenty years ago Mr. Elihu Root wrote some paragraphs which might serve as a text for this book. This is the way he expressed his conception of an experiment in world order:

> The real power behind international as well as national progress toward better conditions is public opinion . . . Public opinion, however, cannot make itself affirmatively effective except by the creation of institutions adapted to give it effect. Mere verbal expressions of opinion get nowhere . . . What is everybody's business is nobody's business. To get things done some human agency must be designated to give effect to the general desire that they be done.

And Mr. Root went on to develop his point in this manner:

> The question inevitably arises, "How is it that nations composed of people who don't want war are continually fighting?" The answer is that opinion against war has been without adequate institutions to give it effect. . . . The important thing is to get the right kind of an institution started, even though it be in the most rudimentary form.

This was what the experiment at Geneva represented: an attempt to get the right kind of institution started, even though it was in rudimentary form.

It is significant that, although the United States was not a

RAYMOND B. FOSDICK, lawyer and well-known public servant, is president and trustee of the Rockefeller Foundation and the General Education Board. He was born in Buffalo. In New York City he served as Commissioner of Accounts and later as a member of the Board of Education. He became in 1916 special representative for the Secretary of War on the Mexican Boarder and in 1918 went to France as special representative for the War Department. He acted as civilian aide to General Pershing in 1919. When the League of Nations was formed, Mr. Fosdick became Under Secretary General and served for a year.

member of the League of Nations, nearly three hundred American citizens participated in one aspect or another of its work. This is in keeping with the tradition of American character. Americans have never hesitated to set up instruments and institutions to give effect to public purposes. Our forefathers who cut down the forests with their broadaxes and planted the clearings with Indian corn were consciously building a new order in human society. They were not frightened conservatives dismayed by the prospect of change. They knew that change awaited them as they sailed over a hazardous ocean, and they faced continual change as they established themselves across three thousand miles of continent. They had the capacity to adapt themselves to the new conditions that confronted them, and they were bold in their devising. The spirit behind the Declaration of Independence was the impulse toward free experimentation, toward detachment from the past. The men of the Revolution did not hesitate to try out a new plan of government. The times demanded it and they rose to the challenge. When they found that the only way to protect their new government was to avoid what were called "entangling alliances," they avoided them. But it was a formula of adjustment to the conditions that existed at the moment. Had the circumstances been otherwise, had the perils lain in another direction, they would have adapted their ideas and their institutions to those circumstances and perils with the same inventiveness and fearlessness which had marked their course from the Mayflower Compact to the Constitution and the Bill of Rights.

This is the American tradition—a capacity to accommodate our ways of life to a changing world. Within recent decades we have shown it brilliantly in our industrial organization. We have risen to it heroically in this cataclysmic war in which we are now engaged. The period which follows the war will be a time of testing. If the pioneering tradition of our forefathers still holds in the hearts of this generation, we shall not be afraid of new plans for cooperative action, even when they run counter to ideas and techniques which have long been cherished. We shall not be timid in adapting ourselves to the new world with which the twentieth century has so suddenly surrounded us. We shall not hesitate to create whatever machinery and institutions are necessary to protect our lives and the lives of the children who follow us from the supreme peril of our time.

This book shows the pioneers at work. The forests have been felled and the clearings have been planted. The time for building is at hand.

CONTENTS

THE FRAMEWORK OF PEACE

BY ARTHUR SWEETSER

THE GOVERNMENTS and peoples of the world will face during the coming months the greatest problems of political and social organization in their history. On their decisions will depend whether the world after this war enters into an era of continuing peace and prosperity, with time and opportunity to work out a long peace, or whether we shall again have only a brief armistice period ending in another world cataclysm.

This is the greatest public question in the individual lives of men and women all the world over. To many it may look remote and out of reach of any effective action on their part, yet actually it underlies and conditions all life. On the world's orientation towards peace or towards war will largely depend its decisions between a world-wide exchange of goods or compartmented national hoardings, between a free or a planned economy, between the consecration of wealth and resources to greater happiness or to greater destructiveness, between an increase or a decrease of armaments, between raising or lowering living standards, and, in the end, between normal life or military conscription for everybody. It is one of the phenomena of human waywardness that a problem which means so much to so many should up to now have agitated so few.

The solution to this problem is probably the most difficult in humanity's long groping towards civilization. There is no royal road, no simple panacea or formula which will immediately eradi-

---

ARTHUR SWEETSER began life as a newspaper man, serving in France for the first months of the first World War and then as Associated Press correspondent at the State Department. On America's entry into the war, he became a captain at the Washington headquarters of the new Air Service. After the armistice, he went to the Peace Conference, where he became assistant director of the Press Bureau and subsequently joined the Secretariat of the League of Nations, serving for twelve years in the Information Section as assistant and eventually acting director, and for ten more as director attached to the principal officers, in charge of general liaison. Shortly after America's entry into the present war, he became a deputy director of the Office of War Information, serving also as Chairman of the United Nations Information Board.

cate the habits of centuries. Mankind has come a long way, through various stages of family, clan, tribe, village, town, city, and state; he stands now a second time at the threshold of the final stage in his social organization. He made one effort to cross it after the last World War, and failed; he is fortunate in having another chance after this second World War.

Although little realized or even commented upon by the general public, the broad framework for the solution of this greatest of all human problems has already been planned and stated by the principal governments. On October 30, 1943, the four great powers, the United States, Great Britain, Soviet Russia, and China, which will for some time after the war hold the future of the world in their hands, joined in issuing the Moscow Declaration for "establishing at the earliest practicable date a general international organization, based on the principle of the sovereign equality of all peace-loving States, and open to membership by all such States, large and small, for the maintenance of international peace and security." On November 5, the United States Senate, which in 1919 was hopelessly deadlocked on just such a project, voted by the overwhelming majority of 85 to 5, in favor of this very proposal. On May 29, Secretary of State Hull, at the conclusion of non-partisan discussions with Congressional leaders, announced plans for informal discussions with Great Britain, Russia, and China, and then with the other United Nations for "the establishment of an international peace and security organization," and on June 15, President Roosevelt issued a statement giving the broad outline for "the post-war security organization program."

These various statements hold out promise of a different kind of world. They give the hope that force, power, and responsibility may this second time be united for stifling further war and cultivating a continued peace.

Just what this pledge means in detail and how it will be worked out in practice, is the great question of the coming months. What precise powers shall such a "general international organization" have? What form shall it take; what shall be its relation to national sovereignty? What shall be its basis of organization, universal or regional, or both; how shall the votes of the nations be assessed; shall it have force at its command? Until these and other key questions are answered and the framework of world relations established, it is incalculably more difficult to settle specific matters such as frontiers, bases, armaments, and even tariffs, which are all intimately related to the kind of world in which they will function.

The nations have at their service, for building the world of tomorrow, the illuminating experience of a similar effort after the first World War. Although great advances were made, that experience was not all on the positive side; on the contrary, its negative lessons are perhaps equally valuable as pointing out the dangers and pitfalls that await the second effort. The past is never an easy or a complacent guide for the future, but it has the virtue of reality as against theory and is grounded on actual test rather than on mere enthusiasm.

The experience of some sixty nations in international organization during the twenty-year inter-war period from 1919 to 1939 represents both in its successes and its failures an experience of infinite value to all thoughtful people, and especially to representatives of government who will be charged with creating the "general international organization" promulgated in the Moscow Declaration and the Senate Resolution. Whatever may be the future of the agencies then created, particularly the League of Nations, the International Labor Organization, the Permanent Court of International Justice, they offer a major contribution at the moment in illuminating out of experience the difficult path ahead. They provide the makers of the coming settlement an opportunity to start their task long leaps ahead of the pioneers who had to draw up the last settlement.

Governments have already begun to make use of this advantage. Both the League and the Labor Office were invited to make their experience available in the creation of the two United Nations agencies of Relief and Rehabilitation and of Food and Agriculture. Officials of both conferred for months and provided numerous memoranda giving the new agencies judgments based on years of trial and error. Similarly, in the wider fields of international organization now under contemplation, foreign offices frequently turn for advice to those who have actually lived through similar problems in the past.

The general public has not, however, had the same advantage, especially in the United States, where there has been a tendency either to pass the League experience by in silence or to strike out on new, dramatic, and super-simplified lines. Our abrupt reversal of policy in 1919–20 from organized international cooperation to isolation and indifference had incalculable effects on American thinking. The government turned its back on the effort which it had induced the other governments to undertake; the country did not "belong" to the League, and although some citizens had twinges of conscience or even of foreboding, Americans generally felt no identification with it and some a definite hostility. Isolationism not only of policy but of thinking ran high; the type of world interest heretofore evinced by such American leaders as John Hay, Theodore Roosevelt, Elihu Root, William Howard Taft, and Woodrow Wilson went under a cloud. Americans set about ingeniously finding alternatives to current world policy, such as the "codification of international law," the Washington Arms Conference, the Kellogg Pact, Pan-American hemispheric isolationism, neutrality and the like—each, it is true, of limited value in itself yet all falling far short of meeting the central world emergency.

Pearl Harbor ruthlessly exposed the fallacy of these partial escapisms, and Americans are now trying to make up for two barren decades of indifference. It is striking that both the grandson of the man who led the fight against the League of Nations in the Senate and the only living ex-President who held office in the subsequent years have recently urged their countrymen to study the experience of the League of Nations for the guidance it offers the future. Senator Henry Cabot Lodge, Jr., has written that "there are very valuable lessons to be learned from the League of Nations which can be of great usefulness to the American people today," while former President Herbert Hoover has stated that, "unless we learn the lessons of League experience, we shall fall into the old disastrous mistakes and unless we realize its successes, we shall not make the best of world organization."

Fortunately and despite the fact that the United States was not a member of the League of Nations, close to three hundred American citizens were actually associated with many branches of League work throughout this inter-war period. Though almost wholly unrecognized by their compatriots at the time, these men are now available to give information and suggestion, as it were, from the inside. This fact in itself is curiously illustrative of America's intimate, even if not formalized or publicized, relations with League work. Some of these Americans were, or are today, officials of the United States government appointed by the government to represent its interests and views at League Conferences, such as the World Disarmament and Economic gatherings. Others were, or are today, government officials or private citizens appointed by the League itself for personal and expert contribution to the common welfare. Between them they cover nearly the whole range of League experience and offer as representative a cross-sectional viewpoint of the "first general international organization" as could be found even in countries which are full members of the League. They cover the Permanent Court of International Justice, the International Labor Organization, the League's Economic Committee and the Opium Board, as well as committees on disarmament, economics, finance, double taxation, world statistics, communications, health, nutrition, housing, child welfare, intellectual cooperation, refugees and international administration. A dozen have been members of the League Secretariat, five of these serving from eight to twenty-two years each in the world's first general international civil service at Geneva.

Over a hundred of these American citizens came together twice during the war at the Institute for Advanced Study in Princeton, once in 1940 and again in 1943, to attempt to apply the lessons of their past experience to present-day problems. A representative group were requested to prepare memoranda drawing out of that experience the highlights they would like to present to the designers of the "general international organization" to follow this war. No attempt was made to give all the answers to all the problems, or even to cover them all, for the future will have special problems of its own. These memoranda, however, constituted a sound introductory starting point for approaching the next settlement in a logical and orderly way, and the authors were invited to revise them for publication in this book as a kind of testament from the past to the future; while the result is a cooperative venture based on a general ground work of agreement, each author is specifically responsible only for the chapter bearing his name.

In addition to the individuals who have given freely of their time both in writing and in conference, five of America's best qualified unofficial agencies have made substantial contributions: the League of Nations Association in initiating the project and carrying much of the organizational work, the Woodrow Wilson Foundation, the Carnegie Endowment for International Peace, and the Millbank Memorial in providing funds and facilities for final publication, and the Institute for Advanced Study in providing hospitality for the two conferences.

OUTSTANDING LESSONS FROM THE LEAGUE

The outstanding summary lesson from League experience in the twenty-year inter-war period might be expressed in the following three-sided formula:

First, that the creation of such a permanent, continuous, international agency as foreseen in the Moscow Declaration and the Senate Resolution is, and has proved to be, entirely feasible and practicable.

Second, that such an agency can do, and has done, invaluable work in improving the relations and contacts of nations.

Third, and conversely, that it has, however, little reasonable hope of averting the world's major calamity of general war unless an almost complete revolution of thought and policy occurs amongst governments and peoples, making prevention of war and continuance of peace the prime object of policy and effort.

The League of Nations, by its success in some ways and its failure in others, proved all three of these points, amply, tragically, yet challengingly. It demonstrated conclusively that it is possible to build a system of organized international cooperation complete in all its parts; that such a system will function effectively as long as it is moderately supported and not too greatly strained; but that it will not be able to withstand the greater shocks unless the world's principal governments give it their full support. The governments and peoples of the world can have peace if they want it, but they cannot hope to get it by default or half-effort.

The League's greatest success undoubtedly lay in the first point —the creation of a complete system of international cooperation ramifying into practically every domain of international interest. It built up a mechanism of conference, consultation, and study, including an annual Assembly of all the member states which met in regular session every September for the whole inter-war period and in extraordinary session on several other occasions; an executive Council of the more important members which held 106 regular and many extraordinary sessions; two autonomous agencies of Permanent Court and International Labor Organization to function in their special fields; a network of special committees on the many interests in international life from the protection of whales to the supervision of armaments; an extensive system of organizing and directing special conferences on various subjects as they matured; and a permanent international staff and civil service in Geneva with a high standard of loyalty and efficiency.

The mere existence of such a central agency with its constant contact, consultation, and conference served greatly to quicken international life and effort. The interchange between men from different backgrounds and parts of the world, cross-fertilization from one subject to another, and even the mere momentum of a continuing agency in periodic conference advanced many international activities more in twenty years than in the entire previous century. There can be no question, from the experience of the League, that the existence of a "general international organization" perceptibly raised the ideals and standards, and, for a while, the practices, of the world community, even despite the final catastrophe of war. Truly it may be said that the League rose above its own source.

But it could not rise very high above that source. There, indeed, lay the tragedy of the League. It was an agency and an organization of governments, which, while expressive of their better spirit was, nevertheless, in the final analysis, dependent on their support. It could carry them a certain distance, but it could not force them beyond the point they were willing to go, nor, being in truth only a league of many nations, could it operate on its own, in an international vacuum, as many people now seem to have expected. There lies the great danger for any international organization based on too broad an interpretation of "national sovereignty," often a cloak for national lawlessness and irresponsibility.

It is utterly vital to the future to appreciate this fundamental fact of the past. People speak of the "failure" of the League of Nations to avert a second World War, as though that failure were not shared to a very large degree by the governments which defaulted the League's principles. Unless the responsibility for the present tragedy is truly placed and unless governments and peoples realize the share of it which belongs to governments, they will be building the new "general international organization" on a wholly false foundation which will again shortly collapse under the impact of reality.

The principal responsibility rested upon the so-called great powers, the very powers being counted upon today to assure peace to the future world. Yet their past record in relation to the first general international organization is plainly bad. Never at any one time were all seven of them, or indeed more than five, even nominally members of the League. The United States, most powerful of all, which had taken the initiative in launching the League, as it now has in launching the United Nations, dealt the League a crippling blow at the very outset by refusing its own membership and then even in the first years appearing definitely unsympathetic. Two other original members, Japan and Italy, flew directly in the face of their solemn obligations to the League, when, in the early thirties they ran amok, in Manchuria and in Ethiopia, respectively. Both were subjected to the shame of a world verdict of aggression and Italy, in addition, to the first world-wide sanctions ever decreed; both flounced out of the League in defiance of all its principles. Germany, held outside the League for the first five years, joined for an uneasy and egocentric few years until Hitler threw aside any pretense of international principle and set out openly to secure his objectives in defiance of the international community. Soviet Russia was not in a position to join until 1934, became for a while the foremost spokesman for collective security, but in 1939, it took unilateral action in defense against Germany, involving invasion of Finland and consequently expulsion from the League. Small wonder that, as first one great power and then another abandoned League principles, Britain and France each began seeking its own safety in isolated action until they reached the inevitable tragedies of Munich, Compiègne, and Dunkirk.

The League's bitter experience demonstrates that, solid though the structural basis may be, it is impossible to create an international agency strong enough to hold back the floodgates of future war unless the member nations, and particularly the great powers, and this means the majority of their citizens, give it far more support than they ever gave the League. If the conditions which followed the last war repeat themselves after this one, and the nations, losing sight of the primary objective of peace, split off in separate pursuit of their individual and often ephemeral interests, the "general international organization" now hailed with such enthusiasm may suffer the same lingering debility as did the League. The outstanding lesson of the inter-war period is that, if there is to be hope of peace, the great powers must continue to exercise that control and not abdicate, abandon, or challenge it.

But merely to stand together, in a kind of negative passivism, will not be sufficient. Peace, as the last experience proved, is not static; it requires constant effort and attention. The great powers, if they really want peace, must will it with all their energies. Last time the nations only played at peace. None made any real effort for it, much less any real sacrifice; none based its domestic or foreign policy on the hypothesis that the greatest national and international boon was the prevention of another war. Recommendations, appeals, even pleas, from Geneva fell often on deaf ears; delegates who in a moment of general enlightenment agreed to some modest advance in the community interest often returned home to find themselves repudiated by their politics-ridden colleagues or certain highly vocal private interests. Not a single government acted on the theory that the "general international organization" created after the last war was its insurance against the greatest modern danger; on the contrary, in the really important questions, they frequently justified inaction on "sovereignty," isolationism, national pride, lack of interest, and eventually downright repudiation. Often, when a crisis came, Geneva was abandoned in a world of unreality, unsupported by those who had created it to defend their most vital interests, and maligned by those "realists" who were destined to get their answer at Pearl Harbor. The natural outcome was war, which broke over the heads of the nations practically by default.

Pursuing for a moment the analogy of an international organization as insurance against war, let us ask what premiums the governments of the world were willing to pay for such insurance. The answer is shattering: slightly more than seven million dollars a year all together, from some sixty governments, to support their only common agencies of peaceful cooperation—the League, the Labor Organization, and the Court! This seven-million-dollar yearly peace budget would meet the war bill of the United States alone for just thirty-seven minutes. Or, conversely, the total American war budget of one hundred billion dollars would have carried the expenses of the entire League of Nations for fourteen thousand years, back to the prehistoric days of the Ice Age! These figures make a travesty of the nations' previous efforts for peace and throw a dazzling spotlight on how little they were willing to do.

The greatest chance of success for the "general international organization" to be created after this war is an almost complete revolution in the philosophy of governments and peoples. They must recognize that the prevention of war and the perpetuation of peace is a fundamental issue to be given preference over such specific questions as an ill-defined "sovereignty," now, in any event, greatly circumscribed; so-called strategic frontiers, which are hardly "strategic" in a world of a single air command; or one-sided tariffs, which can easily ruin our best customers. Simple as this may sound, it is the lesson which the world did not apply last time and which has cost it the agony of this second war. One may safely prophesy that, until the governments and peoples of the world not only recognize but act upon this truth, they will be living in deadly danger of repeating the experience of 1939, with any general international organization powerless to dam the flood.

SPECIFIC SUGGESTIONS FROM LEAGUE EXPERIENCE

Beyond this fundamental lesson, League experience can also offer precise suggestions to those charged with designing the world's new structure. Many of these will be discussed in detail in the following chapters, but certain general observations may be given here.

First of all, the emergency problem of the prevention of war and aggression is so urgent and depends so heavily on the great powers as to be in a special category by itself, to be differently treated from more normal and more slow-moving questions. It is here that both past experience and present tendency suggest the greatest structural change over the League system. An international organization, to be effective in a sudden emergency and to prevent the world's being set aflame again, must have some emergency service, like a fire-engine corps, which can act ruthlessly and immediately. This means that the great powers, which have both the material power and very often the moral obligation to prevent actual fighting, must hold a special position and status for emergency, able to act, as the Moscow Declaration expresses it, "on behalf of the community of nations." Primary responsibility in this contingency would be concentrated with those who have the power to fulfill it; it would not, as was the tendency in the League, be so dispersed into anonymity that in the end no one exercised it.

This raises at once the old conflict which echoed continuously at Geneva between the so-called great and the so-called small powers. Here again, however, experience points towards a solution, or at least a very definite amelioration of the dispute. Any emergency action taken by the great powers would be taken on behalf of the world community, would be reported to that community to assure its support, and would be open to criticism or even—though such a case is almost unimaginable—to repudiation by it. With two world wars in a single generation due largely to great power divisions, it is not likely that the small powers would contest the assumption of responsibility for preventing aggression on the part of those who alone have the power to exercise it.

It is even less likely because the small powers would not and could not be excluded from any part in this responsibility. On the contrary, they will always, in any alignment, have a very real and a double role to play. First, the great powers are almost certain to call upon them in one way or another and would probably give them a direct voice in the decisions, as they scrupulously did in the League. Either as involuntary centers of conflict, or as elements in any projected military or economic action, the small powers will always be important in any scheme of world organization. They will, secondly, carry in world councils that particular moral weight attached to states not seeking their own aggrandizement but able to assess disputes in the light of the interests of the whole world.

Moreover, experience shows ways of alleviating the acerbity which developed around this issue. Whereas the League Covenant set off certain nations by name as always entitled to a predominant situation, thus arousing resentments among the others, the International Labor Organization Constitution found a less invidious formula by giving leadership to the states "of chief industrial importance." This at once removed the discussion from the dangerous idea of "greatness," and transferred it to the less emotional field of statistics and facts. In the future it may be possible to have, instead of perpetual "great powers," powers of "chief military interest," "chief economic interest," "chief colonial interest," and the like.

Short of an emergency police service, for which the great powers would be primarily responsible, there is another possible method of restraint of a recalcitrant nation, namely, economic sanctions. Sanctions bulked large in League discussions but are strangely absent from the plans today. There, League experience seems unfortunately to have been misread. The single case in which sanctions were applied against Italy over Ethiopia was not so unsuccessful and negative as is commonly thought. While these sanctions did not and indeed could not succeed in bringing Italy to her knees, since the military campaign was finished before the sanctions had time to become effective, they demonstrated that it is possible to organize such action on a world scale, and that, as Mussolini's bellowing showed, it can be very painful, in the end probably fatal, to the recalcitrant state. It would, therefore, be well for the future to reexamine this case of sanctions against Italy. From the moral standpoint, nonintercourse with a state branded as an aggressor would seem to be the least that a self-respecting member of the community could do, a procedure increasingly urged on the neutrals in the second World War. Experience, however, suggests two further avenues of exploration: first, that such sanctions, if decreed, be carefully related to the military situation and not, as in the Italian case, kept entirely apart from it; second, that some sort of mutual assistance in sharing the common burden be instituted, as in the League's projected treaty for financial assistance or in the subsequent American lend-lease policy.

Wider vistas of peaceful settlement than were available or even thought of at the last peace conference have been opened up by League experience. The presence of a mediatory body to which any state, even a third party, can present a conflict, of a Permanent Court of International Justice, to which legal cases can be brought, and of other methods of mediation and conciliation provide valuable bases for further progress which were lacking at the last settlement. Experience has shown that such agencies can, and indeed did, settle many disputes which threatened armed conflict; that they are capable of acting very quickly, if need be, within a few days, as in the Greek-Bulgar affair; and that they can, in extreme cases, carry action through to a world verdict condemning a state of aggression, as with both Japan and Italy.

One of the principal differences between the last and the next settlement will probably lie in the field of armaments. While the enemy states may be even more ruthlessly disarmed than before, the same stigma will not again be attached to armaments in the hands of peace-loving states. Recognition will be given to the fact that certain armaments must be maintained to prevent the rise of another threat to the world's peace. The League's experience has two vital lessons in this field. First, after years of effort, the Geneva discussions destroyed the theory, pressed especially by certain American and British sources, that armaments were the cause of political insecurity rather than its consequence, and started an attempt to remove the causes which made armaments seem necessary. Second, these League discussions left a heritage of useful material, particularly in the form of draft treaties, which need only to be brought up to date to meet such serious questions as the control and supervision of armaments, traffic in armaments, budgetary control of armaments, and classification of armaments.

So in almost every field of international interest, as the succeeding pages will show, a vast amount of material remains over from the past, waiting for the nations to reanimate it into further progress. The work of the League's economic, financial and transit departments, which accomplished many precise results in its twenty years and laid down sound philosophies of world trade, suggests ways and means of meeting the colossal difficulties of tomorrow's war-burdened world. The International Labor Organization is even today proposing methods for transferring from a war to a peace economy and for advancing standards of labor in all countries, including the most favored. The League's social, health, nutrition, and other activities open further possibilities, as is dramatically shown by the creation of the United Nations Organization for Food and Agriculture, a direct descendant of the League's nutrition efforts. Its antidrug work, which even during the war has made notable progress, promises greater control over this most terrible of scourges than was ever possible before; its experience with the mandates system permits further progress in the welfare of dependent peoples than was possible when this system was launched against such opposition after the last war.

WHAT KIND OF OVER-ALL AGENCY?

These and many other questions will be discussed in detail in the following pages. What will not be covered in the individual chapters, however, is the kind and type of over-all agency or agencies which will be necessary to handle work of such widely varying character, and what principles of international organization would seem from the experience of the League to be the most practicable. Should there be a single, central agency, perhaps with associated specialized agencies, or should the main interest center, as is sometimes urged, on building up the separate technical agencies in the hope that their sum total would assure good conditions in all fields and hence would remove the causes of war?

Here again the League's experience, contrary to certain views taken in the first disillusionment after the outbreak of this war, points very strongly to a single, centralized, unitary agency—what the Moscow and Senate pronouncements called "a *general* international organization." This could be supplemented with specialized or regional agencies, but should always remain as the ultimate source of authority. The existence of a series of uncoordinated, unassociated, and probably competitive agencies would, from the League's experience, spell administrative and political chaos.

Though all such agencies, after the first war, were supposed to be centralized around the newly created League, as provided in Article XXIV of the Covenant, many did not achieve such integration but went their own separate ways. This was due to a variety of reasons: the non-universality of the League and particularly the absence of the United States, the unwillingness of interested national governments to give up a political or prestige advantage, and even the small-mindedness of entrenched bureaucrats who feared to lose an independent position at the head of a small agency in favor of cooperation in a large agency. Thus, the prewar Postal and Telegraphic Unions remained outside the League's system and tended to block League suggestions in their fields.

The International Air Commission in Paris jealously guarded its own particular domain and was used to keep the League from taking up what was becoming one of the most important international problems. The International Institute of Agriculture in Rome endeavored, until Mussolini killed it, to maintain a monopoly of its subject. The Pan-American Union in Washington had no cooperative relationship to the general world agency and for the first fifteen years it did not even have authority to correspond with it. Even the International Labor Organization, though associated with the League, presented administrative problems which are acute today.

Such division and fragmentation should not be permitted a second time. Specialized agencies, whether regional or functional, should be coordinated into one system which, while maintaining the autonomy of the parts, can provide a free and effective interchange between them. An inclusive system like the League's made it possible, for instance, for Marshal Chiang Kai-shek to appeal to a single agency for experts in economics, finance, communications, health, and education on a coordinated program; for those struggling with the institution of a system of supervision of armaments to call in others who had just established a comparable system for the supervision of drugs; or for those who wished to extend the field of international cooperative effort to begin with certain technical activities which could expand step by step towards the unfolding of a general program.

This does not at all mean that the existence of such "a general international organization" would militate against either regional or specialized agencies. The League's experience was quite the contrary on both points; far from crippling such agencies, it did more to extend them than had ever been done before. In the regional field, for instance, it fostered the development of regional groupings such as the Little Entente and the Balkan, Oslo, Neutral, and Arab groups; its annual Assembly was featured by regular meetings of the states from the Americas. Similarly in the functional field, it could not possibly handle all the multitudinous detail which constantly arose in these widely different fields; more and more it set them up on their own, maintaining only a general coordinating and supervising interest over them and especially over their interrelationships.

The wide sweep of this system has often been overlooked. Its consequences were perhaps most fully described by the Secretary of State of a non-member nation, Mr. Cordell Hull, who wrote in a communication to League members a few months before the war broke out that "The League has been responsible for the development of mutual exchange and discussion of ideas and methods to a greater extent and in more fields of humanitarian and scientific endeavor than any other organization in history."

ACTUAL REMAINING ASSETS

If these are the general lessons of experience, what are the actual assets remaining over from the past, and what is to be done about them and about the existing League?

In the first place, contrary to certain assumptions based on the fact that the League has not been conspicuously active since the nations chose the alternative of war, the League is not, as is sometimes said, "dead." It has continued to exist throughout the war, even if its normal functioning has been in suspense. Forty-five nations, about a dozen more than are included in the United Nations on its second anniversary, have continued as members of the League, technically bound by its Covenant, even if not formally applying it, and many of them continuing their contributions to its treasury, some in full, the majority in part.

While the central political agencies of the League, the Assembly and the Council, have not met during the war except for an extraordinary session of the former in 1939 in connection with the Finnish conflict, a number of other meetings have been held, though unreported by the press. The Supervisory Commission, to which the Assembly had delegated plenary powers over League matters, has met regularly each year in Montreal to vote the budget and take what action was possible towards continuing League work. The Economic Committee met in The Hague before the German invasion of Holland; its members resident in Britain have met in London and those resident in the Americas in Princeton. The antidrug committees have met regularly in

London, a group of fiscal experts in Mexico City, and a group of cultural experts in Washington and Havana.

Essential parts of the League's permanent staff have been maintained throughout the war and kept in as full operation as possible. The Acting Secretary General, Mr. Sean Lester, has remained at headquarters in Geneva, keeping with him about eighty of the original staff, only a tenth of the pre-war organization but so divided as to represent each main branch of League activity and sufficient to maintain the records until the day when the nations start in on the long road to reconstruction.

Two branches of League work found asylum in the United States. At the moment when German occupation of Switzerland seemed imminent, three American educational institutions at Princeton, the Institute for Advanced Study, Princeton University, and the Rockefeller Foundation, united in inviting the League's technical services to establish temporary headquarters in Princeton. In August, 1940, a group of officials of the Economic, Financial, and Transit Department arrived after an adventurous voyage and at once resumed on this side of the Atlantic the reports and studies on the world's economic situation which had given them a world reputation. It was with these experts that governments conferred in organizing the United Nations agencies on Relief and Rehabilitation and on Food and Agriculture.

The League's antidrug enforcement officials, who are charged with executing international treaties signed by over sixty nations, including the United States, have been established in Washington. Throughout their stay, they have kept in touch with the other officials in Geneva and with the directing committees which have met in London; have issued their regular statements on drug requirements and trade; and have had no small part in securing British and Dutch agreement to the policy long advocated in Geneva of abolishing opium smoking in certain Far Eastern possessions as soon as the Japanese are evicted. Similarly, the League Treasurer and Pensions Officer have been headquartered in London, with visits to the United States and Canada, and the High Commissioner for Refugees has also continued in London.

Moreover, after the creation of UNRRA, a third League office, the Health Research Unit, was opened in Washington to bring the League's experience in this field to the service of the new agency and to prevent needless expense and duplication in a work which was purely transitory. The staff at Geneva was to be strengthened and the Far Eastern Epidemiological Bureau, which had been disrupted when the Japanese occupied Singapore, reestablished.

The two autonomous agencies associated with the League, the Permanent Court of International Justice and the International Labor Organization, have also remained in being throughout the war, as will be shown in detail later. The President, Registrar, and offices of the former were transferred to Geneva when the Germans expelled the diplomatic corps and the Court from The Hague, and the Court continues subject to call whenever the nations revert to peaceful messages. The Labor Office has maintained its operation more fully than any other part of the League grouping, having transferred practically all its remaining staff to Montreal and held two plenary sessions in New York and Philadelphia, respectively, with periodic meetings of the Governing Body in London.

The importance of these continuing efforts lies not so much in the actual work accomplished under almost impossible conditions, but even more in the fact that the staff is maintained, the records kept up to date and ready, and the whole made available to fit in any way desired into post-war organization. It will not be necessary this time, as it was last, to start from scratch; a strong connecting link exists from the past to the future.

Another fact little noted in today's plans for the future is the existence of several hundred treaties contracted during the twenty-year inter-war period and conferring on the League many and diverse legal responsibilities. They include numerous treaties on arbitration and conciliation, several disarmament treaties, various conventions on economic and financial matters, the whole chain of mandates treaties, the agreements against the drug and white slave traffics, and others too numerous to mention. The

League has become deeply embedded in the treaty life of the world; provision must be found either for continuing or transferring its obligations.

The question then arises as to how these various obligations, agencies, and individuals will fit into the post-war planning. What will be their relationship to the "general international organization" promised by the Moscow and Senate pronouncements? That question must be faced, and far sooner and more precisely than was anticipated.

At the earliest possible moment, and certainly the very moment the war ends, there must be a full meeting of League members, if only to decide as to these very points. Nations will not want to permit the many obligations and responsibilities, held in suspense during the war, to continue in such an indefinite status. They will have to decide whether they will maintain or denounce their obligations under the Covenant; whether they will resume, transfer, or terminate the network of international organizations which they organized during the inter-war period; whether they will continue the contributions they have made during the war and maintain the staff or terminate or transfer both. They will have to decide as to the continuance of innumerable treaty obligations both as to special matters like mandates and as to particular questions like the future use of the magnificent buildings and grounds making up League headquarters at Geneva. It will be necessary, in short, to end the present anomalous situation and come to a permanent solution of the basic question of the future of the League.

FOUR POSSIBLE BASES OF ORGANIZATION

The answer will obviously depend on the type of "general international organization" which is eventually worked out under the conditions actually prevailing in the post-war era. Considered purely from the viewpoint of theory and without relation to political practicability, which is unforeseeable, there would seem to be four possible bases of post-war organization. Taken in their chronological order, these may be described as follows:

1. *The League of Nations Revised and Strengthened:* This is

undoubtedly the first possibility from the juridical viewpoint, irrespective of whether it is feasible politically. The League is, as shown, an existing agency, with a Covenant binding on forty-four nations, a rich history and precedent, a mechanism of conferences and commissions, a staff, buildings, treasury, and even very definite loyalties, around which the nations could concentrate as much power as they desired. Its continuance, with the necessary amendments, would be the simplest course juridically, would provide a certain valuable historical continuity, and would be easier in some ways than building entirely new. That course, however, has appreciable difficulties, mainly psychological, through association in the public mind with the failure to prevent war and because it is merely a continuation of the old, without the stimulus of the new. Moreover, the League faces special difficulties in several important countries, not only in the United States, where controversial memories smoulder in some quarters, but also in Russia, which was declared no longer a member because of her attack on Finland; in some of the neutral states which felt abandoned in the League during the appeasement days of the Great Powers; and eventually in the Axis countries, two of which, Japan and Italy, were submitted by the League to the first world-wide verdict of aggression and the latter of which was submitted to the first world-wide sanctions.

2. *The United Nations Expanded and Formalized:* The United Nations were launched, not after the war, as was the League, but on January 1, 1942, less than four weeks after Pearl Harbor and the entry of the United States into the war. They did not spring completely into being as a full working agency organized around a specific constitution, as did the League, but began as a group of powers united through the Declaration of the United Nations, a brief document creating, in effect, an alliance for the war, with provisions against a separate peace, but also embodying the promise of a world ultimately organized on the principles of the Atlantic Charter. More and more, as the war progressed, action was taken in the name of the United Nations. While as yet no central agency has been established similar to the League Assembly or Council, nevertheless, even during the

war, three large-scale specialized conferences were called on the vital questions of the organization of world relief and food supply and on financial and monetary problems, and two technical agencies created: the United Nations Relief and Rehabilitation Administration and the United Nations Food and Agriculture Administration. Other agencies tended to develop in other special fields, as the United Nations Commission on War Crimes in London and the United Nations Information Offices in London and New York. The United Nations concept has all the appeal of a new name and method; it is free to develop, even during the war, as occasion offers; and it concentrates power in the hands of those who will have made the sacrifices for the common victory of democracy. It does not have the precedent or the continuity of the League, nor does it have the League's special psychological difficulties mentioned above, though it is fair to recognize, for whatever it may be worth, that it will have its own new difficulties in the ex-enemy countries, which will have been submitted to a stinging defeat by a coalition bearing the United Nation's name.

3. *An Altogether New Agency, Combining the Best Features of Both:* This possibility, which might be known under some such title as the Commonwealth of Nations, has not been widely discussed, but is worth bearing in mind, especially if the present indeterminate conditions should continue for a long time and the creation of the final "general international organization" should be postponed. In that case, probably all existing agencies, both special and general, would be continued in their particular fields and opportunity would be given for careful working out of the ultimate arrangements, with fuller time for consideration of the neutral and even the ex-enemy powers. While it is impossible today to predict the course which events will actually take, it is clear that this method would have both advantages and disadvantages which would have to be set off against each other: advantages in allowing more time for mature consideration of all the elements, disadvantages in continuing an indeterminate situation and perhaps losing the psychological moment.

4. *Two Agencies, One Concentrated Exclusively on the Pre-*

vention of War and Aggression, and the Other Dealing with All Other Problems: This possibility also has not been very much discussed but is wholly feasible from the theoretical point of view and presents certain practical advantages. There is a tendency in some quarters, as previously noted, to separate the specific emergency problem of preventing war and aggression from the other more slow-moving problems of advancing human welfare. This would suggest a double system whereby, for peace and security, the great powers possessing military, naval, and air forces would act within this special field, possibly as mandatories and certainly with the essential collaboration of the others, and, for general welfare and social advancement, a more universal, more democratic, and less emergency agency of all the powers. Even were this method followed, it would be necessary to make a choice among the other alternatives for the ultimate "general international organization."

Each of these methods has advantages. Some time soon, and perhaps sooner than is anticipated, the nations will have to take a decision as to the specific basis on which they wish to organize international security, reconstruction, and the peace of tomorrow. Through the first years of the war so many and often contradictory alternatives and plans were offered the public that many people foundered, confused. But as the broad outlines of the "general international organization" of tomorrow become clearer, the individual pieces will fit together, and a great impulsion should come to specific and constructive thinking.

As to the future of the League itself, some Americans may hold that since the United States is not a member, it has no role to play and no vote to cast on this question. But the United States has in actuality had so many contacts with League work and holds today such a vital place in world affairs that it has not only an interest but a right to make known its views as they crystallize in the public mind.

The launching of the United Nations concept and the Moscow and Senate pronouncement in favor of "a general international organization" express the same general international philosophy as the League and offer the likelihood of bringing about more effective international cooperation than was ever before possible.

The creation of specific United Nations agencies, such as Relief and Rehabilitation and Food and Agriculture which the United States took the initiative in launching, offer instruments and new possibilities to the international cooperation which the League endeavored for twenty years to stimulate. This relationship to existing agencies, such as the League's Economic and Financial Committees and the International Labor Organization, is also of great importance.

Even more specific questions are beginning, and will increasingly continue to arise, as the terms of the settlement become more precise. The future of the World Court was directly brought into discussion when Secretary of State Cordell Hull on September 12, 1943, raised the question as to "the extent to which the existing court of international justice may or may not need to be remodeled." Five days later the whole question of the mandates administration of the League was raised in President Roosevelt's message to Congress that "it goes almost without saying" that Japan would never again be allowed to exercise authority over the Pacific Islands. In due course, practically all activities of the League will come up for review and consideration.

This is as it should be. The past must be harmonized with the future. The nations which will hold the responsibility for the continuance of world peace after this war must bring the scattered ends together one by one. And it is fortunate that this can happen at a moment when certain old difficulties regarding the League have largely vanished in the United States. While remnants of the 1919 bitternesses still linger in a few quarters, the general reaction to the League and what it tried to do is increasingly one of understanding and sympathy.

Fortunately this liberal attitude prevails also in the League itself. The Acting Secretary General, Mr. Sean Lester, speaking in his annual report for 1941–42 of the international agency to follow the present war, went so far as to say that "the form that organization will take will probably be different from that of the first stage of the experiment." League adherents generally recognize that the real purposes for which the League was founded are best served by calling, not for the same old League, but for a Union of Nations which, by taking advantage of both the good and the bad in the first experience, may grant to itself the power to accomplish what the League could not. It is in this spirit that sixteen American citizens who cooperated in many branches of League work offer the following chapters as a contribution from the last settlement to the next. The book has no past cause to defend and no past policy to justify. There is no time now for making dispassionate historical judgments; the past, good or bad, is important only as it bears directly on the policies of today and tomorrow, only as it suggests methods for creating the "general international organization" advocated by the Moscow Declaration and the Senate Resolution, and gives to the world a reasonable chance for sustained peace.

SECURITY

BY JAMES T. SHOTWELL

THE PROBLEM OF SECURITY IN THE COVENANT

It was on the question of security that the Senate of the United States found its chief argument for opposing the adoption of the Covenant of the League of Nations. To the American public, at least to that section of it which followed the debate, Articles 10 and 16 became a kind of shorthand symbol for the chief issue raised by the Covenant: the support to be given by members of the League towards the maintenance of peace. Now, in the final phase of the second World War, public opinion in the United States is apparently moving in absolutely the opposite direction. It is demanding not merely the substance of Articles 10 and 16 of the Covenant, but an even stronger and more definite statement of what America's participation in the maintenance of peace is to be. Wherever this question is discussed the dominant criticism is almost always that the Covenant of the League did not go far enough in the provision for peace enforcement. This paradox grows all the stranger when we look at the history which lies behind it.

First, as to Article 10. The text reads as follows:

The Members of the League undertake to respect and preserve as against external aggression the territorial integrity and existing political independence of all Members of the League. In case of any such aggression or in case of any threat or danger of such aggression, the Council shall advise upon the means by which this obligation shall be fulfilled.

James T. Shotwell is one of America's most eminent historians. He was a member of the famous Paris Peace Conference of 1917 and has subsequently served his country in many international capacities, most recently as consultant to the State Department and as director of the Commission to Study the Organization of Peace. He was for over thirty years professor of history at Columbia University, is a trustee and the director of the Division of Economics and History for the Carnegie Endowment for International Peace, and has served as chairman of the American Committee on International Intellectual Cooperation of the League of Nations. Dr. Shotwell has written many books on historical and international subjects.

This is the one Article of the Covenant which grew out of Mr. Wilson's own experience in dealing with Latin America and which therefore he was unwilling to see modified or changed in the slightest degree. The need for some such international undertaking had been driven home in Wilson's mind as a result of his dealings with Mexico prior to the outbreak of the World War. During the winter and spring of 1914, there had been grave danger of an outbreak of war, following upon a long series of incidents throughout the preceding two years of Wilson's administration. On April 21, 1914, the American Marines had landed at Vera Cruz and taken possession of the Customs House there. On April 24 the mediation of Argentina, Brazil, and Chile was accepted by the United States, their representatives met on the neutral soil of Canada, and by the procedure of conciliation succeeded in warding off the one danger of war which at that time confronted the American Government. The success of this method made a deep impression upon President Wilson. On May 11, in a memorial address for the men killed at Vera Cruz, he took occasion to point out that the victims had been drawn from all the nations of Europe, and implied that his policy had been based not merely upon narrow or selfish national purpose, but on the fundamental principle of a common humanity. This was a thought to which he had already given elaborate utterance in his address to Congress on April 20:

We seek to maintain the dignity and authority of the United States only because we wish always to keep our great influence unimpaired for the uses of liberty, both in the United States and wherever else it was being employed for the benefit of mankind.

It was therefore not an idle phrase or even a sudden inspiration of President Wilson's when, in his address to Congress of January 22, 1917, on the foundation of peace, the address which was the prelude to our entry into the first World War, he summed up his proposals as follows:

I am proposing, as it were, that the nations should, with one accord, adopt the doctrine of President Monroe as the doctrine of the world: that no nation should seek to extend its polity under any other nation or people, but that every people should be left free to determine its own polity, its own way of development, unhindered, unthreatened, unafraid, the little along with the great and powerful.

This is the speech in which, for the first time, President Wilson used the phrase, "If the peace to be presently made is to endure, it must be made secure by the organized major force of mankind," thus definitely throwing down the challenge to American isolation. The challenge was immediately taken up by Senator Lodge in his speech of February 1. The Monroe Doctrine, said Senator Lodge, was purely a document of the United States and "defined our position and defined nobody else's position." To extend it to all the world and put behind it the armed weight of a League of Nations, would, he said, imperil the safety of the United States and would not further the cause of peace, because of the complications of world politics in fields in which the United States would have no direct interest. Senator Lodge summed up his view of the situation in a straightforward phrase: "The first service which the United States can render to the cause of peace is to preserve its own." In reply to the question, "Are you unwilling to use the power and influence of the United States for promotion of the permanent peace of the world?" Lodge's answer was, "Not at all, but we should try within the necessary and natural limits, to extend the use of voluntary arbitration and urge a general reduction of armament by all nations."

In the light of today it seems almost incredible that this program of Senator Lodge should have even temporarily won the day against that of President Wilson. No one knew better than Senator Lodge that we have no arbitration treaties with any other nation which reach beyond the obligation to present to the Senate the question at issue; if the Senate agrees that it is the kind of an issue which might be arbitrated, we then could proceed with arbitration. No poorer provision could exist in a nation for dealing with the grave political issues upon which wars are fought. Moreover, arbitration is not the appropriate method for dealing with the immediate menace of war. The only technique which has been found successful when war threatens is conciliation, of the kind which succeeded in the Mexican incident and which became the chief instrument of the League of Nations for the settlement of dangerous political disputes. To follow Lodge's second suggestion—the reduction of armaments as a preventive measure without having provided alternatives for war and a method for lessening the dangers of aggression—would be the most unreal and misleading of policies. Nevertheless, before the long debate was over, Lodge's point of view had won.

This is not all the background of Article 10 but it partly explains why President Wilson insisted so strongly upon maintaining it in the Covenant. It also partly explains, although not wholly, why the European nations never gave it the attention one might have expected. For them the Covenant itself implied such a guarantee of peace, which therefore did not require specific mention in the terms of Article 10. Moreover, it is a strange and almost unbelievable fact that Article 10 was never invoked throughout the history of the League, down to the last episode, that of the outbreak of war in Manchuria in 1931.

The relation of all of this to the Monroe Doctrine was rather bewildering to the European delegates at the Paris Peace Conference. Article 21 brings the Monroe Doctrine into the Covenant in the following terms:

> Nothing in this Covenant shall be deemed to affect the validity of international engagements, such as treaties of arbitration or regional understandings like the Monroe Doctrine, for securing the maintenance of peace.

When this article was up for discussion, there was much questioning and not a little initial research in American history on the part of the European delegates. From the standpoint of the American delegation, Article 21 was a distinct recognition that the Monroe Doctrine had developed into a second phase, that it was no longer a unilateral doctrine for the defense of the interests of the United States, but a cooperative understanding between American nations.

In other words, the Good Neighbor policy was the application in the Western Hemisphere of the fundamental principle of the League of Nations as envisaged by its chief architect. The dispute with Mexico, which was settled through the helpful mediation of the A.B.C. powers, had brought home to President Wilson the need for both a guarantee against external aggression and a friendly interest in the welfare of neighboring peoples. In his last public address President Wilson concentrated most of his argument upon Article 10 which he called, "the heart of the Covenant." "Article 10," he said, "strikes at the taproot of war. Article 10 is a statement that the very things that have always been sought in imperialistic wars are henceforth foregone by every ambitious nation in the world." The conception of such a definite guarantee against external aggression is distinctly American, the kind of pronouncement which can only establish its validity on the basis of history. There had been no Monroe Doctrine on the continent of Europe.

If Article 10 played so slight a part in the actual history of the League of Nations, that is not because of any lack of interest in the problems of security. From first to last, security held the primacy over all other questions. But the statesmen at Geneva, having to face realities, concentrated more upon the ways and means to prevent war than upon the broad, general obligation of Article 10. This meant transferring the center of interest to the two other articles which called for practical measures in the hour of crisis, Articles 11 and 16. These two articles complement each other, Article 11 dealing with the dangerous situations out of which wars may rise, and Article 16 dealing primarily with the method for stopping action already begun. It is to these two articles, therefore, that we should chiefly look for the principles upon which collective security was worked out by the League of Nations.

Article 11 reads as follows:

1. Any war or threat of war, whether immediately affecting any of the Members of the League or not, is hereby declared a matter of concern to the whole League, and the League shall take any action that may be deemed wise and effectual to safeguard the peace of nations. In case any such emergency should arise the Secretary-General shall on the request of any Member of the League forthwith summon a meeting of the Council.

2. It is also declared to be the friendly right of each Member of the League to bring to the attention of the Assembly or of the Council any circumstance whatever affecting international relations which

threatens to disturb international peace or the good understanding between nations upon which peace depends.

It does not seem to have been fully realized at the Paris Peace Conference that this article was the most revolutionary of all the articles of the Covenant. It was cast in such general terms as to give almost the impression of an abstract statement of international morals. The statement that war or the threat of it "is hereby declared a matter of concern to the whole League," seems at first reading to be a mere commonplace. But actually it was a denial of the sovereign right of a nation to use on its own behalf the oldest instrument of politics—war. International law had never dared to say anything as bold as this before. The first slight step in this direction was taken at the Paris Conference held in 1856 after the Crimean War, when it was recognized that a nation might offer to mediate in a war between other nations without endangering its position as a neutral. The Hague Conferences strengthened this right of mediation both textually and by the moral influence which they exerted, but never before had the nations of the world subscribed to the doctrine that the disturbance of the peace was a matter of such prime interest to the community of nations that the nations meeting in conference could take any action that might be deemed wise and effectual to safeguard it. Here was interference with sovereignty, recognized and accepted on the basis of a common interest in peace.

The fact that this general principle was not tied in with any definite method of action seemed, at first sight, to weaken it, but on the contrary, it was the very basis of its strength. The only obligation of Article 11 was the provision that the Assembly or Council would have to pay attention to any circumstances threatening war, whenever any member brought the matter to the attention of the League. Here was collective security set forth in the broadest conceivable framework. This might have led to confusion and failure if the members of the Council and Assembly had been sufficiently careless of their responsibilities to use each crisis as an opportunity for experimentation in the theory of international government. Fortunately—and this is a matter for which the League has never been given full credit—the crises brought to Geneva were never dealt with in any such trivial spirit, but were faced with realism and a sense of responsibility for securing results. A device was at hand for the application of Article 11 which had every possible advantage for all concerned. It was that of sending out a commission to investigate the source of the dispute in the locality, or at least in the countries, where it occurred. This device of the fact-finding commission was of advantage to the League because it furnished time for negotiations as well as concrete data, which reached Council or Assembly not through the medium of partisan statements but through the reports of neutral observers on the spot. It had also the advantage of offering to the disputing nations a medium for the presentation of any valid claims they might have—as good a guarantee of impartiality as could possibly be found.

The outstanding example of the use of the commission of investigation by the League was in the Greco-Bulgarian incident in the autumn of 1925 when Greek armies moved over the frontier in Macedonia and war was apparently a matter of only a few days. Hurriedly the Council met and secured from both the Greek and the Bulgarian governments an armistice to permit the sending of a commission to the seat of trouble. The result was a peaceful settlement instead of a Balkan war which might easily have spread over the continent of Europe. The most important case in which Article 11 was invoked and an investigating commission requested, was the Mukden incident of 1931. Unfortunately the request was made by China and therefore was at first rejected by Japan as not being designed to produce an impartial report. The commission should have been proposed by some neutral state not interested in the dispute. Moreover, the United States backed Japan in its rejection, and Great Britain was at the time only half-hearted in support of League action. This weakness at the critical moment in Oriental history resulted in the League's taking no action whatever in the first decisive months of Japan's aggression. Then, by one of the strangest paradoxes in history, Japan itself asked for the commission, which eventually went to the Far East under Lord Lytton. Before its report could be seriously considered, however, the military action had proceeded to a point which nullified all possibility of peaceful settlement. The lesson from this is unmistakable. The prevention of war must be effectively planned and speedily carried through, or the plans of the general staff of a militarist nation will carry the day.

It seems at first strange to put Article 11 so definitely in the forefront of a discussion on collective security, which ordinarily concentrates only on Articles 10 and 16, but the only sure way to prevent a war from spreading is to prevent it from starting. When we turn to Article 16, the whole scene has changed. We are dealing with war and not with the threat of it. The problem then is what penalties are to be imposed in order to stop the war in mid-course. The very opening phrase of Article 16 has an ominous sound, and the sentences which follow ring with the stern note of violated authority. Here the League is at last speaking as a sovereign body. Critics of the Covenant who speak of it as weak are thinking not of the terms of the Covenant but of the manner of their execution. No constitution of any country gives a more definite mandate for the maintenance of law and order than these challenging paragraphs:

1. Should any Member of the League resort to war in disregard of its covenants under Articles 12, 13, or 15, it shall *ipso facto* be deemed to have committed an act of war against all other Members of the League, which hereby undertake immediately to subject it to the severance of all trade or financial relations, the prohibition of all intercourse between their nationals and the nationals of the covenant-breaking State, and the prevention of all financial, commercial or personal intercourse between the nationals of the covenant-breaking State and the nations of any other State, whether a Member of the League or not.

2. It shall be the duty of the Council in such case to recommend to the several Governments concerned what effective military, naval or air force the Members of the League shall severally contribute to the armed forces to be used to protect the covenants of the League.

3. The Members of the League agree, further, that they will mutually support one another in the financial and economic measures which are taken under this Article, in order to minimize the loss and inconvenience resulting from the above measures, and that they will mutually support one another in resisting any special measures aimed at one of their number by the covenant-breaking State, and that they will take the necessary steps to afford passage through their territory

to the forces of any of the Members of the League which are cooperating to protect the covenants of the League.

4. Any member of the League which has violated any covenant of the League may be declared to be no longer a Member of the League by a vote of the Council concurred in by the Representatives of all the other Members of the League represented thereon.

There is of course in this the necessary compromise with the sovereignty of states as to the military measures to be taken by the League against a covenant-breaking state, but the economic sanction is absolute. All members of the League must sever their trade and financial relations and prohibit intercourse between their nationals and the nationals of the covenant-breaking states. They must prevent all intercourse even between the nationals of the covenant-breaking state and those of any other state whether a member of the League or not.

This economic sanction did not work in the case of Italy's aggression in Ethiopia. Why? The answer was given by Lord Baldwin, British Prime Minister, when he said that economic sanctions mean war, and emphasized his conviction by refusing to permit his government to embark on any such perilous enterprise. When one analyzes the Baldwin declaration, however, one sees that it is not the economic sanction which he objects to, but its possible consequences. In other words, he was arguing against the military sanction by refusing to take any step which might lead toward it. Thus the refusal to accept the possibility of an ultimate military sanction vitiated the milder proposal. In other words, history has shown that there is only one sanction, not two, and that if the economic sanction is used it must be imposed by nations which are ready to take the consequences of that action. If the aggressor state decides to fight by force of arms against an economic sanction, then we must be ready to take up the challenge. Otherwise there is no sanction at all.

THE PROTOCOL OF GENEVA

The Assembly of September, 1924, was of decisive importance for the history of the League. In it the question of security was, for the first time in League history, faced openly and definitely with all its implications. The result was embodied in the document known as "The Protocol of Geneva," which, although it ultimately failed of ratification, remains a landmark in history which not even the second World War can obliterate.

In the background of this document lies the history of the League's efforts to secure reduction and limitation of armaments. The failure of these efforts had been chiefly due to the fact that the British and American approach to the problem, shared by some of the Scandinavian countries, had been to adopt the slogan of the Washington Naval Disarmament Conference: "The way to peace is by disarmament, and the way to disarm is to disarm." This slogan was countered by the more realistic statement of the French and other continental nations that disarmament would always be proportional to the degree of security which a nation enjoys. The implication in the French thesis was that a greater degree of collective security must replace the separate and individual preparations of nations for their defense. The whole controversy could be narrowed down to the simple alternative: which comes first, security or disarmament? Unfortunately, the nations which have natural security by reason of distance or geographical equivalents for distance, such as mountains or swamplands, have little appreciation of the insecurity of nations living alongside potentially hostile neighbors with no natural protection against aggression. Consequently, the British and American public opinion could not fully appreciate the French reluctance to disarm unless they had from the League of Nations a solid guarantee of cooperative defense against aggression.

This was the problem which was dealt with by the Temporary Mixed Commission, appointed by the League to supplement the ineffective work of the Permanent Military, Naval and Air Commission which it had set up in accordance with Article 9 of the Covenant, but which, being composed purely of military experts, did next to nothing about the problem of disarmament. The Temporary Mixed Commission brought in civilians alongside military members, and under the inspiring leadership of Lord Robert Cecil, produced a Draft Treaty of Mutual Assistance for the Assembly of 1924 which was destined to serve as a basis for real measures of disarmament.

Meanwhile the Council of the League took cognizance of the work of an unofficial American committee which had prepared a "Draft Treaty of Disarmament and Security" containing at least one essential contribution to the discussion, namely, a definition of aggression. The debate in the Geneva Assembly centered largely upon this definition.

The point at issue is this: if there is a plan for collective security against aggression and no general agreement has been reached as to what constitutes aggression (and it was the commonly held opinion at the time that the term had not been satisfactorily defined), then no real progress could be made by the League of Nations toward securing practical measures of peace enforcement, because no one would know when their application would be valid.

The American group brought along the definition that aggression was the resort to force in violation of a given pledge to have disputes settled by pacific means. This test of aggression did not attempt to cover the causes of the dispute, from the point of view of the justice of the case, but "outlawed" the resort to force as the means of settlement. At the meeting of the Assembly, Premier Herriot summarized the whole issue in a single sentence: "The aggressor is the one which refuses arbitration." In his phrasing, the French word *arbitrage* was used in its wider sense of pacific settlement of disputes. But the French Prime Minister had also definitely in mind the settlement of the reparations problem at the recent London Conference and it was this experience which influenced both M. Herriot and Prime Minister Ramsay MacDonald to accept the definition of aggression in their opening speeches at the Assembly. Mr. MacDonald's advocacy of compulsory arbitration was, however, widely interpreted as having reference to the compulsory jurisdiction of the Court and being therefore not so definitely a problem for the League Assembly as was the more general phrasing of the plan of the Prime Minister of France. In any case, it was M. Herriot's address which was regarded as the keynote speech of the Assembly, on the basis of which it set about shaping a document which would outlaw all aggressive war—the famous Protocol of Geneva.

The 1924 *Protocol for the Pacific Settlement of International Disputes,* to give the document its official title, was first of all an effort to "block the hole in the Covenant," in Section 7 of Article 15. This section reserved the right of the members of the League to go to war if the Council failed to make a unanimous (excluding the disputants) report on the question in dispute. This was a recognition in the Covenant itself that in the last resort war was legitimate as an instrument of national policy. The Protocol therefore denied this ultimate freedom of action, admitting the legitimacy of warlike measures only "in case of resistance to acts of aggression or when acting in agreement with the Council or the Assembly of the League of Nations in accordance with the provisions of the Covenant and of the present Protocol." (Article 2)

In Article 3, it accepted the compulsory jurisdiction of the Permanent Court of International Justice, and then went on, in Article 4, to outline the method of arbitration which would cover all other disputes, ending with this unqualified clause: "Should a State in disregard of the above undertakings resort to war, the sanctions provided for by Article 16 of the Covenant, interpreted in the manner indicated in the present Protocol, shall immediately become applicable to it." There were further provisions for the guidance of the League in such cases but all of these culminated in the ringing declaration of Article 10, which is quoted here in full because it is the high-water mark in the history of the efforts of the League to outlaw war:

ARTICLE 10

Every State which resorts to war in violation of the undertakings contained in the Covenant or in the present Protocol is an aggressor. Violation of the rules laid down for a demilitarized zone shall be held equivalent to resort to war.

In the event of hostilities having broken out, any State shall be presumed to be an aggressor, unless a decision of the Council, which must be taken unanimously, shall otherwise declare:

1. If it has refused to submit the dispute to the procedure of pacific settlement provided by Articles 13 and 15 of the Covenant as amplified by the present Protocol, or to comply with a judicial sentence or arbitral award or with a unanimous recommendation of the Council, or has disregarded a unanimous report of the Council, a judicial

sentence or an arbitral award recognizing that the dispute between it and the other belligerent State arises out of a matter which by international law is solely within the domestic jurisdiction of the latter State; nevertheless, in the last case the State shall only be presumed to be an aggressor if it has not previously submitted the question to the Council or the Assembly, in accordance with Article 11 of the Covenant.

2. If it has violated provisional measures enjoined by the Council for the period while the proceedings are in progress as contemplated by Article 7 of the present Protocol.

Apart from the cases dealt with in paragraphs 1 and 2 of the present Article, if the Council does not at once succeed in determining the aggressor, it shall be bound to enjoin upon the belligerents an armistice, and shall fix the terms, acting, if need be, by a two-thirds majority and shall supervise its execution.

Any belligerent which has refused to accept the armistice or has violated its terms shall be deemed an aggressor.

The Council shall call upon the signatory States to apply forthwith against the aggressor the sanctions provided by Article 11 of the present Protocol, and any signatory State thus called upon shall thereupon be entitled to exercise the rights of a belligerent.

Article 11 of the Protocol modified its iron-clad provision only in the sense of making it more practical. "Those obligations shall be interpreted as obliging each of the signatory States to cooperate loyally and effectively in support of the Covenant of the League of Nations, and in resistance to any act of aggression, in the degree which its geographical position and its particular situation as regards armaments allow." This last phrase was inserted because a nation like Denmark, which at that time was almost wholly unarmed, refused to accept an obligation which would force it to increase armaments contrary to the spirit of the Covenant. With the exception of this modifying clause the Protocol was universal in its application. And on the basis of this particular commitment the Protocol then went on to bind the signatory states "to participate in an International Conference for the reduction of armaments" to which all states should be invited.

By the adoption of this Protocol, the League had taken the final step in creating a system of collective security along the lines which had been consistently upheld by the statesmen of the Continent. Although Germany was not as yet a member of the

League, the theory of the Protocol found wide acceptance there. But calling as it did for participation in preventing war under all circumstances by the acceptance of the definition of aggression, it ran counter to the traditional way of viewing international obligations in English and American political thought. Therefore, when a few months later the MacDonald government was replaced by a Conservative government in Great Britain, the Protocol failed of ratification there. This dealt the fatal blow from which the Protocol and the League never recovered.

English public opinion, however, did not rest satisfied with this negative result and in the early months of 1925 Sir Austen Chamberlain, Secretary of State for Foreign Affairs, was happy to accept the suggestion which came from Germany that a limited guarantee could be given by Great Britain against the outbreak of war between Germany and France, a proposal which was developed out of the earlier Cuno proposal of 1922. This was the starting point for the negotiations which culminated at Locarno, in the month of October, 1925, when the same kind of guarantee was extended around the other frontiers of Germany. It seems to have escaped the notice of the negotiators of Locarno that even in its limited application they fell back upon the definition of aggression. The guarantee was to become operative in case of "flagrant aggression," when either Germany or its neighbors invaded the territory of the neighboring state, and also when either Germany or its neighbors went to war in violation of its given pledge to take the case to the pertinent means of pacific settlement indicated in the Treaty.

The years 1924 and 1925 thus offered to the world two theories of security, one a general guarantee and the other a limited one. Owing to British insistence, it was the limited one which was chosen. For a decade Europe accepted the Locarno settlement as the best that could be achieved, a territorial series of guarantees regionally limited to the frontiers of Germany. Then Hitler proceeded to test its reality by a series of acts which finally led to the second World War. First of all, there was the reoccupation of the Rhineland. Technically, this was a violation of Locarno, but it was not the kind of incident upon which Great Britain, or even

France, was ready to make a determined stand. Then came the *Anschluss* with Austria, and again the signatories of Locarno remained passive. The pathway was now open, however, for the aggression against Czechoslovakia, the humiliation of the Munich appeasement and the triumph of a now dominant militarism in Central Europe. Finally, the guarantors of peace along the frontiers of Germany found themselves obliged to take up the challenge to the peace of Europe after the diplomatic battle had been won by Hitler and the Nazi armies were attacking Poland, beyond the reach of the British or the French.

This tragic history of the failure to maintain a guarantee of universal peace thus brings us to the outbreak of the second World War. England did not go to war for the sake of Poland. It said as much at the time. England went to war to maintain a regime of peace in the world, with law and order and respect for the given word of nations. Had it supported the League and accepted the obligations of the Protocol of Geneva, it would not have found itself in the tragic position of a nation fighting too late for the fundamental principles of a civilized society—too late, that is, to escape the vast and terrible cataclysm which followed.

THE CRISES OF THE LEAGUE

In tracing the history of Continental Europe through the Protocol of Geneva to the outbreak of the second World War, we have had to leave aside for the time being that other pathway to the second World War which opened at Mukden in Manchuria, in 1931. It was the month of September and both Council and Assembly were in session at Geneva. At once the Chinese delegation asked that a commission should be despatched to investigate the situation on the spot. The Japanese Government, at that time composed of liberal elements, opposed the suggestion on the ground that it would further weaken its prestige with its own military leaders, and in this they were supported by the government at Washington which, although not a League member, exercised a real influence at the time. The British also gave support to this point of view. It was not until months passed that the Lytton Commission was finally sent to the Orient at the request of Japan.

But it was too late. Never was there a clearer proof of the fundamental fact that the strategy of peace must be as speedy as that of an army General Staff. Once embarked upon its career of conquest, Japan could not be checked without a major military action which the League members were not prepared to take. Japan's final defiance of the League was the almost inevitable consequence of the policies which the members of the League had pursued at the start.

The problems presented by the civil war in Spain are too many and too complicated to be discussed in full here. Domestic war had never lain within the sphere of League action, except when it threatened the peace of other nations. It is now sufficiently clear that that war was not won by Franco's Spanish faction but by the support which he secured from his Fascist and Nazi allies, and that the republicans themselves were the chief sufferers from the blockade maintained by the British and from American neutrality. Moreover, the weakness and divided counsels of the peace-loving nations were correctly appraised by the Axis powers as signs of the inherent weakness of any regional system of security.

Even earlier, the first to exploit this weakness was Mussolini in his invasion of Ethiopia. Had the League imposed a complete embargo on oil, that invasion would have been checked at the start. But the British argued that American oil firms would in any case supply Italian needs, and therefore Britain should not take the risk of blockade measures of any sort which would result in war with Italy. As a matter of fact, Secretary Hull went very far in his direction of American policy toward the imposition of a sanction against Italy. The full story of that chapter of American history has yet to be written and does not belong here. The main point of our discussion is that without a general system of security, any measures taken only on the haphazard lines of the old diplomacy were doomed to frustration.

From this short survey of the problem of security as revealed in the history of the League of Nations we may conclude that collective security did not fail but that it was never tried.

DISARMAMENT

BY LAURA PUFFER MORGAN

Foreword, by Mary E. Woolley

AGAINST THE BACKGROUND of the warring world today, the General Disarmament Conference of 1932 and 1933 and the years spent in preparation for it may seem like a futile and unrealistic gesture, barren of results.

But the question of the reduction and limitation of armaments cannot be relegated to the category of the unrealistic. It is inescapable that the world of the future must concern itself with this problem, for the alternative would be a world-wide armed camp with the peoples of all countries living under the shadow of catastrophe.

Despite the failure of the General Disarmament Conference, much may be learned from its record. In whatever way the future may be made secure through disarmament, the question of method will have to be settled. If the Disarmament Conference had made no other contribution, it would be invaluable as a source book and a record office. Moreover, however unsuccessful its results, the organization and technique of the Conference were beyond

---

MARY E. WOOLLEY was a member of the United States delegation to the Disarmament Conference of 1932. She was for nearly forty years president of Mount Holyoke College, and her influence has contributed to many of the important social and educational movements of the past fifty years in the United States, among them the United States Peoples Mandate for Inter-American Peace and Co-operation, the Federal Council of Churches, and the Institute of Pacific Relations.

LAURA PUFFER MORGAN, observer and press correspondent to the League of Nations, the London Naval Conferences, and the General Disarmament Conference in Geneva, is a member of the Governing Board of the Geneva Research Center and is editor of a news letter: "The World through Washington" issued monthly by the American University in Washington, D.C., in collaboration with the Institute on World Organization. Mrs. Morgan taught in the University of Nebraska, was later on the Board of Education of the District of Columbia, has for years specialized on disarmament, writing and lecturing extensively on this subject. Her paper is based on material originally written for *World Organization: a Balance Sheet of the First Great Experiment*, published by the American Council on Public Affairs, Washington, D.C.

criticism, and this machinery stands ready for use by the next group to study the problem.

Another contribution of the Conference was the movement for moral disarmament, the "disarming of the mind," which it started by setting up a Committee to study the various aspects of the question and to weigh the two schools of thought, one for restrictive and one for educational methods of achieving moral disarmament, the latter upheld by the majority, including the United States. On this subject, there was close cooperation between the Conference and the International Committee on Intellectual Cooperation, and a beginning was made.

"There is available a high income from the making of honest mistakes," said a wise educator. The "honest mistakes" of the General Disarmament Conference of the thirties, demonstrating that the fault lay, not in the machine, but in the lack of power to run it, offer a high available income which our post-war world can scarcely afford to ignore.

Disarmament

THE PROBLEM of disarmament after the present war will differ in many ways from the situation which faced the Allied and Associated Powers in 1919. Current tendencies were reflected in the remarks of Winston Churchill made to the House of Commons on August 24, 1941, in interpretation of the Atlantic Charter:

> There are, however, two distinct and marked differences in this joint declaration from the attitude adopted by the Allies during the latter part of the last war, and no one should overlook them. The United States and Great Britain do not now assume that there will never be any more war again. On the contrary, we intend to take ample precaution to prevent its renewal in any period we can foresee by effectively disarming the guilty nations while remaining suitably protected ourselves.

It may be assumed, then, that there will be no immediate repetition of the promise that the disarmament of Germany would be followed by a general reduction and limitation of armaments, as was implied in Clemenceau's letter of July 16, 1919, to the

German delegation; in the preamble to Part V of the Treaty of Versailles; and in Article 8 of the League Covenant. On the contrary, a clear distinction will be drawn between the United Nations and the "guilty nations," and, if plans now being put forward in the American Congress are an indication of future trends, Mr. Churchill's phrase "suitably protected" may be regarded as a typical example of British understatement.

The Cairo declaration regarding the treatment of Japan after the victory of the United Nations, and all the official statements from Britain and the United States regarding the treatment of Germany, point to a policy of complete disarmament of the Axis Powers. Should the announced policy of "unconditional surrender" be modified in any respect, all signs seem to indicate that this modification would not permit any measure of rearmament. So far as armaments are concerned, it will be a dictated peace. It will also be unilateral disarmament, enforced for a period of years, perhaps for a generation. While the Atlantic Charter spoke in terms of the disarmament of these nations "pending the establishment of a wider and permanent system of collective security," the ruthlessness of Axis methods since that declaration, has so stiffened the opposition that, after the establishment of the general international organization envisaged by the Moscow Declaration, a considerable period of probation will very probably be demanded in the interests of security, although this cannot be regarded as a permanent solution.

Both the Atlantic Charter and the Moscow Declaration, however, recognize that for the anti-Axis nations—"the peace-loving peoples"—a problem of armaments remains. The Atlantic Charter (Art. 8) envisages "all other practicable measures which will lighten . . . the crushing burden of armaments." The Moscow Declaration pledges on behalf of the four governments

> that they will confer and cooperate with one another and with other members of the United Nations to bring about a practicable general agreement with respect to the regulation of armaments in the post-war period.

This means that two problems of armaments will confront the world after the war: first, the problem of insuring the continued disarmament of the Axis Powers and their satellites; second, the problem of limitation and reduction of armaments of all the others, United Nations and neutrals, without endangering security.

The first will be comparatively simple so long as it is treated on a purely technical basis, for, as will be shown later, the technical problems of disarmament have already been solved. It was political considerations which allowed German rearmament in the last decade, and it was Germany's aggressive intentions, and the speed with which rearmament was accomplished, not the secrecy, which took the world off its guard. This time that danger will be minimized if, in addition to demilitarization, Germany is deprived of her armaments industry. No such step was taken in 1919.

It is the second problem of a general agreement on armaments which will remain to be solved. Practically all military power—land, sea, and air—after this war, will be concentrated in the hands of three, or at most, four great powers, as was not the case after the last war. Post-war agreements on armaments, therefore, may be of two kinds: one between the three great powers which have major responsibility for keeping the peace, the other to include all other members of the United Nations. These two agreements might be incorporated into one instrument.

It may be expected that each of the great powers will assume specific obligations. Areas and functions might be apportioned to them as trustees of the United Nations or of a future international organization, whether it be the League or some similar body. Any reduction or limitation of armaments would be subject to these obligations. Agreements will have to cover not only armaments but naval and air bases. Here some obligations might be assumed by the smaller states. This might be an international police force in embryo.

Probably no substantial reduction in armament can be expected immediately after the war, except as voluntarily carried out by the states, acting individually to lighten budgets. But regulation is necessary, and may be interpreted to cover limitation of armaments, at least qualitative and perhaps quantitative, together with limitation of expenditure. Supervision under an international authority, including inspection on the spot, would be an indispensable condition of such regulation, not only for the Axis Powers but for all states subject to the agreement. Such a general agreement could be concluded even before the cessation of hostilities. Eventually, as confidence is restored, limitation of armaments should be followed by reduction, until equality of rights in a system of security for all becomes possible.

Without discussing the question of an international army or air force, which may be regarded as the fundamental solution of the problem raised by national armaments, it should be pointed out that either would involve, as a preliminary step, the total or partial disarmament of national forces.

There is still another way in which the post-war problem of armaments will not repeat that of 1919. It is now generally recognized, as it was not after the last war, that the problem is not primarily technical but fundamentally political. Disarmament—the objective of the peace movement since its early beginnings—has been a history of failures, due to the attempt to isolate the problem of armaments and treat it technically without regard to the political background. In other words, governments will not get rid of their armaments until they are convinced that they will not be obliged to use them in defense against aggression, or in order to secure release from a position of injustice regarded as insupportable. Today the recognition of this fact is reflected in the acceptance, as expressed in the Connally Resolution, of the principle of "international authority with power to prevent aggression and to preserve the peace of the world."

This is merely the logical conclusion to be drawn from experience. The record of the various attempts made by governments to meet the problem shows that in no case was agreement on reduction or limitation of armaments reached without a previous political agreement. The first Hague Peace Conference, called to put a stop to the dangerous race in armaments and convened on May 18, 1899, succeeded only in formulating the rules of war. The second Hague Conference (1907) made no progress in disarmament, and the third, planned for 1915, never took place.

President Wilson's Fourteen Points again pointed out the necessity for reduction of armaments. In his campaign for the League in 1919 and 1920, he explicitly recognized the connection between armaments and their alternative—an international organization to prevent aggression and do away with war. "The United States must either join the League," he said, "or build the biggest navy in the world." The United States did not join the League, and when the naval bill for that year was introduced in the House of Representatives, it called for appropriation of an unprecedented sum.

Mr. Wilson's reasoning was not grasped by the legislators. Under the leadership of Senator Lodge, the Republicans repudiated the League, and then, led by Senator Borah, espoused the cause of disarmament. Meantime, it is true, a naval race had developed, joined by the three great naval powers, which produced a dangerous political situation between the United States and Japan. The Washington Naval Conference checked the arms race, effected a tremendous saving in naval expenditures, established the principle of parity between the United States and the British Empire, and changed the atmosphere in Japan almost overnight. But it is useful to remember that, although this Conference was backed by a tremendous movement of the peace forces of the country, unaware of all the political implications, it was, in its inception, the Republican answer to Woodrow Wilson and the supporters of the League of Nations. The League had already taken its first steps to deal with disarmament, but no reference was made to these, nor was there any offer of cooperation—this in spite of the fact that eight of the nine participants in the Washington Conference were members of the League.

In fact, because of American nonmembership in the League and refusal, in the early days, to cooperate with it, the world's disarmament efforts were forced to follow two different channels: The first, the series of naval conferences, Washington, Coolidge, and London, initiated primarily by the United States on a ship for ship, gun for gun basis until it was forced to abandon that method; and the other, the League system, based predominantly on the organization of peace and collective security, from which disarmament would naturally flow as a consequence.

The Washington Naval Conference, the first step in the American approach, which convened on November 11, 1921, and resulted in the Washington Treaty of February 6, 1922, stands to date as the only really successful effort in the specific field of limiting and reducing armaments. But the method adopted, instead of being the model of disarmament which it has long been considered, was actually of limited application, the armaments results were temporary, and the political results at least doubtful. The limitation applied only to the largest categories of ships—capital ships and aircraft carriers; moreover this accord would not have been reached had there not been a prior political agreement on the area in which competition in this particular type of ship existed. The Four-Power Pact, together with the Nine-Power Pact, provided the political background without which the Five-Power Naval Treaty would not have been ratified by the United States Senate. In fact, negotiations on the naval agreement were held up for several weeks until the terms of the Four-Power Pact were publicly announced. This Pact, the first achievement of the Conference, provided for the termination of the Anglo-Japanese Alliance declared by Senator Lodge to be "necessary to the successful conclusion of the naval treaty." By way of compensation to Japan, it also virtually pledged the British Empire and the United States not to intervene jointly in the Orient (Article I.). Furthermore, the agreement on the part of the British Empire and the United States not to increase their fortifications or naval bases in Hong Kong, Guam, or the Philippines, contained in the Naval Treaty itself (Article XIX), was the condition demanded by Japan for accepting its naval inferiority in the ratio 5:3. These two provisions were intended to render it impossible for either the United States or Japan to make war against the other in its own waters, that is, to commit an act of aggression.

Finally, the Nine-Power Treaty, promising to respect the sovereignty, independence, and integrity of China as well as the principle of the open door, was an attempt to stabilize conditions in the Far East and thus to deal with the political causes of the tension between the United States and Japan, reflected in the naval race between the two countries. But no provision was made for regular consultation or conference, or for collective defense, only for "full and frank communication" (Article VII). Consequently on the one occasion when the treaty was invoked, at Brussels, November, 1937, lack of provisions for its enforcement resulted in a conference without issue. In spite, therefore, of the immediate beneficial effects of the Washington Naval Treaty, its ultimate result was to give Japan a position of supremacy in the Far East, of which she has subsequently taken advantage.

The Geneva Naval Conference of 1927, the second step in the American program, was called by President Coolidge to extend the Washington limitation to the smaller categories—cruisers, destroyers, and submarines—in which a new naval race had already developed between the British and American navies, as well as between the French and Italian. This conference was a complete failure, partly because France and Italy refused to participate. Both countries were rapidly increasing their navies, France in submarines and Italy in light surface ships. While Britain could not ignore this fact, it meant nothing to the United States. The second cause of failure lay in the differing cruiser needs set forth by the British Admiralty and the American Navy. To satisfy each of these, and at the same time the demands for parity, would have involved a fantastic increase in tonnage of cruisers for both navies. It was on that question that the Conference broke down.

The Geneva Naval Conference is the best possible example of the futility of attempting to isolate disarmament from its political background. The lesson was learned, and after a change of government in both countries, followed by a preliminary agreement between President Hoover and Prime Minister Ramsay MacDonald, a new effort was made.

The London Naval Conference of 1930, the third step in this series, succeeded in extending the quantitative limitation to auxiliary naval craft, but the number of signatories to the resulting treaty was narrowed down to the three great naval powers. France and Italy refused to sign it because it was in these types of ships that they were competing with each other, and their political differences had not been resolved. Italy claimed equality with the French Navy, which the French denied.

If some concession had been made to this political situation, relating especially to colonies in Africa; if, for example, a treaty had been drawn along the line of the Four-Power Pact which made the Washington Naval Treaty possible, providing for consultation and conciliation in case of dispute, the naval difficulties might have been solved. The United States held the key to this situation. In fact, the United States delegation, headed by Secretary Stimson, was prepared to agree to a consultative pact, but at the crucial moment President Hoover withheld, or withdrew, his consent. Ramsay MacDonald was unwilling to guarantee the peace alone, and the Five-Power limitation agreement proved impossible. This left only the British Empire, the United States, and Japan as signatories to the limitation provisions of the new treaty (Part III).

The other parts of the treaty, which were signed by all the powers, were not without value. These included limits in tonnage and gun caliber for individual ships, later known as qualitative limitation, and an agreement upon the method of limitation of navies, a more important technical achievement than appears on the surface. Furthermore, the definitions and rules covering countless technical details were later accepted as standard by the General Disarmament Conference at Geneva and were incorporated into the draft disarmament convention.

It was anticipated at the London Naval Conference of 1930 that before the Washington and London naval treaties expired in 1936, they would be supplanted by a general disarmament convention, but, in default of this, the parties agreed (Article XXIII) to meet again in 1935 to conclude a new treaty. This was the fourth and last step under the American approach. The Second London Naval Conference convened in December, 1935. By this time, however, Japan had violated the Nine-Power Treaty and had been declared an aggressor by the League of Nations. As she obviously intended to continue her war policies, there was no longer a political basis for a naval agreement. Under these circumstances, when Japan demanded equality with the other naval powers, presumably to be reached by scrapping on their part, she was met by refusal. Accordingly, she denounced the earlier treaties and refused to be a party to the London Naval Treaty of 1936. This treaty was then signed by France, the United States, the British Empire, India, Australia, Canada, and New Zealand. As a consequence of the Japanese withdrawal and denunciation of earlier obligations to restrict her naval building, the new treaty of 1936 contained no provision for quantitative limitation, but it preserved the principle of naval limitation on a qualitative basis, including the reduction, limitation, and standardization of size of ships and caliber of guns. A valuable new provision, however, was the agreement to give advance notification of annual building programs. The two previous treaties had provided for an exchange of information after building, but the principle of advance notice was new, and was considered very important, tending to reduce suspicion and uncertainty among governments.

With the idea that a new method of naval limitation had been found which might prove acceptable to all countries, the London Treaty of 1936 was communicated to all League members through the Secretary General. The adherence of Germany, Soviet Russia, and Italy was secured through bilateral agreements concluded with the British Government, the first two coming into force in 1937, while Italy adhered in 1938. With the outbreak of war the obligations under the treaty were suspended by all the signatory powers and it expired in 1942. Thus, nothing more remains of the naval limitations save Part IV of the 1930 treaty restricting the use of submarines, which is still legally binding on forty-seven states.

These efforts toward naval disarmament were carried on outside the League and parallel to the League steps toward general disarmament. Within the League itself, there was a general recognition, from the outset, of the obligation of the great powers to reduce their armaments in accordance with Article 8 of the Covenant. To meet this obligation, the Council in May, 1920, appointed a Permanent Advisory Commission of technical experts. The First Assembly, however, meeting in September, 1920, viewing disarmament as more than a technical question, provided for the Temporary Mixed Commission, composed of accepted authorities on the political, social, and economic as well as the military aspects of the question.

Recognizing that governments would not reduce their armaments without a guarantee against aggression, this new Commission tackled the political end of the problem first. In 1923 it brought to the Assembly a Draft Treaty of Mutual Assistance, to come into effect after a disarmament treaty had been accepted. Adopting the principle that security and disarmament must proceed hand in hand, the draft denounced "aggressive action as an international crime," which the parties to the treaty would agree not to commit; they would moreover furnish assistance to any party which became the victim of an attack, provided it had conformed to the disarmament provisions of the treaty. The draft combined a general system of collective security with supplementary regional pacts; for example, no signatory would be required to cooperate in military action except in the continent where its own territory was situated. There followed certain disarmament clauses:

> The scheme of the treaty was to confine the guarantee of assistance to those who disarmed, believing that thereby sufficient inducement to disarm would be given. Certainly it was the view of the authors of the draft that, without an effective guarantee of security, there could be no hope of disarmament and that, without a reduction and limitation of armaments, a guarantee of security was impracticable. I am still of the opinion that these propositions are vital to the solution of the problem of disarmament and, therefore, of peace.[1]

The report and Draft Treaty were adopted by the Assembly and sent to the governments for ratification, but the death blow was administered by the British Government. The first MacDonald government was then in power, with a pacifist, the late Lord Parmoor, in the Foreign Office. Certain other reasons were given officially, but the real reason for the refusal was that Lord Parmoor believed that all international questions could be settled without force. He could not support the promise of military

[1] Viscount Cecil, *A Great Experiment; an Autobiography* (New York, Oxford University Press, 1941), p. 152.

assistance. The next year, 1924, Ramsay MacDonald and Premier Herriot of France took the lead at the Assembly in negotiating the Geneva Protocol, which added arbitration to the conceptions of security and disarmament and attempted to set up a complete system of compulsory arbitration and common action against aggression, all this being conditioned upon disarmament.

Again the Assembly accepted the plan with enthusiasm, but once more the British Government—this time a Conservative government with Sir Austen Chamberlain as Foreign Minister—refused it, principally on the ground of "no commitments in advance." Thus the second attempt to take steps toward disarmament had failed. Sir Austen, however, realized the necessity of coming to some arrangement with Germany and proposed the alternative that special arrangements to meet special needs should be added as a supplement to the League Covenant. With Herr Stresemann he negotiated the Locarno treaties, which came into effect in 1925 and were followed by the entrance of Germany into the League in 1926. This made steps toward disarmament imperative, and the Assembly of 1925 ordered the appointment of the Preparatory Disarmament Commission, which was instructed to prepare for a general conference to meet the next summer. The Commission was composed of representatives of the principal military and naval powers, whether or not they were members of the League, in addition to the states then members of the Council, and included the United States and Soviet Russia as well as Germany.

Baffled by both political and technical obstacles, the Commission made little progress until the London Naval Conference of 1930 had settled the Franco-British controversy over the method of naval limitation. France wanted a "global" or over-all limit, while Britain insisted upon limitation by categories of ships. In London a compromise was found which combined both methods. This released the deadlock in Geneva and permitted the Council to fix the date for the disarmament conference.

Meantime, however, there was beginning to be a tendency to forget that this was to be primarily a political conference, one of a chain of steps toward liquidating the last war. In addition to the German demand that the Allies should honor their promises, the peoples of every country were clamoring for relief from the danger of overgrown armaments and the burden of military expenditures. The record of the whole first session of the General Disarmament Conference, ending in the resolution of July 23, 1932, is a history of the attempt to skate over underlying political issues, and to solve disarmament by technical means.

Germany would not sign a treaty without equality of treatment, that is, without abrogation of the disarmament clauses of Versailles and without a promise of ultimate equality in armaments, either by reduction or rearmament. France would not agree to equality without some compensation in political security, such as watertight guarantees or other safeguards against German aggression. These it was impossible to secure until it is too late.

Moreover, the General Disarmament Conference opened on February 2, 1932, to the accompaniment of the bombardment of Shanghai. The fact that Japan had been allowed to proceed with her aggression in China shattered confidence in the whole peace system, a confidence vital to any agreement for the reduction of armaments. The French thereupon made even more insistent demands for security, although France herself had failed to live up to her obligations to the League with respect to Japanese aggression as well as in other matters.

Nevertheless, the picture of the General Disarmament Conference which the cynical press has made popular—a gathering of diplomats with tongue in cheek seeking to deceive the people with fine words but really blocking all efforts for disarmament—is quite false. It was rather an assemblage of diplomats seeking disarmament without undue loss of political advantage for themselves or of security for their country. Where it would entail such loss, compensation was demanded. It came down to a problem of bargaining between those who demanded certain compensation for disarmament, and those who were unwilling to pay the price—specifically, between France, which demanded certain guarantees of security, and Great Britain and the United States, which were unwilling to pay the price.

An equally wrong conception of the Disarmament Conference is that it was doomed from the outset to failure. On several occasions agreement seemed near but the opportunity was missed. One of these was the introduction on June 22, 1932, of the Hoover plan proposing the abolition of aggressive weapons, with a resulting reduction in armaments by approximately one third. For a time hopes ran high, but the Hoover plan proposed disarmament without paying the price. It left questions of security for subsequent treatment. In consequence, the French refused to recognize the German demand, which at the outset had been a demand for reduction by the heavily armed powers but had now become a claim for equality. Thereupon Germany refused to participate further in the Conference until this demand should be faced.

Attention now of necessity became focused upon the real issue. In the fall of 1932, a new start was made, with the result that the Declaration of the Five Powers, accepting the principle of equality in a system which should give security to all, was signed on December 11, 1932. But in the attempt to translate principle into practice, the same maneuvering under the guise of technical questions went on. It was then that Salvador de Madariaga said: "There are no technical questions. They are only political questions in uniform." By this time Hitler had been made chancellor and the political situation had become correspondingly worse.

The real hope of success came with the announcement by Mr. Norman Davis, head of the American Delegation, in May, 1933, that President Roosevelt was willing to agree to consultation in the event of a breach of the peace, and also not to interfere with any collective action on the part of the other powers, if the United States agreed with their designation of "the aggressor." This was the price the United States was willing to pay for disarmament, and, together with American acceptance of the principle of effective supervision, including local inspection, as part of the disarmament treaty, this satisfied France. Success might have been reached had not progress been interrupted by the World Economic Conference in London. When the delegates gathered again in the week preceding October 14, despite a more tense political situation, hopes of an agreement were never so high. A treaty was actually taking shape, when the attempt to condemn Germany to a probation period of four years before any steps toward equality should be taken led to her final withdrawal from both the General Disarmament Conference and the League.

This did not, however, bring the conference to an end. The gap between France and Germany was being slowly narrowed through private negotiations until the spring of 1934. Then signs of German rearmament led to the French note of April 17, 1934, abruptly breaking off the negotiations. Thereafter Germany's rearmament became open and rapid. On June 8, after ten days of tense discussion, the General Commission decided to continue the Conference, but from that time no attempt was made to discuss the main issues of equality and security, which had been successfully narrowed down to the question of French acceptance of a measure of German rearmament. It was failure by a hair's-breadth. Whereas France had begun by demanding guarantees of assistance—a military alliance with the British Government, at least—under the Daladier government in 1933, it had agreed to accept instead a strict system of supervision and guarantees of the execution of the disarmament treaty, in addition to the American promise of consultation and waiving certain neutrality rights. This agreement, representing the minimum condition for reduction of armaments, is important for the future.

Certain other approaches to the problem of disarmament were made through the Conference which, should reduction fail, may point the way to the next steps after the present war is over. In November, 1934, it was decided, pending the solution of the main political issue, to proceed at once to frame, sign, and put into effect as soon as possible a separate treaty or protocol covering three points—the regulation and control of the manufacture of and trade in arms, publicity on national-defense expenditures, and the establishment of a Permanent Disarmament Commission to follow and supervise the execution of the treaty. At the same time a text covering these points was formally submitted to the Conference by the United States delegation, elaborating a proposal made some months earlier, when it was accepted in principle by the delegates of the chief arms-producing countries.[2] Such a

[2] *Report of Special Committee*, July 23, 1934, League of Nations Documents, Conf.D.C.G. p. 171.

treaty, though a far cry from the General Disarmament Convention envisaged when the Conference opened, would nevertheless constitute a very real step toward the control of armaments. But even that proved impossible of achievement. After two months of intensive work in the winter and spring of 1935, the Special Committee on the Manufacture of and Trade in Armaments adjourned on April 13, having finished only the first reading of that part of the treaty, and leaving many controversial points unsettled.[3]

Except for a meeting of the Bureau (Steering Committee) on May 31, 1937, when an attempt was made to carry forward these special subjects, this was the last act of the Conference. The Disarmament Conference, however, remains technically in existence. The office of president has been vacant since the death of Arthur Henderson, but it could be filled at any time by the Council of the League, and the Conference could be convened without further formalities should the occasion arise.

In spite of its spectacular failure to bring about a general reduction and limitation of armaments, with the political repercussions that are now so familiar, the achievements of the Disarmament Conference should not be underrated. In the first place, it served to clarify the problem and to determine the conditions upon which nations will agree to reduce their armaments, as it proved, in the second place, that with political obstacles removed, the technical problems involved in disarmament could be solved. The Conference actually did solve these problems through its various technical commissions and committees. A statement often made by Mr. Henderson and generally accepted was that the Conference had covered all the technical work necessary for a disarmament convention (in the state of technical development then reached) and that once agreement had been reached on political principles such a convention could be concluded within a comparatively short time.[4]

[3] *Report of Special Committee,* April 13, 1935, League of Nations Documents, Conf.D. p. 168.

[4] A preliminary report on the work of the Conference prepared by the president and published in July, 1936, presents a short chronological record of the proceedings, a summary of its technical work on specific problems, and a general view of the results achieved. Conf.D.171 (1).

Finally, the experience of the Conference showed that international confidence, and especially confidence in the observance of treaties, must be restored before the technical solutions reached by its various committees can be utilized. The problem is one of finding effective guarantees for the execution of a disarmament agreement, and the first essential guarantee is an effective system of supervision and control. This principle, always urged by the French Government, was agreed to only with some reluctance by the other great powers, but it was finally accepted *in toto* by the United States Government and embodied in the proposals submitted to the Conference in 1934. While the British Government was not ready to go so far at that time, later indications showed a change of attitude.

The disarmament of the future, however, will not necessarily be approached along the same lines as in the past. The method of quantitative limitation, at first partially successful in the field of naval armament and envisaged by the Draft Convention drawn up by the Preparation Commission, had become so involved with questions of prestige that it appeared doubtful if it could ever again serve as the basis of any disarmament measures. As Norman Davis, head of the American delegation, said at the London Naval Conference in 1936, quantitative limitation "is not possible without fixing ratios; and . . . except for Great Britain and the United States, none of the parties were willing to be bound any longer by ratios." It is hardly necessary to point out that the prestige of the two great powers was not impaired by parity. The French delegation, however, found quantitative limitations after fourteen years' experience "arbitrary in character, and irritating in their effects."

The method of qualitative limitation—the complete prohibition, as aggressive weapons, of certain types of armaments, such as ships and tanks over a certain caliber, and even certain categories of armaments, such as bombing planes, instruments of chemical warfare, and submarines—seemed at one time more hopeful. It was adopted in principle by the General Disarmament Conference and was, in fact, as has been shown, utilized in the London Treaty of 1936, together with a provision for exchange of information. But this method, if not combined with quantitative limitation, or extended to them specifically, leaves entirely untouched whole fields of deadly weapons—such as the machine gun and the small tank, even if a definition of aggressive weapons could be reached.

A third method, the limitation of national defense expenditure—commonly known as budgetary limitation—was advocated by the French Government at an early stage of the disarmament discussions and agreed to later by the British and other delegations. The United States Government, however, while accepting the principles of both quantitative and qualitative limitation, and indeed going extremely far in both these directions in its proposals to the Conference, was never won over to a limitation of budgets. The main reason alleged for this attitude was that since American wages and prices were on a scale so much higher than those of other countries, a comparison of national expenditures would inevitably be made, to the disadvantage of the United States. As a result, although the National Defense Expenditure Commission had elaborated in all its details a scheme of publicity, supervision, and limitation of budgets and expenses,[5] the Conference unanimously agreed and formally accepted the proposals concerning publicity and supervision, but rejected those concerning limitation.

A fourth method which would lead to eventual reduction could be instituted as a first step before other measures became possible. This is limitation upon acquisition of new armaments by either manufacture or importation. It has been advocated by certain experts as the only practical means by which armaments can be restricted. It is at the "source," either in the manufacturing plants or at the customs barriers, that the supervision and control regarded as a necessary condition for the general acceptance of any disarmament provision, can be made most effective.

Three of these technical questions were embodied in separate protocols that might come into force without waiting for the conclusion of a general convention, following the decision of November, 1934.

[5] League of Nations Documents, Conf.D.C.G. p. 160.

The technique of the system of supervision incorporated in the arms control Protocol was an adaptation of the system for the supervision and control of narcotic drugs through the execution of international treaties which had been developed by the League of Nations over a period of years.[6]

The analogies between the traffic in narcotic drugs and the manufacture of and trade in arms are striking. Armaments, like drugs, have two uses, legitimate and illegitimate—armaments for defense and armaments for offense. Whereas the problem of drug control is to draw a clear-cut line between legitimate and illegitimate traffic, to limit production and manufacture to the amounts required for medical purposes and by strict supervision to prevent products of legitimate manufacture from being diverted to illicit traffic, so the problem of control of armaments is to draw a line between those necessary for defense and those which by their nature or quantity are a threat to world peace, to restrict their manufacture to the types and quantities allowed, and, by the strict application of measures of supervision, to insure the observance of the restrictions adopted.

The international administration of the control of armaments would be entrusted to a Permanent Disarmament Commission, which would operate under the authority of the League of Nations, or whatever world organization is established in its place. As in the case of drugs, the international administration would have to work through national administrations set up in each country. One of the original features of the American plan was that the national governments were made responsible for all manufacture and trade in armaments within their territory, thus paving the way for the necessary supervision by national and international authorities and putting upon the governments themselves the responsibility for dealing with private manufacturers. Supervision would apply to public and private plants alike.

Given agreement upon the measures of limitation to be put into effect, quantitative or qualitative, as already discussed (this includes the prohibition of certain types of arms), the next question

[6] See "Dangerous Drugs," p. 182.

is that of effective supervision. Here the technique already perfected for narcotic drugs may be practically lifted over to armaments. This would include licenses to manufacture; certificates for export, import, and transit; and a system of reports in complete detail from the manufacturer and the exporter to the national governments and from the governments to the Permanent Disarmament Commission, which would watch all the stages of the proceedings. One essential feature of arms supervision, however, which has no counterpart in the drug system is inspection by the international authority on the spot—that is, inspection at the factory or arsenal to insure that the amount of war material being produced is not excessive and that it otherwise conforms to the conditions laid down.

The fact that during the discussions in the Special Committee at the Disarmament Conference at least three of the great powers —the United States, France, and Soviet Russia—accepted this system suggests that it will be put into operation at a future time. The British Government accepted it in principle but not in detail, being unwilling under the conditions prevailing at that time to agree to inspection on the spot, but this is no reason to suppose that agreement would not be reached now. Moreover, the United States showed its good faith and made a practical application of the principle by passing legislation establishing the National Munitions Control Board. This Board put into effect nationally, so far as possible without an international treaty, the provisions of its own proposal.

Such a system of international supervision of both the manufacture and the export of armaments, accompanied by measures of publicity scrupulously followed, would afford the best guarantee against the risk of violation of the treaty or of secret rearmament. It was pointed out to the Special Committee at Geneva by the French delegate that

> Aggressive intentions or a threat of aggression would, in the majority of cases, take the form of increased orders and greater activity in the armaments industry, and it was highly probable that a system of international supervision directed by a permanent commission at

Geneva—a system of permanent automatic supervision based upon both documentary evidence and local investigations—would detect such intentions or threats from their inception.[7]

The intention or threat thus detected could be dealt with at once automatically by technical or diplomatic measures. Should these fail, an embargo against the state guilty of violation, as well as the granting of favors and facilities to the threatened state, are a possibility, even before the danger of war is directly involved.[8]

Here again the drug control system furnishes useful examples of collective action, even of the imposition of embargoes. An embargo on armaments would be fully effective only against a non-manufacturing country, which would hardly plan an act of aggression. But an embargo on certain essential war materials—as, for example, nickel or some other material whose production is geographically limited—might be applied with decisive effect to any country, especially if the production and exportation were internationally controlled, to prevent stocking of supplies in advance.

An example of a treaty providing collective action for granting assistance and facilities to a threatened state is furnished by the Convention on Financial Assistance drawn up under League auspices. It was adopted by the League Assembly and opened for signature on October 2, 1930, but was to come into force subject to two conditions, namely, that at least three governments providing specific assistance should have ratified and that a plan for the reduction of armaments should have come into force. In this form it was signed by thirty states, of which three, Denmark, Finland, and Iran, had ratified it prior to December 31, 1937. This treaty could be put into effect without further formalities, once the necessary conditions have been fulfilled.

The General Convention to Improve the Means of Preventing War is another treaty which, if in force, would be extremely use-

[7] Minutes, Special Committee, Seventeenth Meeting, July 2, 1934, Conf.D.C.G. p. 171.

[8] Such interim measures on a graduated scale are proposed in a memorandum, submitted to the Conference by its Committee on Guarantees of Execution, which analyzes the problem and contains the main outlines of solutions. Conf.D.C.G. p. 170, July 5, 1934.

ful as an interim measure in case of a threat of aggression. This Convention, approved by the Assembly on September 26, 1931, and circulated for ratification by the governments, was signed by twenty-two states. It was subject to the condition that it would come into effect ninety days after the ratification or accession of ten members or non-members of the League, as between these states. Up to December 31, 1937, the Convention had received four ratifications—Netherlands, Nicaragua, Norway, and Peru—and nineteen signatures subject to ratification.

The Convention provides for conservatory measures of a non-military nature to be prescribed by the Council, for example, withdrawal of forces to a fixed line or evacuation of a demilitarized zone or the territory of the other party. The parties undertake to carry out without delay the measures so prescribed and any violation of them resulting in war is then regarded as calling for collective action. This Convention would have been directly applicable to the Manchurian case. Had it been in effect then it would have altered radically the legal position and might have changed the whole course of events.

Certain other treaties providing for demilitarized zones concluded by the League and dependent upon the League for their execution should be considered in connection with disarmament. The first is the Convention Relating to the Non-Fortification and Neutralization of the Aaland Islands, signed at Geneva, October 20, 1921. The purpose of the convention is to guarantee that these islands may never become a source of military danger. The League of Nations is given the task of assuring the execution of the treaty.

The Regime of the Straits of the Dardanelles, demilitarized under the Treaty of Lausanne, was modified by the Montreux Convention and a Protocol was signed July 30, 1936, the principle of freedom of transit and navigation being, however, reaffirmed. Under the new treaty the Turkish Government is given the right to supervise the execution of the convention but must render an annual report to the League. The convention is to remain in force twenty years.

The territories subject to the mandate system are also demilitarized. Article 22, paragraphs 5 and 6, of the Covenant provide for the "B" and "C" mandates that the mandatory power must be responsible for the prohibition of the arms traffic, prevention of the establishment of fortifications or military and naval bases, and of military training of the natives for other than police purposes and the defense of territory. Paragraph 7 provides that the mandatory shall render an annual report to the League Council on the territory under its charge.

The obvious violation of the mandate restrictions by Japan in the Pacific Islands was brought to the attention of the Permanent Mandates Commission in 1939, reported to the Council, and discussed, but without further action. This is another instance of the political situation's preventing appropriate action. In this case action would have proved extremely difficult without the cooperation of the United States, which was then bound by the Neutrality Act.

If these zones and territories are to remain subject to the restriction of demilitarization in the future, some method must be found of continuing the supervision exercised by the League and authorized by the conventions, or a new machinery must be established.

THE WORLD COURT

BY MANLEY O. HUDSON

THE ESTABLISHMENT of the Permanent Court of International Justice may go down in history as a great turning point in international relations. It represented the triumph of a whole generation of earnest and intelligent effort and it brought to realization ideas which had been stirring in men's minds for centuries.

In the course of the nineteenth century, remarkable progress had been made in the arbitration of international disputes. The success of the Alabama Claims Arbitration between the United States and Great Britain in 1872 was a landmark in that development and it compelled responsible statesmen to take serious notice of a movement which they had previously been disposed to ignore. Numerous arbitration treaties were concluded in the ensuing years, and at the close of the century, a Peace Conference at The Hague took up the task of facilitating and systematizing various methods of pacific settlement.

The Permanent Court of Arbitration, created in 1899, has served as the foundation stone of a new structure. It is not in reality a *court*, nor does it justify what is implied in the descriptive term *permanent*. Instead, it is a panel from which arbitrators may be chosen to constitute tribunals as they may be needed for the arbitration of particular disputes. As each of more than forty states may appoint four members of the panel, about one hundred

---

MANLEY O. HUDSON has been a Judge of the Permanent Court of International Justice since 1936. He is also a member of the Permanent Court of Arbitration and has long been the Bemis Professor of International Law at the Harvard Law School. Born in Missouri, he had a varied legal experience in the United States, serving at one time as secretary of the National Conference of Commissioners on Uniform State Laws. After the Paris Peace Conference, where he was attached to the American Commission to Negotiate Peace, he entered the legal section of the Secretariat of the League of Nations and was the legal adviser to the International Labor Conferences of 1919, 1920, and 1924. His numerous publications include International Legislation World Court Reports, and a recent treatise on the Court. For each of the past twenty-two years, he has published an annual article on the Court in the *American Journal of International Law.*

and fifty men are usually listed as members. In forty-five years men have been selected from the panel to constitute nineteen tribunals, which have dealt with twenty-one cases. The Permanent Court of Arbitration survived the World War of 1914, and it may survive the present war.

Useful as it has been, the Permanent Court of Arbitration falls short of supplying the world with a really permanent judicial institution. This was appreciated even when it was launched, and in 1907 a second Peace Conference at The Hague endeavored to create, by its side, a true court of arbitral justice. That effort failed. It failed chiefly because the more powerful states insisted on being represented on the bench and the less powerful states sought to maintain equality in their position. The world came to 1914, therefore, with no advance beyond the Permanent Court of Arbitration, but the struggle of those four years produced a determination to begin the effort anew.

The Covenant of the League of Nations called for the establishment of a Permanent Court of International Justice, and in February, 1920, the first decision taken by the Council of the League was directed to preparation for the drafting of a statute under which the Court might be organized. A committee of eminent jurists labored through many months to elaborate a draft. To escape from the *impasse* of 1907, the Committee took account of the existence of an Assembly in which all members of the League were to be represented and of a Council in which the more powerful states were to have permanent seats, and proposed that judges of the new Court should be elected by these bodies. The Committee's draft was debated at length in the Council and Assembly of the League, and on December 16, 1920, a protocol with the Court's Statute annexed was opened to signature.

It is one thing to launch a satisfactory plan for an international institution; it is another thing, however, to get that plan adopted. The Statute of the Court did not project itself; governments had to proceed to give it life. Some governments acted promptly, so that the Statute was brought into force within eight months. Other governments permitted themselves to delay, usually for reasons unconnected with the merits of the Statute, for its provisions became the subject of protracted debate only in the United States of America. In the course of twenty years, the Court protocol was signed by fifty-nine states, and fifty-one of them proceeded to its ratification. The result was to give the Court a broad base, to justify its description as a World Court.

On the whole, the 1920 Statute worked with general satisfaction; the amendments which were drawn up in 1929, and brought into force in 1936, effected relatively unimportant changes. It brought into being a viable, a living institution which functioned with surprising success down to February, 1940, when a hiatus was imposed upon it by the conflict which has engulfed the world.

The Court consists of fifteen judges—formerly it consisted of eleven judges and four deputy-judges—who are elected for nine-year terms. They must be of different nationalities. General elections of the whole bench were held in 1921 and 1930, but a general election due in 1939 was postponed because of the war. In addition nine by-elections have been held to fill vacancies. In later years, states not members of the League of Nations but parties to the Court Statute participated, with the Assembly and Council, in the process of election. Despite the forebodings of earlier years, that process worked smoothly. There were no untoward incidents. Of course, it was not giant supermen who were selected. Yet the working of the system supplied the Court at all times with a bench which, on the whole, was outstanding in both competence and prestige, which united many varieties of experience, and which had no local complexion. If one may question the outstanding superiority of some of the judges, many others had world-wide reputations as leaders in international law.

The great advance was made in getting away completely from the idea of government representation. The candidates whose names were on the ballot in the elections were nominated not by governments but by national groups in the older Permanent Court of Arbitration, and in consequence the electors' failure to support a particular candidate could not have the appearance of a disregard of the wishes of the government of which he was a national. Within this system, however, there was some room for informal understanding as to the number of judges to be selected from various parts of the world; in 1930 Latin American states procured the election of three judges from Latin America, and in 1939 they were disposed to seek a greater number. The Islamic states also united in 1939 to request the election of a judge trained in Islamic law.

Only the rudiments of the Court's procedure were prescribed in the Statute, and it proved to be a wise course to leave the elaboration of rules of procedure to the Court itself. The judges bestowed great care upon the rules which they adopted, and the rules of 1922 were revised in 1926, in 1931, and in 1936. In retrospect, one must say that it is remarkable that these rules produced such general satisfaction to litigant states. Almost no serious criticism was ever made of them, except by the judges themselves, and the criticism within the Court has been revealed to the interested public by the publication of the complete minutes at sessions devoted to the rule-making function.

The jurisdiction possessed by the Court derives from various sources. The Covenant envisaged a Court "competent to hear and determine any dispute of an international character which the parties thereto submit to it"; four classes of disputes were declared to be "generally suitable" for submission to arbitration or judicial settlement, but neither the Covenant nor the Statute purported to require their submission to the Court. The proposals made by the 1920 Committee of Jurists would have given the Court a wide measure of compulsory jurisdiction, but many states were not then prepared to go so far. Hence the Statute provided for optional declarations by states, conferring on the Court compulsory jurisdiction over any or all of the four classes of disputes described in the Covenant. For a time few such declarations were forthcoming, but by 1928 a general movement in this direction was under way, and eventually declarations, on varying terms and in many cases for limited periods, were brought into force by forty-seven states. The declarations of twenty-nine of these states are still in force.

Quite as important as a source of the jurisdiction of the Court are the many treaties concluded during the past twenty years.

Some are treaties of pacific settlement, entered into for this express purpose; for example, twenty-three states bound themselves by the Geneva General Act of 1928. Others are treaties relating to a variety of subjects, containing provisions for resort to the Court in event of a dispute as to their interpretation or application. Most of these treaties have not been suspended by the war, and indeed some of them have been negotiated during the war. Some four hundred treaties have been concluded which in one way or another relate to the Court's functioning. With all of this development, one may say that the Court has been given a central place in the vast structure of the world's treaty law. Almost all of the states of the world conferred some jurisdiction on the Court—all except a few inactive states like Nepal and Saudi Arabia and diminutive states like San Marino and Vatican City.

The Court has power, also, to give advisory opinions at the request of the Assembly or Council of the League of Nations. It does not serve the function of an ordinary legal adviser to those bodies, for the Court has exercised its power only within the strict limitations of judicial process. Indeed it has gone very far, some people think too far, toward assimilating advisory to contentious proceedings.

Only states may be parties before the Court. Individuals, private companies, even international organizations are excluded. This is in line with the conception of the Court as an organ of international law which applies, primarily at any rate, to the relations of states. Throughout its jurisprudence, the Court has insisted that the consent of a state is essential to the Court's having jurisdiction over it, but that consent may be manifested in various ways. Two states may by special agreement submit a particular case for the Court's judgment; or if all the parties to a dispute are subject to the compulsory jurisdiction, one party may initiate a proceeding by application.

When the Court was first organized, the opinion prevailed in some quarters that it would have little to do; but the record of eighteen years did not vindicate this anticipation. In that period, sixty-five cases came before the Court. It handed down thirty-two judgments, twenty-seven advisory opinions, and several hundred orders. A full record of each proceeding is published, so that the whole world has been kept apprised of what the Court was doing as it was being done.

The contentious proceedings before the Court have related to a wide variety of cases, in fact they run almost the whole gamut of international law. Each of them was important to the states immediately concerned, while some of them possessed a general interest. In some cases, the matters involved related to questions of national honor and vital interest—the type of question which earlier treaties excepted from the obligation to arbitrate. A passing reference to some of the cases will illustrate their range.

In its first judgment in 1923 the Court gave an interpretation of provisions in the Treaty of Versailles concerning Germany's obligations with respect to the freedom of the Kiel Canal. In the *Lotus Case* between France and Turkey, the Court pronounced upon the jurisdiction of Turkish courts to take cognizance of crimes committed on the high seas, in connection with a collision between French and Turkish vessels.

In the *Free Zones Case*, between France and Switzerland, the Court upheld Switzerland's contention that France was still bound to maintain the zones around Geneva which were established under treaties going back to 1815 and before. A territorial dispute of first magnitude was carried to the Court by Denmark and Norway when a threatening situation arose out of their conflicting claims to East Greenland; an enormous documentation was submitted, and the oral arguments in the case consumed the time of the Court during fifty-seven half-day sessions. In the *Meuse Case* between Belgium and the Netherlands, the Court construed a treaty of 1863 to find that neither party could complain of the other party's diversion of water from the Meuse River. In the case relating to *Phosphates in Morocco*, the Court found that France was not subject to the compulsory jurisdiction which Italy was invoking.

Some of the advisory proceedings before the Court were as important as the cases presented for judgment. In a case relating to certain *Nationality Decrees in Tunis and Morocco*, France and Great Britain had asked the Council to request an opinion because their negotiations had been bogged down by the French insistence that the dispute related to a domestic question. In the *Eastern Carelia* dispute between Finland and the Soviet Union, the Court declined to give the opinion requested. In several cases—the *Jaworzina* dispute between Czechoslovakia and Poland, the *St. Naoum Boundary* dispute between Albania and Jugoslavia, and the *Mosul* dispute between Great Britain and Turkey—phases of territorial disputes came before the Court, and in each of them its opinion aided in the settlement of the dispute. In a number of cases the question related to the functioning of international organizations, particularly the International Labor Organization. The Court's opinion in the *Austro-German Customs Regime Case*, given by a bare majority, provoked a wide discussion, but later events may be thought to have vindicated the result which was reached.

The judgments and opinions given by the Court led to the settlement of a large number of disputes. None of them was flouted; in no case was challenge offered to the Court's authority. No one can say that any of the disputes might otherwise have led to armed conflict, yet some of them at any rate might have proved disturbing if they had been permitted to simmer. By its advisory opinions, the Court was also able to facilitate the working of other international institutions. Its jurisprudence now assumes a prominent place in the corpus of materials of international law, and its influence has greatly encouraged the development of the law concerning pacific settlement. The world over, the contribution of the Court has been acclaimed by the legal profession, and from the general public there has been only that measure of criticism which any public institution must expect.

On this record, it may be said that the Court has earned its salt, and quite clearly it must be continued in the future. Fortunately this conclusion is shared by the various governments which are now giving intensive study to the problem. With the creation of a "general international organization" as an effective agency "for the maintenance of international peace and security," as promised in the Moscow Declaration, a new prospect will open for the usefulness of the existing Permanent Court of International Justice.

The reanimation of the Court will require that attention be given to a number of difficult problems.

It is essential, first of all, that the great progress which has been achieved should be preserved. The Court now exists, under a Statute which has proved to be quite satisfactory. More than fifty states have accepted that Statute, and other states may accept it. This is a great advantage. The work of a generation does not need to be repeated. Of course, some improvements could be made in the Statute, but none of them is urgently needed, and the advantage of effecting them would not outweigh the disadvantage of sacrificing achieved gains.

The Court's Statute does not need to be redrafted, but it may have to be adapted, however, to the new situation which will exist at the end of the war. In many ways the Court is linked to the League of Nations. The "general international organization" of the future, which may supersede and succeed the League of Nations, may make some departures. It may differ from the League in both function and structure. If this is to be the case, practical problems will arise in the continuation of the Court and they should be faced at the outset.

The chief of these problems relates to the election of the judges. The Court now has twelve judges, whose normal terms expired at the end of 1939 but who continue in office, under a provision in the Statute, until the selection of their successors. Some of them have served continuously since 1922, having been reelected in 1930; some are advanced in years. Even if the Court were activated with its present bench, a new election cannot be long postponed, and the method of conducting it may require attention immediately at the close of the war. If the Assembly and Council of the League of Nations, with the participation of other states parties to the Statute, are available for this purpose, the problem will be simple; otherwise, substitute agencies must be devised.

It would seem desirable to continue to entrust the nomination of candidates to the national groups in the Permanent Court of Arbitration. If the Assembly and Council are not available as electoral bodies, similar bodies in the General Organization, or a body similar to the Assembly, should discharge the function of election. Or an *ad hoc* conference of states' representatives could be relied upon. A mere voting by foreign offices, by mail, should be avoided, for it would lose the advantage of consultation.

A second problem will relate to supplying funds for meeting the expenses of the Court. In normal years these expenses have ranged around $650,000. They cover the salaries of the judges and of the Registrar and his staff, the rent of the premises maintained in the Peace Palace at The Hague, and the costs of administration and of publications. Funds were supplied to the Court by the League of Nations—a total of about $10,000,000 in eighteen years. Each state which was a member of the League of Nations was bound to contribute, whether or not it was a party to the Court's Statute; and on several occasions contributions were made by states which though parties to the Statute, were no longer members of the League. In this way, from 1922 to 1940, the Court was never lacking in funds for meeting its expenses. Its budget, framed by the Court itself, was alimented by the League, the proportion of states' contributions being determined by the League and the collection of the contributions being made by League officials. The system worked well, and without the slightest impairment of the Court's judicial independence.

If such assistance by the League should no longer be available to the Court, some other way must be found to meet its financial needs. The expenses of the Permanent Court of Arbitration, recently about $40,000 a year, have been met by the Netherlands Government, subject to reimbursement by the states parties to one or both of The Hague Conventions, according to the proportions fixed for the International Bureau of the Universal Postal Union. That system would not suffice, however, for the much larger budget of the Permanent Court of International Justice. Allocation, collection, and management of funds of such magnitude present difficult problems which require continuous attention. The Court might be given its own financial administration, but it should be spared that responsibility. No one state should have charge of its finances, and if the League should be no longer available, it seems desirable that the General International Organization should take over the functions which it has performed in supplying the Court with the needed funds.

Other problems would arise, also, which might necessitate the adapting of the Court's Statute; particularly, the problem of the source of requests for advisory opinions. If contact with the Assembly and Council of the League was no longer possible, power to make such requests should be lodged elsewhere, preferably in organs of the General International Organization.

The task of making it possible for the present Court to resume its useful activities under the existing Statute should present no insuperable difficulties. It should be approached with appreciation of the supreme importance of continuity in judicial organization and with a desire to preserve what has been gained by generations of fruitful effort. Neither the Court's Statute, to which many states are now parties, nor the hundreds of treaties now in force which refer to the Court need be sacrificed. It is not necessary to make a fresh start, and it is not desirable to reopen old controversies for which reasonably satisfactory solutions have been found.

The "reestablishment of law and order," forecast by the Moscow Declaration of October 30, 1943, is not merely an ultimate goal. With the close of the war, it will become an urgent and immediate need. A world conflict carries in its wake vast possibilities of interstate disputes, and, freed from the present travail, the world will yearn for a speedy return to justice according to law. Restored to its normal role, the Court can serve as a powerful agency for the reestablishment of law and for engendering confidence in orderly methods.

If we are to advance in this century toward an organized world, if we are to engage in a serious effort to safeguard peace and security for the generations to come, the preservation of the Permanent Court of International Justice must be one of our principal objectives. Yet such an institution cannot be our sole reliance. Many things will need to be done which a court, operating within the limitations of the judicial process, cannot do. Legislative agencies will be needed, also, and other agencies and methods of adjustment. Too much should not be expected of judges on the bench. The chief responsibility for the maintenance of peace must rest with statesmen, not with judges. The statesmen's task can be made easier, however, and the success of their efforts can be better assured if a court is at hand, open to all the states of the world, ready to declare the law applicable to any dispute that may be brought before it, encouraging through wise judgements the development of international law, and serving as a stabilizing influence in an ever-changing world.

INTERNATIONAL CIVIL SERVICE

The Secretariat of the League of Nations

BY FRANK G. BOUDREAU

EXPERIENCE TEACHES that success in international cooperation depends to a considerable extent upon the method of organization. It is clear that the kind and degree of international cooperation needed in the modern world cannot be assured by diplomatic negotiations carried on by correspondence or cable between national foreign offices. Responsible statesmen must meet face to face, as they have been doing for years whenever serious problems require solution by international agreement. And they must also bring together experts in the different questions at issue, to advise the delegates and to counsel together. But such conferences are only the beginnings of international cooperation. They provide the necessary authority for action but there must also be ways and means of preparing the ground and of implementing the decisions. From 1851 until 1907 international sanitary conferences were held nearly every four years in Europe, but no real agreements were reached nor was the march of epidemics prevented until a permanent international organization was set up to prepare the work of the conferences and to carry out the conferences' agreements and decisions.

Preparation for councils or assemblies of responsible statesmen calls for the services of authorities or experts in the questions at issue. For example, if the subject is prevention of the interstate

---

FRANK G. BOUDREAU has for many years specialized in epidemiology and public health. He was a medical officer in the United States Army during the first World War, and in that capacity spent nearly two years abroad. In 1925 he was appointed to the Health Organization of the League of Nations in Geneva, acting successively as epidemiologist-statistician, chief of the Bureau of Epidemiological Intelligence and Public Health Statistics, and medical director. In 1937 he returned to this country to become executive director of the Milbank Memorial Fund, a position he now holds. He is also chairman of the Food and Nutrition Board of the National Research Council and has taken part in the international conferences held at Hot Springs and Atlantic City, on food, agriculture, and relief.

spread of disease, which involves shipping, the views of authorities in transport as well as in health and medicine are needed. Statesmen will consult with their national health and shipping authorities, who will study the problem from the standpoint of their own countries. But national authorities will not see the problem from the point of view which is of first importance internationally: that the interests of the whole are greater than those of any of its parts. Hence in addition to national experts there must be committees of experts acting as such, not representative of governments but of the subject itself; speaking not for any country, but in behalf of the whole community of nations. Failing this, international cooperation in technical fields will never advance very far. For it is essential to have an unbiased report on the ultimate possibilities of international cooperation in a given field and then attempt to advance as far as national conditions, interests, and prejudices will permit.

Meetings of experts need just as careful preparation and guidance as any others. Experts seldom adopt an international point of view without guidance. Their discussions must be properly oriented. This is the task of the third essential element in the organization of international cooperation; the secretariat or international civil service.

Visitors to Geneva frequently remarked upon the efficiency of the Secretariat of the League of Nations. Those who were familiar with the difficulties in international cooperation were loudest in their praise. They saw meetings running smoothly, translation and interpretation rapidly and accurately made, documents multigraphed and distributed without delay, material arrangements so convenient and efficient that they passed almost without notice. What the casual observer failed to see was the dominant influence of the Secretariat in bringing to bear on every question the international point of view. Thoroughly international in outlook and devoted to the ideals and principles of the League of Nations, the Secretariat of the League was a far more potent instrument than the makers of the Covenant had anticipated.

There were secretariats of international organizations before the League of Nations came into existence, for a number of intergovernmental agencies had been set up to deal with such subjects as health and postal matters. But no attempt had been made to organize an international secretariat of the type that was built up by the League of Nations. The Secretariat of the Office International d'Hygiène Publique was wholly French, and that of the Universal Postal Union wholly Swiss. Nor did the Covenant of the League of Nations throw any light on this subject, providing simply that "the Secretariat and staff of the Secretariat shall be appointed by the Secretary General with the approval of the Council." (Article VI.)

There were two possible methods of reorganization: the Secretariat might be composed of national delegations (suggested by Sir Maurice Hankey) or it could be made a real international civil service. Sir Eric Drummond (now the Earl of Perth), the first Secretary General, made the momentous decision "to organize his staff as an international civil service, each official being supposed to act only on the instructions of the Secretary General and in the interest of the League, without regard to the policy of his own government." [1]

"There is hardly any disagreement regarding the wisdom of Sir Eric's momentous decision, and it is extremely unlikely that any future international agency would revert to the system of national representation." [2]

It was probably not the desire of the delegates who drafted the Covenant to confer large powers upon the head of the Secretariat. During the conference the title of chancellor had been suggested, but in the end the name Secretary General was adopted. Mention of the Secretary General in the Covenant is restricted to the following paragraphs:

> The Secretariat shall comprise a Secretary General and such secretaries and staff as may be required.
>
> The Secretariat and staff of the Secretariat shall be appointed by the Secretary General with the approval of the Council.
>
> The Secretary General shall, on the request of any member of the League, forthwith summon a meeting of the Council.

[1] F. P. Walters, *Administrative Problems of International Organization* (London, London University Press, 1941). Barnett House Paper No. 24.

[2] Egon Ranshofen-Wertheimer, "Problems of Postwar Reconstruction," *American Political Science Review*, XXXVII (October, 1943), 872–88.

It is evident that no one expected the Secretary General to play an important role in the high political work of the League. But experience soon showed that he was in a key position, and if he chose to do so might enjoy a prestige and exercise an influence far beyond anything that had been anticipated. He alone of those sitting around the Council table was in a position to work and speak for the community of nations; he could, if he so desired, represent the conscience of mankind in crises in which governments sought to avoid or evade the obligations they had assumed under the Covenant. He could obtain the clearest view of every important problem coming before the League, enlightened on the one hand by the representatives of the contending and neutral powers and on the other by a zealous internationally minded Secretariat. He alone was bound by no instructions of a national government; it was his right and his duty to interpret without prejudice or bias the high principles of the international charter. Statesmen came and went, the Secretary General remained at the center, familiar with the usages and methods of international co-operation, and with a potential grasp of current international events seldom equaled and never surpassed by that of any member of the Council or Assembly. Moreover, in the eyes of representatives of the smaller powers, he could stand for the interests of all states-members of the League, and might, if he would, utilize the authority arising from this belief. However able and powerful, most representatives of governments were novices in international affairs as conducted at Geneva when compared to the Secretary General, who had the opportunity to sit in on the preparation of every item on the agenda, to attend every private meeting, to hear all the discussions, and to take a hand in the drafting of every important report. He could therefore orient every discussion without exceeding his authority, and he could constantly hold up before the national representatives the League view, the international aspect, of every problem. The exercise of such powers depends entirely upon the character and ability of the individual. While the first Secretary General made the momentous decision to organize a real international civil service, a decision which influenced favorably the work of the League for years to come, information now available does not show that in other respects either he or his successor fully lived up to the high potentialities of their key position. Everything went well when the tide was flowing with the League; everything went badly when the tide turned. No one can say whether a more courageous policy on the part of the Secretary General would have led on to fortune. But when such critical hours come to the future general international organization, one may hope that the Secretary General and his staff will utilize to the full the great potentialities of their special knowledge and opportunities.

Two distinct types of official were recruited for the staff of the League at different stages in its existence. In the first years, when no one could foresee how the League would succeed, it appealed to persons imbued with the spirit of adventure. It took courage to give up good positions at home for the unknown abroad. Hence early recruits to the staff possessed the attributes which are commonly found in those of an adventurous disposition. They were devoted more greatly to the cause of the League than to their own advancement; they brought to their work all the energy and enthusiasm of the pioneer, and what some of them may have lacked in training and knowledge they made up for in zeal and devotion. It was fortunate that much excellent material of this type was available in the various interallied agencies then existing.

When the League was at the high tide of its success, a new type of recruit emerged. Service of the League had become an accepted career. It was safe, well paid, and agreeable. So the League began to receive new staff members who lacked the zeal and enthusiasm of the first comers but who made up for this lack to a degree by the excellence of their training and the scope of their technical knowledge.

However, the character of the Secretariat in the second stage was being molded by many other factors. Toward the end age and fatigue had begun to condition the zeal and energy of the first recruits. Some governments which had looked with favor upon the League when there seemed no danger that it would interfere with their national policies, began to regard it as a potential enemy. Most serious of all, the integrity of the international civil service was threatened by the slow infiltration into its ranks (against the protests of the Secretary General) of officials who held the interests of their countries above those of the League and who boldly acted upon the instructions of their governments.

The Secretariat was of course never wholly international, never wholly national. But the rule in the beginning that the staff owed primary allegiance to the League was toward the end so weakened that a more cynical attitude began to appear among the staff.

The experience of the League Secretariat teaches one lesson which should be cherished by all future international organizations: that there *is* such a thing as international loyalty, and that this is indispensable to the success of an international secretariat. Sir Eric Drummond [3] and some of his associates have defined international loyalty as "the conviction that the highest interests of one's own country are served best by the promotion of security and welfare everywhere, and the steadfast maintenance of that conviction without regard to changing circumstances."

To this should be added C. W. Jenks' definition of the international outlook: [4]

> The international outlook required of the international civil servant is an awareness made instinctive by habit of the needs, emotions and prejudices of the peoples of differently circumstanced countries, as they are felt and expressed by the peoples concerned, accompanied by a capacity for weighing . . . these elements in a judicial manner before reaching any decision to which they are relevant.

League experience does not explain how international loyalty can be secured among recruits. I suspect that it might be taught to suitable young men and women by proper courses of post-graduate type and by traveling missions. Failing such methods, the ideals and spirit of candidates must be assessed by personal interviews. There is nowadays a tendency to filter all applications

[3] *The International Secretariat of the Future.* Pamphlet published by the Royal Institute of International Affairs (London, Oxford University Press, January, 1944), p. 18.

[4] C. W. Jenks, (legal adviser of the International Labour Office): "Some Problems of an International Civil Service," *Public Administration Review,* III (1943), p. 95.

through masses of forms in the hope that ingenuity in devising questions will compensate for the lack of insight on the part of the employer. While it may be necessary to obtain a minimum of factual data from the candidate, this should be restricted to essentials and never for a moment allowed to take the place of impressions gained in the course of personal interviews.

Factors other than loyalty and zeal influenced in minor degree the success of the League Secretariat. Salaries were relatively high, there was security in tenure and generous retirement allowances. Nevertheless, as in most administrations the burden of the work was not shared equally by all. This was partly, but only partly, due to the fact that English and French were the official languages, and that those who had spoken one or the other from infancy had the best grasp of this important tool. More important factors influencing the Secretariat were the desire to recruit staff from many countries and the pressure from governments for the employment of their sometimes unqualified nationals. No matter how hard an international civil service may fight against this kind of pressure, the result is bound to be a compromise. However, the fight to keep down the number of such inefficient staff should never be given up, for the incapable recruits themselves suffer as much if not more damage than the service.

A special plea should be made to keep the staff as small as is compatible with the proper performance of its work, for League experience shows that the best results are secured from a small, carefully selected, highly paid, well-qualified staff.

A large staff seems to call for the routine application of general rules affecting the employment, salaries, promotion, and retirement of human beings and this is bound to have bad results, for the differences among them are greater than any common denominator. In general, young men and women are most useful in an international civil service, but physical and mental age are not always matters of years. Staff members should be retired when they have lost their enthusiasm for their work. Frequent missions to their own and other countries pay big dividends, for actual contact with the life and problems of the people and the governments is refreshing and brings relief from a sense of isolation, from the pressure always present in an undertaking which is breaking new ground, and from the difficulty of using a language other than one's own. Above all, the staff should be given the greatest possible liberty in planning and carrying on its work. They should be given definite responsibilities and left to handle them in their own way, for the assumption of responsibility in an atmosphere of freedom promotes growth.

In 1929, when the League was at its height, there were in all 630 employees in the Secretariat and 371 in the International Labor Office. A slightly larger staff might have been an advantage, but no one would have dreamed of a staff four or five times as large. One primary reason for a small staff is that the decisions of the League were carried out by the cooperating governments. Moreover, it was always possible to persuade the greatest authorities in a given field to work for the League for a limited period on a specific assignment for an honorarium only slightly larger than necessary to cover the expense of traveling and subsistence. This is a method which worked out well in practice and is to be recommended in future.

Many thought that a Secretariat made up of the nationals of forty or fifty governments would become a veritable Tower of Babel, with national differences and prejudices arousing strife which would end in the destruction of all efficiency. Nothing could have been further from the truth. In the League's good years a very high proportion of League officials found the atmosphere congenial and a real *esprit de corps* developed which continued, without much abatement, even after the war broke out in 1939. Many of those who spent years on the staff of the Secretariat look back upon them as the happiest and most productive years of their professional life. Work in an international civil service certainly compares favorably with work in a department or bureau of a single government, at least for those who have the proper bent.

It is a matter for congratulation that the Council of United Nations Relief and Rehabilitation Administration, at its first meeting in Atlantic City on November 10–December 1, 1943, should have taken due account of League experience by adopting the following resolution:

Resolution No. 37

WHEREAS

The Council desires to promote the concept of a truly international civil service; and,

WHEREAS

It recognizes that the success of the Administration will in large part depend upon the vision, competence, integrity, and loyalty of the men and women who will become its administrative officers, and comprise its technical staff; and that the vesting, by the Agreement, of full executive authority and responsibility in the Director General, requires that he act with the greatest possible freedom in the selection of personnel and the establishment of personnel standards . . .

RESOLVED

1. That the staff of the Administration should be of an international character selected upon the basis of individual competence, character, and integrity, without discrimination on the grounds of sex, race, nationality, or creed, and recruited upon as wide a geographic basis as is possible, compatible with efficient administration; and that salary standards be established at a sufficiently high level to make it possible for the Administration to secure the employment of persons possessing the highest qualifications within their own field of endeavor; et cetera, et cetera.

The work of the League of Nations was done with an extremely small budget. For the League proper and the two associated but autonomous organizations, the International Labor Organization and the Permanent Court of International Justice, the budget never exceeded eight million dollars annually. Funds were received from the Rockefeller Foundation for the library and for the work of some of the technical organizations, and some smaller grants were made by other private agencies.

On adopting the Budget for 1944 the Supervisory Commission of the League of Nations declared that the International Labor Organization, the Permanent Court of International Justice, and the Secretariat of the League constituted

> . . . the one great storehouse of experience in international cooperation and administration. For more than twenty years a network of international technical committees has been built up in the most important fields of human activity; over this long period, staffs have been trained to undertake, organize and direct international work. Nowhere else can this experience be found.

It is essential that the Secretariat and the International Labour Organization should be ready and able to render assistance to international conferences and to individual Governments on all those matters in which they have acquired, over long years, this unique knowledge and experience . . . a knowledge and experience gained at once from their daily concern with these affairs and from the systematic and continuous collection and sifting of information relating to them.[5]

It is gratifying that present or former members of the Secretariat have been used in the preparation of the first meeting of the Council of United Nations Relief and Rehabilitation Administration, in the preparation and conduct of the United Nations Conference for Food and Agriculture at Hot Springs, and in the work of the Interim Commission which is laying the foundation for the Permanent Organization in Food and Agriculture.

The League's experience in the development of the first real international civil service should be fully utilized in planning and setting up the several functional organizations which will be needed to attempt the solution of the world's social and economic problems when the war is over.

Official League documents freely available in this country constitute a rich source of information on this and other subjects of special interest to those who are concerned with the future organization of peace. These documents may be consulted conveniently at the library of the Woodrow Wilson Foundation in New York City, or at almost any large public library in other centers of population. They may be purchased from the Columbia University Press, International Documents Service, 2960 Broadway, New York 27, N. Y.

Many former Secretariat officials are filling important positions in government or private business in the different countries. But a number still remain at work for the League in Geneva, London, Princeton, Washington, and Montreal. The work of the recent International Labor Conference in Philadelphia was prepared mainly by officials of the International Labor Office with headquarters in Geneva and Montreal. Publications on subjects of

[5] *Report on the Work of the League 1942–1943*. C.25.M.25.1943. Series of League of Nations Publications General, 1943, I.

world-wide interest in economics are now being issued by the League group in Princeton, and Washington is now the headquarters of the international campaign against the illicit traffic in opium and other narcotic drugs. Although much reduced in numbers the trained, experienced civil service is still capable of organizing and guiding international cooperation efficiently and wisely.

THE INTERNATIONAL LABOR ORGANIZATION

BY CARTER GOODRICH

THE CONFERENCE of the International Labor Organization met in Philadelphia from April 20 to May 12, 1944. Official delegations were present from forty-one member states, including responsible government officials and prominent leaders of labor and industry from every continent. The fact that they came together at a time when the tempo of the war was mounting toward the climax of invasion, indicated a realization that the social problems of the peace settlement and of reconstruction could not wait and that their solution called for international planning and discussion. The extraordinarily full coverage given to the Conference by the press of the United States and other countries may be taken as a sign of widespread popular interest in such discussion. The deliberations—both the early disagreements in the Conference and the conclusions which it finally reached unanimously or by overwhelming majorities—were fully reported by a corps of correspondents who were on the whole notably well-informed and, though free from any undue reverence, distinctly friendly toward international cooperation in labor and social fields.

The occasion of the Conference, therefore, provides an appropriate time for considering the past work and the future program of the International Labor Organization. Certainly the delegates were conscious both of continuity with the past and of the challenge of the new time. It was the Twenty-Sixth Session of the International Labor Conference, and it was followed immediately by the Ninety-Third Session of the Governing Body. These

---

CARTER GOODRICH is chairman of the Governing Body of the International Labor Office on which he has represented the United States Government since 1936. He is an American economist, born in New Jersey, who has since 1931 been professor of economics at Columbia University. He acted as consultant to the Social Security Board, was for three years United States labor commissioner in Geneva, and was in 1941 special assistant to the American Ambassador to Great Britain. His chapter was written following the closing of the International Labor Conference in Philadelphia.

phrases have a traditional ring. In more ways than the casual observer realized, the methods by which the Conference worked—documentation and current record, arrangements for interpretation, relation between Office proposals and Conference decisions, type of cooperation between members of the staff and members of the delegations, methods of accommodation between government, employer, and worker groups—were methods which had been developed during the long series of meetings at Geneva. By normal constitutional procedure, the Conference adopted formal recommendations, which were a direct continuation and expansion of previous work in the same fields, on organization of employment, on social security, and on social standards in dependent territories.

With so many post-war problems to be solved, however, no merely traditional meeting would have been called for the spring of 1944. On the proposal of the United States Government, adopted without opposition at the meeting of the I.L.O. Governing Body in December, 1943, the Conference was asked to make "Recommendations to the United Nations on Present and Post-war Social Policy." It discharged this responsibility by adopting a series of resolutions on "social provisions in the peace settlement" and on "economic policies for the attainment of social objectives." From this point of view, the Conference takes its place with the international food conference at Hot Springs, the UNRRA meeting at Atlantic City, and the Monetary Conference at Bretton Woods. Delegates to the Labor Conference were aware that it was taking part in the preparation of the peace settlement. At the same time, they were attempting to shape and reach conclusions on the future of their own Organization. Indeed, the first item on the agenda of the Conference and in the minds of many the most important was that of "The Future Policy, Program and Status of the International Labor Organization."

This problem the Conference approached with complete confidence not merely in the survival but in the expanding usefulness of the I.L.O. The first message read on the opening day was a letter from President Roosevelt which said: "Within the field of your activity the United Nations have no need to extemporize a new organization." As its first major decision, the Conference adopted after prolonged discussion but by unanimous vote a Declaration of the Aims and Purposes of the International Labor Organization, known as the Declaration of Philadelphia.[1] Less dramatically, but no less significantly, the Governing Body of the International Labor Office, meeting immediately after the Conference adjourned and taking into account its decisions and its spirit, adopted an I.L.O. budget for the year 1945 that is more than double that of 1944 and larger than that of any pre-war year.

The occasion is therefore appropriate for examining the contributions to world order that may be expected from the International Labor Organization on the basis of its record in peace and in war and of the decisions of the Philadelphia Conference.

THE I.L.O. IN PEACE

A really adequate account of the activities of the International Labor Office during the twenty years from its foundation in 1919 to the outbreak of war in 1939 would make a book in itself, with a special chapter for each of the three technical subjects dealt with by the 1944 Conference: the organization of the labor market, social security, and the problems of colonial labor.

The first would begin with the provisions for public employment offices in the Unemployment Convention of 1919, would refer to the public works recommendations of 1937, and would perhaps conclude with a comment on the International Public Works Committee, which held one meeting before the war and has just been revived by decision of the Governing Body. The second would analyze the comprehensive series of conventions and recommendations on workmen's compensation and social insurance worked out in successive conferences at Geneva and the program of aid and advice to individual national administrations, including that of the United States, under which experts from the International Labor Office have assisted in devising and perfecting national systems of social security. The third would deal with the four "native labor" conventions, aimed at the grosser abuses of colonial labor exploitation: forced labor, penal sanctions, and

[1] The text of the Declaration is given in Appendix 1.

chicanery in the recruitment of native labor. These conventions are now largely in force throughout the great colonial areas; they provided the basis from which the 1944 Conference was able to proceed to a wider program of labor standards for dependent territories.

In such a volume, a rather longer chapter would recount the maritime activities of the Organization. These resulted in a comprehensive code of standards for conditions of work of seamen—thirteen Conventions and eight Recommendations, worked out in a series of special maritime conferences which in the vigor and realism of their discussions have on the whole surpassed the ordinary—or as the seamen would say—the "land" conferences of the Organization. Here the center of activity has been a specialized Joint Maritime Commission, consisting of shipowners and seamen. This body met in 1942 to draw up a series of rules for safety of seamen in wartime—a number of which were promptly put into effect by the United States Coast Guard and the British Board of Trade. It is expected to meet again in September, 1944, to make plans for post-war improvements in maritime labor conditions.

So the story might go on for other specialized phases of the I.L.O.'s work, but space permits only a very general account. Fortunately there are three authoritative books to which the reader may turn. The background of the Organization and the processes by which it was created at the Paris Peace Conference are fully covered in the two volumes on the *Origins of the International Labor Organization* [2] edited by Professor Shotwell, who himself, as a member of the United States delegation, played a large part in the negotiations. This book shows how the somewhat vague desire to "do something for labor," at a time when all Europe was seething with unrest, found expression in the creation of a continuing organization. It tells how the constitution was formulated in a Commission which sat under the chairmanship of Samuel Gompers. It shows the origin of the most unique feature in the I.L.O. constitution—unique in 1919 and still unique in 1944, for

[2] James T. Shotwell, ed., *The Origins of the International Labor Organization*, New York, Columbia University Press, 1934.

all the many constitutions now under discussion—placing representatives of employers and workers on an equal footing with representatives of governments in the councils of an official international institution. Dr. Shotwell's book explains how agreement was reached on the form which international labor standards were to take and the authority to be given them. It was agreed that these standards should be embodied in *conventions* adopted by a two-thirds vote of the Conference and submitted without delay to the competent national authorities, but that the final decision regarding ratification should remain the function of the individual nations. The Commission developed at the same time the alternative device of the *recommendation.* This was originally intended to meet the problem of federal countries, but in practice it has proved more useful as a way to put the weight of international opinion behind certain measures not suited to binding treaty obligations between states but serving as model legislation to be followed in a number of countries.

The early years of the International Labor Office have been described by its first employee and its present acting director, Edward J. Phelan.[3] This is not only a memoir of the work of the dynamic first director but also an acute commentary on the problem of building an international administration. It emphasizes the importance of the tradition established by Thomas which expects the director of the International Labor Office to make definite proposals, on his own responsibility and on the basis of the work of the permanent staff, concerning the questions brought before those representative bodies which decide the policy of the Organization. Significant parts of the story are continued in the thoughtful chapters of *The Lost Peace* [4] by Harold Butler, second director of the Office and now British minister in Washington. Mr. Butler handed over the responsibility of the International Labor Office to John G. Winant at the end of 1938, when the shadow of approaching war already lay heavily over the work of the Organization.

To the International Labor Conference each member nation

[3] London, Cresset Press, 1936.
[4] London, Faber and Faber, 1941.

is entitled to send two government delegates, one workers' delegate, and one employers' delegate, together with advisers. The non-government delegates are "chosen in agreement with the industrial organization, if such organizations exist, which are most representative of employers or of work people, as the case may be, in their respective countries." The same proportion is followed in the composition of the Governing Body which sets the agenda of the Conference and exercises supervision over the work of the International Labor Office. Since 1934 it has consisted of the representatives of sixteen governments, of whom eight are elected and eight are "the states of chief industrial importance"; eight workers and eight employers.

During the years between the wars, the International Labor Conference met each June at Geneva. The core of its business was the formulation and adoption of conventions or labor treaties setting minimum standards of labor conditions. For these, draft proposals were presented by the permanent staff of the Office on the basis of questionnaires previously circulated to governments. These were then subjected to debate and amendment in tripartite committees, usually at two successive sessions. If they emerged successfully from this international crossfire of government, employer, and worker opinion, they were then adopted by two-thirds vote in the full Conference and sent on to the national authorities of the member states, which alone had the power to give them the binding force of law.

This process, like others that involve the winning of democratic consent, is a slow one and has certain definite limitations. The provisions adopted could rarely go beyond those already in force in the most advanced countries; more often, indeed, the principal effect of the conferences has been gradually to spread these standards to other countries. Those who frame conventions for "universal" or quasi-universal application must necessarily steer between the two dangers of standards so detailed that they can be applied only in a few countries and of standards so general that they provide no real guidance. Yet by this painstaking method and in spite of these limitations, a substantial and useful body of international labor legislation was built up during the twenty years ending in 1939. Its subject matter followed closely the list of measures for the improvement of labor conditions referred to in the Preamble of the Constitution:

The regulation of the hours of work, including the establishment of a maximum working day and week, the regulation of the labor supply, the prevention of unemployment, the provision of an adequate living wage, the protection of the worker against sickness, disease and injury arising out of his employment, the protection of children, young persons and women, provision for old age and injury, protection of the interests of workers when employed in countries other than their own, recognition of the principle of freedom of association, the organization of vocational and technical education and other measures.

On these the degree of accomplishment varied from item to item. Certainly the I.L.O. could not claim that it had achieved "the prevention of unemployment," though the measures already referred to make a useful contribution toward a better organization of the labor market. Again, no way was found to make a frontal attack on the central problem of the amount of wages, although one convention laid down standards for the establishment of machinery for fixing the minimum wage. A series of conventions on the almost equally controversial question of the hours of work, however, had widespread influence. Reference has already been made to the important work done on maritime labor, on social insurance, and on colonial labor. Other sets of standards adopted provide for the prohibition of child labor, the protection of women and children, industrial health and safety, and the protection of migrants.

The International Labor Code varies not only in scope but also in the extent to which it has been applied. No nation is obliged to ratify a convention or follow a recommendation. Some nations have ratified many, others few. Moreover, some nations are far more meticulous than others in the fulfillment of obligations they have accepted. The International Labor Organization has no rights of inspection; it exerts pressure for the enforcement of conventions by moral suasion rather than by the use of an elaborate set of sanctions provided for in its Constitution. Each member state must furnish annual reports on the conventions which it has ratified. These are first scrutinized by a committee of experts and then brought before the bar of international public opinion as represented by the government, employer, and worker members of a committee of the annual Conference.

In all, sixty-seven conventions and about the same number of recommendations have been adopted. The total number of national acts of ratification has been brought to 887; the last three have been added within the past year by the action of the British and Belgian governments in accepting the obligation of certain colonial labor standards. Of the conventions in force when war broke out, twenty-eight had been ratified by fifty or more nations, and of these, ten had been ratified by thirty or more nations. No fewer than fifty nations had accepted the obligations of some part of the code. Our own Senate has ratified five maritime conventions. "There was thus in existence at the outbreak of war a far-flung though highly uneven network of international obligations in respect of labor and social questions. . . . Gradually but surely, international standards of labor and social policy were being built up and international obligations to maintain these standards were being increasingly accepted by the members of the International Labor Organization." [5]

These were by no means the only results of the I.L.O.'s work. The delegates who came to the conferences did not confine themselves to the drafting of conventions. Each year the discussion of the director's report ranged over a wide field of social and economic questions. From contacts made and experiences shared in Geneva, delegates carried home many intangible gains, never set down in formal documents, with which to influence policy in their own countries.

Meanwhile, the International Labor Office, with its Geneva headquarters and a network of branch offices and correspondents throughout the world, became the recognized center and clearinghouse for information, publication, and research in the fields of

[5] International Labor Office, *The International Labor Code, 1939* (Montreal, 1941, p. xiii). This volume arranges by subject matter the provisions of all conventions and recommendations adopted.

labor legislation and administration. Its experts were frequently called upon to give technical advice to individual governments.

Finally, the Organization had started and was continuing to develop a series of specialized organs for dealing with particular problems. Among these were the Joint Maritime Commission and the International Public Works Committee, mentioned above, which were set up to assist in synchronizing the public works programs of different countries. The organization of a Permanent Committee on Migration for Settlement had been completed just before the outbreak of war. A World Textile Conference held in Washington in 1937 brought the employers and workers in this international industry together for the first time in a discussion of their social and economic problems. An equally important precedent for regional gatherings was set at the Conference of the American members of the International Labor Organization held in 1936 in Santiago de Chile.

THE I.L.O. IN WARTIME

The I.L.O.'s preparations for wartime work began the month after Munich. At its London meeting in October, 1938, the Governing Body came unanimously to the conclusion that the activity of the Organization should be maintained at the highest possible level even if war should break out. At its next meeting, the Governing Body appointed an Emergency Committee, which would make administrative plans for wartime and if necessary, should the emergency come, take the place of the full Governing Body. When war did break out, work was carried on in the spirit of these decisions. The Emergency Committee came to Geneva for meetings in September and in October, 1939. A second American Regional Conference, which had been scheduled for Havana, Cuba, in November, 1939, was held according to plan and with great success. A well-attended meeting of the full Governing Body was held in Geneva in February, 1940; and the notices of the cancellation of the annual Conference of that year did not go out to the member states until the day the Germans launched the invasion of the West.

As long as a democratic France stood at one of the three borders of Switzerland, the Office remained at work in Geneva. After the fall of France, effective action from Geneva appeared no longer possible, and the director decided to move the principal working center across the Atlantic. The cordial welcome of the Canadian Government and the hospitality of McGill University set the location at Montreal. In the report he issued at the time of his resignation, Mr. Winant explained the transfer in the following terms:

It was my clear duty to avoid all danger that the International Labor Organization, the repository of the traditions of a world-wide effort at tripartite international co-operation to promote social justice, should become the tool of political forces which would have attempted to use it as a mask for policies of domination rather than as a spearhead of social and economic freedom.[6]

In its new location there could be no doubt of its democratic orientation.

The veteran staff which moved to Montreal was only a fraction of the pre-war membership. Just before the war, the Labor Office, like the Secretariat, had undergone severe budgetary reductions as the result of the successive withdrawals of Germany, Italy, and Japan; the emergencies of war and transfer still further reduced its staff. The network of international communications, however, was well maintained. The Geneva building remains open, and branch offices in Washington, London, Chungking, and New Delhi, together with correspondents in fourteen other countries, provide for a constant exchange of information.

One consequence of the transfer was to facilitate a notable increase in the technical services rendered by the Office to the nations of Latin America. I.L.O. experts, particularly in the field of social security, have rendered special assistance to the governments of a number of countries, and an official of the Office participated, at the request of the two governments concerned, in the work of the Joint Bolivian-United States Labor Commission.

[6] John G. Winant, *A Report to the Governments, Employers and Workers of Member States of the International Labour Organisation* (Montreal, International Labor Office, 1941), p. 9.

One result of these efforts was the formation of an Inter-American Committee on Social Security, autonomous in character but closely linked with the I.L.O., whose first conference was held at Santiago, Chile, in September, 1942.

From the new working center in Montreal, the Office promptly resumed its series of publications. The *International Labor Review* published a series of descriptions of social conditions under totalitarian rule and put even greater emphasis on analyses of the methods by which the democratic nations were organizing their labor supply in the war effort. The titles of the Office's Studies and Reports reflect this concern: *Studies in War Economics; Labor Supply and National Defense; Labor Conditions in War Contracts; Lifesaving Measures for Merchant Seamen in Time of War; Wartime Developments in Government-Employer-Worker Collaboration;* and three volumes interpreting British experience in *Food Control*, *The Wartime Transference of Labor*, and *Joint Production Machinery*.

In spite of the interruption to ordinary meetings, these were not wholly reports produced in isolation. The life-saving study was the result of a meeting of the Joint Maritime Commission. The studies of labor supply were produced for, and in many respects guided by, a series of seven informal Canadian-American discussions in which government officials, labor leaders, and employers from both sides of the border met to consider the organization of manpower.

The study of tripartite collaboration was a part of the preparation for the Conference of the International Labor Organization held in New York and Washington in October and November, 1941. As President Roosevelt has recently said: "Representatives of governments, workers, and employers had the boldness to come together from all parts of the world to formulate plans for reconstruction." Five weeks before Pearl Harbor, and at a time when the majority of the thirty-four nations represented were still neutral, the Conference prefaced its major resolution with the statement that: "The victory of the free peoples in the war against totalitarian aggression is an indispensable condition of the attainment of the ideals of the International Labor Organization." The Resolution listed the tasks of reconstruction for which plans should be ready at the close of the war. It is hardly going too far to say that this Conference, which met before the United Nations had even come into being, sketched the broad outlines of the very program which the United Nations are now following through their own functional agencies. The Resolution asked the governments to associate the I.L.O. "with the planning and application of measures of reconstruction." It directed that the work of the I.L.O. itself should be organized in such a way "that the International Labor Organization shall be in a position to give authoritative expression to the social objectives confided to it, in the rebuilding of a peaceful world upon the basis of 'improved labor standards, economic advancement and social security.' "

As a result of this decision and of the discussions at the meeting of the Emergency Committee in London in the spring of 1942, the attention of the Office has been more and more devoted to preparation for post-war problems. This has been reflected in the contents of the *International Labor Review* and in the series of Studies and Reports. One of the most notable of these is *The Displacement of Population in Europe*, a careful and authoritative study of the tremendous wartime dislocations, intended to help in the solution of the immediate post-war problems of the resettlement and redistribution of the scattered population. A longer-range problem is faced in *World Economic Development*, a book which poses the question of the effect on established industrial areas of the industrialization of less developed countries. It offers pertinent suggestions as to the measures called for in both types of areas to make the process of benefit to both. Other aspects of postwar problems are dealt with in *Cooperative Organizations and Postwar Relief*, in the introduction to the collection of *Inter-Governmental Commodity Control Agreements*, and in the documents prepared for the 1944 Conference.

The decision to call the Philadelphia Conference was made by the Governing Body at a meeting held in London in December, 1943. The British Minister of Labor, Ernest Bevin, and the Foreign Secretary, Anthony Eden, both addressed the Governing Body and gave strong support to the proposal. In his address Mr.

Eden declared that if the United Nations did not have the International Labor Organization, they would have to invent it now, and with employers and workers playing the same part in its structure and function.

THE I.L.O. LOOKS FORWARD

Mr. Winant's Report to the International Labor Conference of June, 1939, contains a passage which is as challenging today as it was when he wrote it on the eve of war. In it he spoke of "the determination of the Member countries to protect themselves against aggression and to preserve these democratic institutions which are the hope of mankind." He said there was still a chance that that very determination might make it possible for the nations to arrive, without war, at an agreement that would "pave the way toward the enduring peace that was hoped for so fervently in 1919 by a weary soldiery and a war-torn world." He continued:

> For this too we should be prepared. It may mean for us the opportunity to clarify the social objectives of a lasting peace. The workers will measure the value of any settlement by the improvement that it brings to the conditions under which they live and work. It should be our part to have ready a practical social program that would assure to the common people recognition of their ultimate needs. If the opportunity is given, we should accept it with the faith and determination of which Albert Thomas spoke, and use to the full all the great resources and potentialities of the International Labor Organization.[7]

The opportunity was not given without war. To this responsibility the International Labor Conference returned five years later at Philadelphia. It could do so, as it declared, because of "the prospect of the complete victory of the United Nations." As one of its major acts, the Conference adopted a resolution concerning "Social Provisions in the Peace Settlement." In this, it put forward a set of principles which it said were "appropriate for inclusion in a general or special treaty between nations." These included the Declaration of Philadelphia and the statement that:

[7] International Labor Office, Geneva, *The World of Industry and Labour; Report of the Director to the Twenty-Fifth Session of the International Labour Conference*, pp. 10–11.

"Each government recognizes its duty to maintain a high level of employment." The proposed agreement declares that employment and other labor objectives "are of international concern and should be among the social objectives of international as well as national policy," and goes on to provide ways and means for fuller international consultation on these matters through the agency of the I.L.O. The same resolution adds that "the exceptional opportunity of the negotiations of the peace settlement should be taken to secure a concerted advance in the acceptance of binding obligations concerning conditions of labor" and suggests that "throughout the peace settlement, the United Nations should wherever appropriate include provisions for labor standards." Some of these might well be taken from existing I.L.O. conventions. Negotiations regarding shipping and regarding colonial possessions are mentioned among the cases in which specific labor standards might well be applied. For the framing of such standards, the resolution recommends that the Governing Body should appoint, and the United Nations should utilize, "a consultative committee on labor provisions in the peace settlement."

At the same time the Conference adopted a resolution concerning the economic policies, international and national, that should be followed "for the attainment of social objectives." This action was an illustration of the point of view embodied in the Declaration of the Aims and Purposes of the International Labor Organization. In part this Declaration was a restatement and reaffirmation of the principles laid down in Part XIII of the Treaty of Versailles. It declares, for example, "that experience has fully demonstrated the truth of the statement in the Preamble to the Constitution of the International Labor Organization that lasting peace can be established only if it is based on social justice." There are, however, significant differences in emphasis. Where the 1919 Preamble declared that "the failure of any nation to adopt humane conditions of labor is an obstacle in the way of other nations which desire to improve the conditions in their own countries," the Declaration broadens this idea and puts it in bolder and more positive form, stating that "Poverty anywhere constitutes a danger to prosperity everywhere."

The Preamble referred to "the principle of freedom of association." The Declaration goes on from "the effective recognition of the right of collective bargaining" to the cooperation of labor and management "in the continuous improvement of productive efficiency" and "in the preparation and application of social and economic measures." Moreover, it emphasizes the part to be played in "the war against want" by "continuous and concerted international effort in which the representatives of workers and employers, enjoying equal status with those of governments, join with them in free discussion and democratic decision with a view to the promotion of the common welfare."

The most significant development reflected in the new Declaration is the recognition of the linkage of social and economic problems. At the head of the list of objects to be achieved it places "full employment and the raising of standards of living." It asserts the right of human beings "to pursue both their material well-being and their spiritual development in conditions of freedom and dignity, of economic security and equal opportunity." The attainment of such conditions "must constitute the central aim of national and international policy." From this it follows that economic and financial measures, as well as others, "should be judged in this light and accepted only in so far as they may be held to promote and not to hinder the achievement of this fundamental objective." On this basis the Declaration goes forward to its most discussed paragraph:

> It is a responsibility of the International Labor Organization to examine and consider all international economic and financial policies and measures in the light of this fundamental objective.

What does this mean? Certainly not that the I.L.O. will itself set exchange rates, make loans, hold buffer stocks, or do any one of many other economic tasks for which international machinery is being or may be prepared. What, then, is the intention? A figure of speech which passed from mouth to mouth among the delegates to the Philadelphia Conference answers this question. The I.L.O. was constantly referred to as "watchdog." The High Commissioner for India, Sir Samuel Runganadhan, said in a plenary session: "It must be the watchdog in the world of international policy in the interests of social policy and full employment." The qualifications the I.L.O. can offer for this guarding role are its concern with social objective and its character as the one international forum in which labor and employers have equal official standing in the formulation of international policy.

The Conference realized that to accomplish these aims, the Organization and the Office must be strengthened and the methods of work and relationships with other organizations must be reconsidered. It therefore asked the Governing Body "to appoint a committee as soon as possible to consider the future constitutional development of the Organization." Meanwhile, it authorized the Governing Body "to take appropriate steps to assure close collaboration with and a full interchange of information between the I.L.O. and any other public organizations which now exist or may be established for the promotion of economic and social well-being." It is significant that the resolution, which was presented jointly by the government delegations of the United States and Canada, noted that these steps were to be taken "during the period of the deliberations of the Committee . . . and of the development of an overall pattern of international institutions."

At the same time the Conference indicated its opinion that the strengthening of the Organization called for further development of specialized activities, region by region and industry by industry, to perform functions that cannot be carried out on a "universal" basis. Resolutions were adopted proposing that regional conferences should be held as soon as practicable, both for the Near and Middle East and for Asia, and the acting director spoke of the desirability of an early resumption of the series of American regional conferences. The Conference also approved in principle the proposal, originally put forward by the British Minister of Labor, Ernest Bevin, for the creation of a series of industrial committees which might do for other world industries what the Joint Maritime Commission has done for the shipping industry.

The morning after the Conference adjourned, the Governing Body met and appointed the Constitutional Committee, renewed certain of its old committees, set up a Committee on Employment, made plans for a September meeting of the Joint Maritime Commission, and adopted a budget for 1945 of 11,600,000 Swiss francs (about $2,500,000), more than twice that of the preceding year. These were the first steps toward carrying the decisions of the Conference into action. The reality of its accomplishments will be measured by the work of these continuing agencies, by what the member countries do at home in carrying out the technical recommendations of the Conference, by what use the United Nations make of the I.L.O. in the organization of the peace, and by the degree of understanding and support that is developed among the peoples of the world.

In the difficult period of readjustment and new decision that lies ahead, the International Labor Organization—born out of the last peace settlement—faces its greatest opportunity and its severest test. The test began at Philadelphia. To those who took part in the decisions of the Conference, the challenge was urgent and the direction was clearly forward.

NOT IN ISOLATION

The International Labor Organization was founded by the Paris Treaties, as their French text says, as "part of the ensemble of the institutions of the League." Its original members, as its Constitution provided, were the original members of the League of Nations. Yet, by a precedent that was already old in 1934 when the United States joined the I.L.O. by joint resolution of Congress, nations not members of the League may be and are members of the International Labor Organization. At the present time, the membership of the I.L.O. comprises, in addition to the members of the League of Nations, the United States, Brazil, Peru, Venezuela, Hungary, Chile, Costa Rica, and Haiti, which are not members of the League, and the French Committee of National Liberation, whose relationship to the League has not yet been established. The states named contribute over thirty percent of the 1944 budget of the I.L.O.

From the beginning, the I.L.O. has carried on its work with a high degree of autonomy and independence of action. Of the constitutional ties which link the I.L.O. to the League, the most important are those that concern finance. For the League members, their share of the expenses of the I.L.O. figures as one part of the total budget of the League, and their assessment to the I.L.O. is paid as part of a single payment to the Treasurer of the League. On the other hand, the United States and other non-League members pay directly to the International Labor Office, and their part in the financial decisions is carried on solely with and through the Governing Body. The director of the I.L.O. draws up a proposed budget which is carried first to the Finance Committee of the Governing Body and then is adopted by the Governing Body after scrutiny by its government, employer, and worker members. The League part of the budget is referred, like those of the Secretariat and the Permanent Court, to the Supervisory Commission of the League for its observation. It then goes forward for discussion in the Fourth Commission of the League Assembly and for final adoption by the Assembly itself. During the war the Supervisory Commission, under its emergency powers, has acted for the Assembly.

The relationships are involved, and the system has worked less by logic than by a sort of mutual accommodation under which the scrutiny of the Fourth Commission has in fact been largely nominal. The arrangements are particularly awkward now that the non-League states play so large a role in the work of the I.L.O. Even if the membership of the two organizations were identical, they would be by no means satisfactory. The effect would still be to leave decisions on I.L.O. policy in the hands of the Conference and the Governing Body, in which workers and employers play an active part, and yet to leave at least nominal control of I.L.O. finances in the hands of another body in which employers and workers are not represented.

It was therefore natural that the Philadelphia Conference should include in the terms of reference of the Constitutional Committee the specific point, "the methods of financing the Organization," as well as the more general question of "the relationship of the Organization to other international bodies." It was, however, clear that the spirit of the Conference was opposed to any suggestion that the I.L.O. should attempt to do its work in isolation from the other international institutions. In replying to the debate on the Director's Report, Mr. Phelan made the following statement:

Nothing said in the Office Reports about the autonomy or independence of the International Labor Organization suggests or can reasonably be construed as suggesting that the International Labor Organization should occupy a position of isolation. We have never had and we have not today any such intention or desire.

The same point had been made in somewhat greater detail by Paul van Zeeland, the head of the Belgian delegation and a former prime minister:

The International Labor Organization has always been an autonomous institution. It was attached to the League of Nations by close and organic links, but it had its own Constitution and its own methods, adapted to its particular purposes. Experience has shown that it has a vitality which has enabled it to pursue its work, to act and to confirm its existence while the League remained in the shadows. This autonomy has proved its worth, and it must at all costs be maintained. There might even be serious arguments for increasing its autonomy, in budget matters in particular, but neither its isolation not its absolute independence or detachment are desirable. On the contrary.

Mr. van Zeeland went on, with an eloquence heightened by the experience of an occupied country, to a statement of the most fundamental reason for the I.L.O.'s concern with a general international organization:

There is no enduring peace, it is said in the proposed declaration, without social justice. This is profoundly true. But the contrary is also true. We cannot hope to promote social justice unless we can work in the certainty that peace will be effectively secure this time.

It was obvious to those who took part in this and previous Conferences that a continuing advance in the standard of living could not be expected in a world torn by war or suffering under the threat of further wars. The hope of such advance rests on the success of efforts to build a world structure that will guarantee security against war. Full attainment of the objectives of the

I.L.O. depends, in the writer's judgment, on the triumph in some form of the League idea, though not on the maintenance of the particular constitutional ties that now link the League of Nations and the International Labor Organization. The work of raising labor standards can best go forward as part of a concerted effort of world cooperation. The I.L.O. must therefore function in close and harmonious working relationship not only with the various specialized agencies established by the United Nations but also with the "general international organization," in whatever form it may take, that is promised by the Moscow Declaration and the Connally Resolution.

The precise place of the I.L.O. in the "overall pattern of international institutions" cannot yet be determined. The pattern itself is only beginning to emerge. From the side of the I.L.O. a special negotiating group, proposed by the Conference on May 12 and set up by the Governing Body on May 13, stands ready to assist in the working out of these relationships. It is in the writer's judgment imperative that they preserve for the I.L.O. its essential freedom of action. The élan of a vigorous existing agency should not be sacrificed for the sake of formal symmetry. In particular, we should make sure that the workers' and employers' groups have a full share in all the decisions, of finance as well as policy, in the Labor Organization to which they contribute so much of its unique strength. But the I.L.O. should not work in isolation. The writer is confident that cooperative relationships can be established in the spirit of the comment made by President Roosevelt, who, after the close of the Philadelphia Conference, said to the delegates that they had

"Wisely provided for the further development and reorganization of the International Labor Organization itself so that it may be broadened and strengthened for carrying out these social objectives, and at the same time integrated on a cooperative basis with whatever new international agency or agencies are created by the United Nations."

CONTROL OF SPECIAL AREAS

BY SARAH WAMBAUGH

THE EXPERIENCE of the League of Nations in the years between the wars has greatly enriched the resources of political science. Faced by many obstacles, chief among them the refusal of the United States to take part in collective security, the League could not prevent the second World War. But the fact that the League was "not universal," to use the Geneva phrase, did not prevent it from solving many lesser political questions with notable success. This was especially true of territorial problems.

When the United Nations do, in fact, set up "the general international organization based on the principle of sovereign equality of all peace-loving States," large and small, which was agreed to at Moscow in November, 1943, they will have four most useful devices at hand with which to make such political changes as they may desire on the map of the world, in the interests of permanent peace. These possible devices are: the international plebiscite, the exchange of populations under an international commission, the convention for economic unification of an area politically divided, and the creation of an international civil administration for special areas. The variety offered by these four devices, already perfected by the League, is wide.

In areas where the United Nations may think it advisable to draw a new frontier or to make other territorial changes "in accord with the freely expressed wishes of the people concerned,"

DR. SARAH WAMBAUGH is an American of Dutch and Scotch descent, many generations back. She is the recognized authority on international plebiscites, not only because of her three books on the subject but through her actual connection with several such votes regarding sovereignty. Her experience with international administration began in 1920 when she was for a time the expert on the Saar and Danzig in the Administrative Commissions and Minorities Section of the League of Nations Secretariat. Some years later she was called in by the Peruvian Government as expert adviser for the Tacna-Arica plebiscite. In 1934 the League appointed her as one of the three experts to draft the Saar Plebiscite Regulations and then as technical adviser and deputy member of the Saar Plebiscite Commission. It is on this long experience with the international administration of the Saar Territory that she bases her chapter.

as the Atlantic Charter recites, the general international organization can administer a plebiscite so fairly and carefully that the results will be above doubt. For, with its great reservoir of member states in every continent, the organization can hold the plebiscite under completely international auspices. For the necessary preliminary period it can place the political administration of the area, as well as the several processes of registration and voting, under the administration of an international commission composed, both Commissioners and staff, of citizens of countries with no selfish interest in the outcome of the vote; it can send in a truly international force to secure order; and it can establish complete confidence in the secrecy of the ballot by importing a sufficiently large number of officials from disinterested countries to preside over every voting bureau and to count the ballots with their own hands, safe from the penetrating eye of any local inhabitant. Only the existence of an organization like the League made possible in the Saar these great improvements in the technique of the international plebiscite. In the future only international plebiscites so held will be convincing.

In areas where no plebiscite, however perfect in technique, can yield a useful result, where two or more nationalities are so mingled that no appropriate frontier can be drawn, and yet where the situation is a constant danger to peace and order, the general international organizations can carry out an exchange of populations under an international commission, aided by an international loan negotiated by the international organization. The uprooting of people is always painful. Hitler has shown us how criminally cruel it can be, and, of those whom he has uprooted, all who are still alive must be restored to their homes. But such transfer can be comparatively merciful if done by the international organization with the same care and foresight expended by the League in the exchange of populations between Greece and Turkey and Greece and Bulgaria in 1923 and 1924. That this can then be a real solution is shown by the fact that Greece and Turkey, formerly enemies for centuries, are now at last friends.

In an area which is an economic unit, yet through which, for imperative political reasons, a frontier must be cut, with or without a plebiscite, the Allies can secure from the states to which the parts are to be awarded, a convention, to be administered by the general international organization, sewing up the region again in its economic life so that services of water and electric power can be maintained, railroads can still serve the entire area, trade can prosper, and the inhabitants can cross and recross on their daily business almost as if no line existed. In addition, under this convention an effective mechanism can be set up to protect the political, social, and religious rights of the minorities on both sides. For the fifteen years of its existence the German-Polish Convention regarding Upper Silesia, secured by the League in 1922, served to protect the area in a remarkable degree from evil consequences of the division. Had the governments of Germany and Poland placed concern for the interests of the inhabitants of Upper Silesia above their jealousy over sovereignty, they would not have allowed the Convention to lapse. This device of a convention for economic and social protection should have careful consideration by the United Nations, for it would make possible the healing of many economic and social fissures, old and new.

Lastly, in areas of vital concern to the interests of international society, the United Nations can use the device of international civil administration by commissions appointed by the general international organization. Where the geographic situation of a region, perhaps an island or an isthmus or a port, makes it strategically vital to the safety of several countries—as is the Kiel Canal for instance, and, possibly, Danzig—or necessary to the trade of several States, as is Trieste, the international administration might well be permanent. Where a people are not yet ready for independence, as in mandates, or where they have long since set up a sovereign state but are so backward politically as to menace world peace and to require supervision over order and education, as in Germany and Japan, temporary civil administration by the general international organization, for a definite period, or for an indefinite one depending on the degree of cooperation by their people and their leaders, could be used to handle the problem.

Should the United Nations wish to make use of international civil administration for any purpose, or for any period of time, they will find the experience gained in the Saar Territory during the fifteen years from 1920 to 1935 both useful and encouraging. The handicaps were great. The Territory, though covering only 730 square miles, was a highly industrialized area in the heart of Europe, and determined efforts to discredit the League regime were constantly made by the Saar leaders, supported by the Reich. This effort was due largely to the desire to win at least a 99 percent vote for return to Germany in the plebiscite which was to be held in 1935. Yet in spite of these obstacles, the administration of the Saar Territory through the international Governing Commission appointed by the Council of the League, was successful in all aspects save only that of winning popularity. While the population of the Territory numbered at the time only about 828,000, the system followed there was so simple that it would seem capable of application to a much larger area.

The Saar Territory was a new political entity, established by the Treaty of Versailles, out of parts of Prussia and Bavaria, in order to enable France to enjoy full ownership of the coal mines as reparation for Germany's destruction of the mines in the north of France, and as a prelude to the plebiscite which at the end of the fifteen years was to decide the fate of the area.

The device of an international regime in a highly industrial area for such purposes and for so long a period was completely novel. It represented a compromise between the claim of the French delegation at the Peace Conference and the position of President Wilson and Premier Lloyd George. France demanded annexation of the Saar area or at least a special regime, while Wilson and Lloyd George, though they wished to enable France to exploit the mines, were opposed to annexation, the President favoring the maintenance of German sovereignty and Lloyd George proposing a mandate under the League.

By the Treaty, Germany renounced the government of the Territory "in favor of the League of Nations, in the capacity of trustee." Under the "Saar Statute," as the Treaty provisions are usually termed, the League was to entrust the government of the area to a commission, consisting of five members chosen by the League Council, one to be a citizen of France, one a native inhabitant of the Saar not a citizen of France, and three from countries other than France or Germany. Decisions of the Governing Commission were to be by majority vote. The appointment of each member was for one year and each might be reappointed or replaced. The salaries, fixed by the Council, were to be charged to the local revenues. At the end of fifteen years the inhabitants were to indicate the sovereignty under which they desired to be placed.

The voters in this plebiscite, insisted on by Mr. Wilson, were to decide among the three alternatives: maintenance of the League regime, union with France, or union with Germany. It was Mr. Lloyd George who proposed the insertion of the vote for the League, in order, he said, to stimulate the Commission in its work and also, in case the German Spartacists should triumph and Germany become a proletarian dictatorship like Russia, to enable the Saarlanders to escape a Communist Germany without being forced to put themselves under France. By 1935, however, the situation in Germany had so changed that this third alternative was supported not by the right but by the left and some of the Catholics, in order to avoid union not with a Communist but with a Fascist Germany.

The treaty gave to the Governing Commission all the powers of government within the Territory which had hitherto belonged to the German Empire, Prussia, or Bavaria, including the appointment and dismissal of officials and the creation of such administrative and representative bodies as the Commission might deem necessary. All the laws and regulations in force in the Territory on the date of the armistice of November 11, 1918, except those enacted in consequence of the state of war, were to continue to apply. If it should become necessary to introduce modifications, these were to be decided on and put into effect by the Governing Commission, after consultation with the elected representatives of the inhabitants in such a manner as the Commission might determine. In fixing the conditions and hours of labor, the Governing Commission was to take into consideration the wishes expressed by the local labor organizations, as well as the principles adopted by the League of Nations.

The civil and criminal courts existing in the Territory were to continue, but they were cut off completely from the higher courts in the Reich and appeals were to be heard by a civil and criminal court of eleven judges to be established in the Saar by the Governing Commission. Justice was to be rendered in the name of the Commission.

The Governing Commission alone was to have power to levy taxes, and these were to be applied exclusively to the needs of the Territory. The existing fiscal system was to be maintained as far as possible and no new taxes except customs duties might be imposed without previous consultation of the elected representatives of the inhabitants.

Under the control of the Commission the inhabitants were to retain their religious liberties, their schools, language, and local assemblies. The right of voting, which was to belong to every inhabitant over twenty years of age, without distinction of sex, was not to be exercised for any assemblies other than these local ones.

Military service, compulsory or voluntary, was forbidden in the Territory, and for the maintenance of order only a local gendarmerie was to be established.

The Governing Commission was given the power to decide all questions arising from interpretation of the Treaty provisions, and France and Germany agreed to abide by its majority decisions.

Of the Saar Statute, Sir Geoffrey Knox, the last chairman of the Governing Commission and the man of all others best qualified by experience to give judgment, writes in his recent book, *The Last Peace and the Next,* "that it . . . enshrined a bold and entirely new conception. . . . Technically, too, the Statute was a remarkable piece of work. It showed astonishing foresight in meeting problems for which there was no precedent, great administrative acumen and a broad good sense—the whole embodied in a brief and lucid text."

When, some months before the treaty came into effect, the Secretariat of the League was established *in embryo,* the work on the Saar, like that on Danzig, was entrusted to the Administrative Commissions and Minorities Section under a Norwegian director.

In February, 1920, a month after the Treaty came into force, the League Council appointed the "Governing Commission of the Territory of the Saar Basin." The French Government had designated a *conseiller d'état* as the citizen of France, and the Council, no doubt on French recommendation, appointed the Landrat of Saarlouis as the native inhabitant of the Saar. To fill the other three seats, the Council appointed citizens of Belgium, Canada, and Denmark.

The directions and resolutions adopted by the Council to guide the Governing Commission required that no important decisions should be taken except in full Commission, and that the chairman should report to the Secretary General of the League on all questions of special interest. The Council was not to intervene in the administration, however, except for reasons of the highest importance.

The Governing Commission itself took the place not only of the German, Prussian, and Bavarian governments, but also of the Prussian and Bavarian ministers of the interior and of the Oberpräsidenten and Regierungspräsidenten, under whose control and direct orders the administrative services had lain. The Commission divided these services among its members, the chairman taking the departments of the Interior, Foreign Affairs, Commerce, Industry, Labor, and Control of Mines; the Saar member, those of Agriculture, Health, Charity, and Social Insurance; the Canadian, those of Finances and Economic Questions; the Belgian member, those of Public Works, Railroads, Post, and Telephone and Telegraph; and the Danish member, those of Education, Justice, and Religious Matters. As the years passed and the personnel of the Commission changed, these departments were retained, although reapportioned among the members.

To serve as directors of the departments under the respective Commissioners, and in other important offices, the Commission brought in seventy-three men from outside. Forty-three of these were of French nationality, mostly from Alsace and Lorraine. The general organization of administration was left unchanged, however, for, faced by the utter impossibility of finding enough trained men in the Territory to replace the mass of public officials, the Commission requested the German, Prussian and Bavarian

Governments to place the existing ones at its disposal. This they did, regarding the officials as "on leave." The seven Landräte and the other Kreis officials who controlled the public services continued in office in most instances. By 1934 the original 8,500 state officials had increased to more than 12,000, of whom about one half were new, appointed by the Commission. The system of communal administration also remained practically as it had been under Prussia and Bavaria, although, as the services became permanently organized and the communal administration developed, the Commission gradually introduced inhabitants of the Saar into these services also.

As the treaty required, the lower courts were retained. The Saar Supreme Court, provided in the treaty to take the place of the higher courts in the Reich, was established at Saarlouis. Throughout the fifteen years the Chief Justice was Swiss, the other ten judges being from the Saar, Belgium, Czechoslovakia, France, Luxembourg, the Netherlands and Switzerland.

Except for the seventy-five upper officials, all the administrative personnel of the Saar were German, as they remained throughout the fifteen years. But this did not satisfy the Reich and Saar leaders, who at once condemned the Commission for appointing or employing any non-German at all. Against the introduction of foreigners as heads of the administrative services, and other administrative details, in July, 1920, all the German officials and employees in the Saar went on strike and were supported by a twenty-four-hour sympathetic strike of all Saar labor. The strike, which synchronized with the advance of the Soviet troops in Poland and a railroad strike in the Ruhr, was reported to the League Council by the chairman of the Commission as a deliberate effort to demonstrate that the League regime could not be established. The Commission declared martial law and expelled the leaders. The strike ended and the officials accepted the statute involved, took the required oath of loyalty to the Governing Commission, and thereafter, until the advent of Hitler in the Reich and the approach of the plebiscite period in the Saar, fulfilled their duties "tactfully and conscientiously," as Sir Geoffrey Knox reported to the Council in 1933.

Sir Geoffrey, who had already had experience in dealing with Germany and the Germans while in the British Embassy in Berlin, gives in his book, published in 1943, an interesting glimpse of the attitude of the Saar officials. While a diplomatist stationed in Germany, he writes, must examine most critically the implications of every word spoken to him:

In the administration of the Saar things were different. There, in daily discussion with German officials of practical matters of administration in which both parties had the same interest—the good government of the Territory,—barriers of nationality tended to disappear and relations in most cases became those of the normal close collaboration between the civil servant and his chief. When others, such as the representatives of political parties, trades-unions and masters' associations, came to see one, it meant that they had something to ask for and that their rivals were probably asking for the opposite; thus questions were discussed on a basis of plain and ascertainable fact, and there was little chance of giving or receiving false impressions. In Germany, too, authority, in itself, has a prestige that it enjoys nowhere else, so that not infrequently Germans would seek out the holder of authority, albeit a foreigner, to ask his advice on their personal problems—even on those of national conscience.

Although most of the officials remained loyal, with the coming of the Hitler regime in the Reich the picture began to change. Owing to pressure and intimidation by the Nazis in the Reich and in the Saar, to fear for their own future careers, or to growing sympathy with Nazi doctrines, a considerable number of the officials were now guilty of unneutral conduct, and the Governing Commission was forced to take special measures.

From the beginning the prospect of the plebiscite had given a political aspect to every administrative decision, however much this decision might concern the economic or social welfare of the Territory. Unfortunately, all the original members of the Governing Commission except the Canadian were regarded by the Germans as Francophile. Moreover, the Council in 1920 had designated the French member as chairman, on the ground that close collaboration with France was necessary in the interests of order and welfare in the Territory. This appointment would have been unwise in any case; in a plebiscite area it naturally aroused bitter criticism not only in Germany but in the outer world. But even action clearly required by the Saar Statute was criticized by the Germans for political ends. The Governing Commission rightly considered that its duty under the Treaty was to effect a complete separation, political and administrative, of the Saar from the Reich. Each step to achieve this end, however, was opposed by the German Government on the ground that Germany had not renounced sovereignty but merely the right to govern. Determined on winning at least a 99 percent vote for return to the Reich in 1935, the leaders of the Saar political parties, of the unions, of the chambers of commerce and all other organizations of the territory, were determined to defeat every effort to make the Saar independent of the Reich and to prove that the League regime was impossible, inefficient, and partisan. In this they were supported not only by many of the Saar officials, teachers, and clergy, the higher industrial and commercial classes, and the Saar press, heavily subsidized by Berlin, but also by the Heimatdienst and the Saarverein in the Reich. In almost every important action of the Governing Commission, the Saar chambers of commerce, the political parties and the other associations availed themselves of their right of petition to the Council and registered protest.

The chief grievance against the Governing Commission was that it retained for ten years the French troops, as "garrison troops" under the orders of the chairman. Their retention had been authorized by the League Council until such time as the local Saar gendarmerie, which the treaty stipulated should be the only force to be established to maintain order, had reached a proper size. The Germans, already alarmed by the propaganda bureau set up by the French military authorities and retained by the French Mines Administration, feared that retention of the troops meant an effort to intimidate the inhabitants into voting for France, and complained that the Commission was intentionally slow in recruiting the gendarmerie. The force was finally recruited in sufficient numbers in 1930, and the French troops were finally removed. The grievance second in importance was the setting up by the French Mines Administration of French schools, to which, so the Germans charged, the Administration forced the miners to send their children. Like all other questions, this grievance was greatly sharpened by the prospective plebiscite. The third grievance concerned the lack of representative government. The Commission began by consulting the separate Kreistäge regarding changes in the laws, but, finding this unsatisfactory, in 1922 it established an elected Landesrat of thirty members whose competence was limited to expression of views on any questions submitted to them by the Commission. The Germans dubbed this a "Scheinparlament" or a parliament in name only, and demanded that it be given an effective vote on laws and taxes, the right of interpellation, and the right to elect the Saar member of the Governing Commission. The League Council, in answer, took the position that such powers were impossible to grant if the authority of the Governing Commission under the treaty was to be maintained. This attitude was justified by the fact that throughout the fifteen years the Landesrat rejected practically all the draft decrees of any importance submitted to it for expression of views.

The tension of the early years was brought to a head when in January, 1923, a general strike, lasting one hundred days, broke out in the Saar, ostensibly over wages but actually over the Franco-Belgian occupation of the Ruhr. The Governing Commission's use of two drastic decrees and numerous deportations in order to break the strike greatly irritated the Germans and alarmed liberal groups in the outer world. But the intervention of the League Council brought about by the representatives of Britain and Sweden relieved any fear that the Governing Commission's apparent efforts to establish itself as an autonomous body would meet with no effective check by the League. The action of the Council, the changes in personnel of the Governing Commission which occurred in the following years, and the choice of a Canadian to replace the Frenchman as chairman of the Commission greatly improved the situation. From this time until the end of the League regime the successive chairmen were British, and the other members of the Commission, aside from the French member required by the Statute, were under no charge of partisanship. Nevertheless the leaders in the Saar and Germany continued to teach the Saarlanders that the League regime was an intolerable dictatorship and kept up their stream of protests to Geneva. However, after 1923 the situation improved greatly, and after Locarno, in 1926, it remained reasonably calm and harmonious until the advent of the Hitler regime in the Reich in 1933 and the consequent measures which the Governing Commission was forced to take to protect the Jews in the Saar and to maintain freedom of speech and assembly in view of the approaching plebiscite.

The economic aspect of the League regime was very favorable to the area, for under the Treaty and by subsequent agreements between the French and German governments, the Saar obtained freely from both France and Germany the implements and raw materials necessary for its industry and possessed in both countries an almost unrestricted market. Owing to this special position, the Territory profited greatly by the world prosperity of the late twenties and escaped the worst of the world depression in the early thirties. During the depression unemployment was serious but the percentage was far lower than in the Ruhr. This fact was ignored by the Saar leaders and so brought no credit to the League regime which they blamed for any increase at all. The people of the Saar, backward politically and unaccustomed to independent thought, were docile followers of their German leaders.

It is noteworthy that from the time Germany became a member of the League, in 1926, until its departure in 1933, the German representative on the Council never brought before the League any complaint whatever regarding the Saar. The truth is that for fifteen years the Governing Commission gave to the Saar inhabitants an excellent administration, fulfilling its more than thankless task with skill and devotion. During that most difficult period which followed the first World War and included the four years of world depression, the Saar Territory was well and conscientiously governed, order was maintained, the officials were well paid, many new roads were constructed and the whole transportation system kept in good order, many new churches were built, as well as schools, the education system was carefully nurtured and the teaching kept at a high standard, the taxes were lower than those of the Reich or of France, and the finances were so brilliantly managed that the Territory at the end was handed back to the Reich with no public debt and with money in the treasury. While the Saar did not enjoy a parliamentary government, the Catholics possessed an unaccustomed degree of religious equality and tolerance and the Jews were protected until the end of the League regime.

The Saar record of success in spite of great odds would seem to show that, given the necessary machinery, international administration is possible for any area. It would, of course, be far easier if the region were not highly industrialized, if no plebiscite were in prospect as to sovereignty, and if no one country or group of countries were to enjoy special rights therein.

The Saar experience shows that the machinery of international administration need not be cumbersome, as, for the sake of the finances, it should not be. An international governing commission is essential, its size depending on the area. Thereafter all the members should be carefully chosen from countries not immediately concerned with the territory to be administered. It is imperative that each of the public services have neutral directors. It would be well to increase the number of key positions filled by neutrals and include among them the most important lower administrative officials, such as the Landräte in Prussia. Further, it is of particular importance that there should be enough outsiders in the police force to assure its effective neutralization. For the sake of confidence and harmony, as well as efficiency, the international authority must exercise a close supervision over the administration.

That the document under which the Governing Commission acts should be clear, comprehensive and precise is imperative. This point is emphasized repeatedly by Sir Geoffrey Knox. He writes of the Saar Statute:

> Thanks to this precise charter, the governing body of five men of different nationality, a Briton, a Frenchman, a German, a Jugoslav and a Finn, were able, even in the most difficult times, to work together in harmony. In normal circumstances the Statute met every need of the administration, and it never hemmed or hampered our efforts to govern after adverse conditions had arisen which could not have been

foreseen when the Treaty was concluded—a severe economic depression, the premature evacuation of the neighboring Rhineland by the Allied armies and the advent in their place of a German Government of gangsters with every opportunity to intrigue and intimidate in the Territory.

Again he states:

In the Saar I had three years' daily experience of an international administration in which five men, although of different nationality, education, outlook and profession, worked together in remarkable harmony. But that harmony was only possible, I am convinced, because we worked on the basis of a precise charter. However well domestic affairs may be conducted with an unwritten constitution and uncodified laws, these things, in the conduct of international affairs, are clearly indispensable.

When in the Atlantic Charter the Allies expressed their desire to see "no territorial changes that do not accord with the freely expressed wishes of the peoples concerned," they were making a statement against the handing of peoples about from one national sovereignty to another. They were not denying the right of organized society to set up an international administration in special areas where only such a solution will assure world peace.

If international administration is to be permanent, those inhabitants who may wish to leave should be allowed to do so, taking their property with them. Society might even exercise the right, if circumstances seem to require it, of moving out all the inhabitants who do not pledge loyalty to the new regime and replacing them with others who wish to settle there, the exchange being carefully administered by an international commission.

With the permanent international organization once agreed to, we shall find at hand many a device, already tested, for building the foundations of the edifice of peace.

DEPENDENT PEOPLES AND MANDATES

BY HUNTINGTON GILCHRIST

For the first time in history, during the twenty years from 1920 to 1940 millions of "dependent peoples" [1] were governed under a system of international responsibility—the mandates regime of the League of Nations. Since 1939 the practical operation of this system has been suspended by the war. Geneva has been largely isolated from the rest of the world and many organs of the League of Nations have been unable to meet. Japan violated the mandate agreement by fortifying and using as naval and air bases the islands in the Western Pacific mandated to her for peaceful administration. Some of these are now occupied by the United States, and Japan will certainly not be allowed to administer them again. New Guinea, a part of which was mandated to Australia, was occupied by Japan and then reoccupied by the United Nations.

These are the actual war situations of these territories, but legally their position remains unchanged. The mandatory nations to which they were assigned a quarter century ago are still responsible to the League of Nations for their government.

In the peace settlement to come, the question of these "backward territories," [2] as well as the whole larger issue of govern-

---

Huntington Gilchrist, after teaching and carrying on research in government in the Far East from 1913 to 1915, joined the United States Army as a private in the first World War and served later as a captain, General Staff, A.E.F. Headquarters, France. He was one of the first members of the Secretariat of the League of Nations, acting successively from 1919 to 1928 as personal assistant to Raymond B. Fosdick, Under Secretary General, as Chief of the Department of Administrative Commissions, and as Assistant Director of the Mandates Section. Since 1928 he has been in the chemical industry in England and the United States. He was consultant to the Department of State in 1943 in connection with the formation of the United Nations Relief and Rehabilitation Administration and Secretary of the Second Session of the UNRRA Council in 1944.

[1, 2] The terms "dependent," "backward," and "colonial" peoples and territories are as a rule used interchangeably in this chapter and no attempt will be made to define them.

ment of colonies, protectorates, and other dependencies, will doubtless be raised and may require reconsideration.

The mandates system never pretended to cure all problems of administration or completely prevent abuses in the treatment of natives but it did establish the principle of international responsibility for the government of dependent peoples and provide a practical method for putting that principle into practice, and it not only called to public attention many weak and unsatisfactory situations involving the welfare of natives in the mandated territories but helped bring about a remedy. The mandates system does represent progress and no alternative has ever been tried.

The mandates system is a part of the League of Nations, and there should be no great difficulty in bringing it to life again if the League continues to function along pre-war lines. If, on the other hand, a new United Nations organization takes the place of the League, some arrangements for transfer of powers and functions must be found, and in view of the legal position, this may not be as simple as might at first appear.

Whatever is done is bound to affect, at least indirectly, all the "colonial world," which covers between one fourth and one third of the world's land surface and contains more than one eighth of the population of the earth. In fact, since the growth of colonies, following the discoveries of the fifteenth to the eighteenth centuries, wars between European powers have usually caused greater territorial changes in outlying regions than within Europe itself.

The colonial peoples have generally had little or nothing to do with either the causes or the settlements of these wars which have so affected their destinies. They have been pawns in the imperial struggles of European and Asiatic powers. Commercial enterprises in "backward" areas were sometimes undertaken by private groups without national support, but as soon as political protection appeared necessary, the British, French, German, or other flag usually followed after the businessman.

In modern times the greatest incentives for acquiring and retaining colonies have been military strategy and economic advantage. The latter, of course, includes the control of supplies of raw materials, special marketing opportunities for home-manufactured goods, new territories for the settlement of surplus home populations, and, especially, opportunities for investment.[3] National prestige and the opportunity for administrative positions in government offers further incentive. Desire for special position in missionary or cultural work has in some cases doubtless influenced a movement toward colonial control.

At the end of the first World War, the rights and interests of dependent peoples were clearly recognized. The Allies forswore annexation of backward territories which had been taken from the enemy and, individually as trustees and not as sovereigns, undertook the government of these territories under the supervision of the League of Nations. This resulted from the fifth of President Wilson's Fourteen Points, which reads:

> A free, open-minded, and absolutely impartial adjustment of colonial claims, based upon a strict observance of the principle that in determining all such questions of sovereignty the interests of the populations concerned must have equal weight with the equitable claims of the governments whose title is determined.

Article 22 of the Covenant of the League of Nations translated this point into action. The principles embodied in these texts, however, were not fully carried out by the League or by the mandatories. Syria and the Lebanon, for instance, were mandated to France although it is probable that the population would have preferred some other mandatory power. Moreover, the allocation of the mandates by the Principal Allied and Associated Powers and not by the League followed the general lines already established by military occupation. The actual system used was a compromise between "imperialism" and the idealistic solution of direct international administration in the interests of the inhabitants alone.

The former enemy territories were divided into "A," "B," and "C" groups, roughly corresponding to the presumed degree of independence or autonomy which might eventually be accorded as a result of political development. The "A" mandates, for areas recognized as approaching the time when they could be granted

[3] Lawrence K. Rossinger, *Independence for Colonial Asia* (New York, Foreign Policy Association), Foreign Policy Reports, February 1, 1944.

independence, comprised the Turkish dependencies in the Near East: Iraq (mandated to Great Britain), Syria and the Lebanon (France), Palestine with Trans-Jordan (Great Britain). Iraq was granted independence in 1932. Syria and the Lebanon have been granted independence recently but, as explained below, the legal position is not clear. Palestine has always been in a difficult position because of the problem of the Jewish National Home in this predominantly Arab country, but in June, 1944, Britain promised a more autonomous post-war regime to Trans-Jordan.

The "B" and "C" mandates, for areas not expected to be granted independence in the foreseeable future, comprise all the former German possessions in Africa and the Pacific. The only important difference between "B" and "C" is that in the "C" territories, the mandatory power is not obliged to grant economic equality to the other members of the League of Nations. The "B" territories are: Cameroons, under British mandate; Cameroons under French mandate; Ruanda-Urundi (Belgium); Tanganyika (Great Britain); Togoland under British mandate; Togoland under French mandate. The "C" territories are: Nauru (British Empire); New Guinea (Australia); Pacific Islands under Japanese mandate; Southwest Africa (Union of South Africa); Western Samoa (New Zealand).

The principle of international responsibility in administration was maintained by requiring each mandatory power to submit a report every year for examination by the Permanent Mandates Commission (a committee of colonial experts appointed by the Council of the League of Nations, the majority of whose members were not nationals of mandatory powers), and then to act on the resolutions from the Council of the League, which were usually based on the Commission's advice.

What will happen to this whole situation at the end of this second World War? Territorial changes affecting backward peoples will certainly take place. The Marshall Islands will not be allowed to remain under mandate to Japan. How will Italian Somaliland in northeast Africa be governed? Will the Western Pacific possessions or mandated territories of Australia, France, Great Britain, Holland, Portugal, or other countries merely return to their pre-war political allegiance and status irrespective of the military occupation to which they may have been subjected? There may be a reversion to the pre-1919 practice, with each power acquiring and retaining full ownership of all "backward" territories which it occupies and to which it can obtain legal title. At the Paris Peace Conference of 1919, Australia, New Zealand, and South Africa insisted vigorously, though unsuccessfully, on this solution in regard to territories which their forces had wrested from Germany.

So far, except for a movement toward autonomous self-government in certain cases like the Dutch East Indies, not one of the United Nations in this war has indicated any willingness to yield or share internationally any of its past rights as to ownership and control of its own colonies or other dependencies. Although various schemes have been proposed, largely in the United States, for world government or international regional administration, whereby structure and control of the government of backward territories would be profoundly affected, none so far has received the open official support of any of the United Nations.

Between the extremes of annexation and entirely new schemes lies the possibility of continuing, extending or modifying the mandates system created at Paris in 1919 and still legally in existence, or of adopting some other compromise program.

A continuation of the League of Nations system would naturally be the simplest solution. Some legal problems will have to be dealt with anyway—especially regarding the disposition of the Japanese Mandated Islands—but, if the entire regime for the mandated territories is to be abandoned or altered or transferred to some other "authority," the legal complications might be numerous. Any decision to effect a change would presumably be made in the first place by the more powerful members of the United Nations. Objections by Axis Powers could easily be disposed of, but some smaller allied or neutral power on the Council or in the Assembly of the League of Nations might conceivably raise difficulties, legally justified but perhaps actually motivated by political reasons unrelated to mandates.

THE LEGAL POSITION OF THE MANDATES SYSTEM

A brief review of the principal steps taken to inaugurate the mandates regime, allocate the mandates, and prescribe their terms will illustrate the complexity of the legal position. No attempt is made here to analyze, or to solve, the much mooted problem of "sovereignty" over mandated territories. Over fifty international lawyers of many countries have covered pages with ramifications of this point to support their preferences for the "sovereignty" of the mandatory powers, or the Principal Allied and Associated Powers, or the territories themselves, or the League of Nations, or a division of some sort. This question, however, may prove of practical importance if the Permanent Court of International Justice should ever be called upon to decide some fundamental issue as to the status of one or more of these territories.

The territories formerly belonging to Germany were renounced by Articles 118 and 119 of the Treaty of Versailles (which came into force in January, 1920) in favor of the Principal Allied and Associated Powers, and by Article 22 of the same Treaty the mandates regime for administration of these territories under the general control of the League of Nations was set up. The territories formerly belonging to Turkey were renounced by the Treaty of Lausanne (which came into force in 1923), "the future of these territories . . . being settled or to be settled by the parties concerned" (presumably the Principal Allied Powers who had already acted as explained below).

The Principal Allied and Associated Powers (France, Great Britain, Italy, Japan, and the United States), acting through the Supreme Council at the Paris Peace Conference on May 7, 1919, allocated the mandates for the former German possessions. The United States, represented by President Wilson, then made a reservation regarding Yap; and later, despite its failure to ratify the Treaty of Versailles, it maintained, largely on the ground of its contribution to the defeat of Germany, that there could be no valid or effective disposition of these territories without its assent, which had not been given in the case of Yap.

As the United States did not ratify the Treaty of Versailles it was not legally one of the Principal Allied and Associated Powers in so far as that phrase refers to rights under the Treaty. But the United States contended in February, 1921, that it was included therein and that the texts of the mandates stating that the "Principal Allied and Associated Powers" had agreed to the provisions thereof were inaccurate because the United States had not so agreed. Political consideration for its claims from the Principal Allied Powers appears to have been what the United States desired. With the exception of the case of Yap, the mandatories and the League of Nations Council appear to have been ready to accord this and thus in fact to treat the United States for this purpose and subsequent to this date (February-March, 1921) as one of the Principal Allied and Associated Powers. The position of Yap in relation to the United States was cleared up later.

The Treaty of Versailles contains the League Covenant, and Germany, as a party to the Treaty, "would seem entitled to a fair application of all its terms." [4] No claim or right of protest by Germany in regard to the mandates system was ever recognized by the Principal Allied and Associated Powers or by the League of Nations although Great Britain pointed out that Article 22 constituted a pledge by the Allied Powers to Germany and to their own peoples "to recognize and to accept the special role and function of the League of Nations in connection with the mandates." [5]

The Principal Allied Powers (France, Great Britain, Italy, and Japan), acting through the Supreme Council at San Remo on April 25, 1920, allocated the mandates for the former Turkish territories. This was after the United States retired from the Supreme Council. In August, 1921, the United States (Secretary Hughes) maintained that American approval was necessary for the allotment of these mandates, but there does not appear to have been objection by the United States at any time to the choice of mandatories made at Sam Remo.

The Treaty of Lausanne does not contain the Covenant of

[4] Quincy Wright, *Mandates under the League of Nations* (Chicago, Chicago University Press, 1930), p. 494.

[5] British note to the United States, Dec. 22, 1921, in *Mandate for Palestine*, Dept. of State, 1927.

the League of Nations and makes no mention of the mandates over former Turkish territory. Turkey has never claimed any rights as to the disposition—except for the special question as to frontiers of Iraq (Mosul)—or administration of these former Turkish territories, and it would appear that she has no such rights.

Thus, in view of the provisions of the Treaty of Versailles (Articles 118–119), the Covenant of the League of Nations (Article 22), and the text of the mandates, the Principal Allied and Associated Powers, having accepted responsibility for the institution of the Mandates Regime and having allocated the mandates in the first place, might contend (and this is the view of certain important authorities) that they have the power, and they alone, to change the status of a mandated territory by terminating the mandates regime otherwise than by grant of independence to the territory. These Powers might also contend that their consent is required for any fundamental change in the regime and for any reallocation of a mandate. This view has the advantage of simplicity especially if action is required at the present time, for instance in the case of the Japanese mandated islands because only a few governments need to act and because the Council and Assembly of the League of Nations are not functioning.

The interests and claims of Japan and Italy can be disposed of in the treaties of peace with them. Thus, France, Great Britain, and the United States, which would doubtless still be recognized for this purpose as the Principal Associated Power, would alone be required to act.

Another view, also supported by experts, is that the Principal Allied and Associated Powers were entrusted with a transitional function, and that once they had placed the territories under the regime of Article 22 of the Covenant they passed out of the picture [6] and that thereafter the League of Nations was alone competent not only to reallocate mandates, which is more generally agreed, but also to effect any such change in the status of the territories as was not contemplated by the Covenant. Some experts

[6] Quincy Wright, *op. cit.*, p. 487.

maintain that an amendment to the Covenant would be required for such a change. In any event the Assembly would doubtless insist that it should approve such action or at least be consulted. The Council might decide that it alone had all necessary power. Unanimity would be required in either body, and a reconstituted Council would seem necessary rather than the Council as composed at its last meeting nearly five years ago. It is not clear, therefore, which states would participate in action on the matter. France and Great Britain as permanent members of the Council would certainly do so. The right of the United States to participate would doubtless also be recognized in view of its part in the winning of both wars, and of its separate treaties in regard to most of the mandated territories as mentioned further below. Whatever fundamental legal strength this solution possesses, from the practical and procedural points of view there are complications and uncertainties which might cause considerable delay.

Each mandatory power normally continues to retain its rights under its mandate until the territory is ready for independence or quasi-independence, unless it consents to a transfer of the mandate or to a change in its terms or is convicted of serious violation of its own obligations as mandatory. It is doubtful whether a mandatory power has the right to resign the mandate unilaterally.

The terms of the mandates were proposed by four of the five Principal Allied and Associated Powers (France, Great Britain, Italy, and Japan) acting as a group, as they did in allocating the mandates. The United States insisted, as early as May 12, 1920, upon participating in the decisions of this group as to the provisions of the mandates and on November 20, 1920, requested of the British Government that the draft mandates be submitted to the United States before submission to the Council of the League of Nations. On February 21, 1921, the United States declared that its approval of the form of the mandates was essential to their validity. Before the United States claimed this right of intervention, the terms of the "C" mandates had already been proposed by the above-mentioned Principal Allied Powers and confirmed by the Council of the League of Nations. They were not reconsidered, but the texts of the other mandates were reviewed with the United States and were proposed by the same group only after agreement had been reached with the United States.

The mandatory powers individually (Australia, Belgium, British Empire, France, Great Britain, Japan, New Zealand, and South Africa) agreed to accept the various mandates and undertook to exercise them on behalf of the League of Nations in accordance with the provisions of the proposed mandate texts.

The Council of the League of Nations, on behalf of the League of Nations in accordance with Article 22 of the Covenant, defined the terms of the mandates as they had been proposed by the Principal Allied Powers and confirmed them.

The United States negotiated separate treaties with certain of the mandatory powers (Belgium, France, Great Britain, Japan). These treaties set forth the view of the United States as to its legal rights in regard to each mandated territory and consented, on behalf of the United States, to the administration of the territory concerned pursuant to the mandate (which was quoted in the Preamble) and subject to the treaty with the United States. These treaties also provided: that the United States and American citizens should have the same rights under each mandate as if the United States were a member of the League of Nations; that vested American property rights should be respected; that extradition treaties with the mandatory should apply to the territory (not in treaty for Syria and the Lebanon); that a duplicate of the annual report of the mandatory power should be sent to the United States, without whose consent modification of the terms of the mandate should not affect American rights. The treaties regarding Palestine and Syria, also provide that Americans are permitted to establish and maintain educational, philanthropic, and religious institutions in the territories and to teach the English language.

The treaty with Japan, the first of the series, dealt especially with the island of Yap and provided that, in respect to cable stations and communications and rights connected therewith, the United States and its nationals should be treated as Japan and its nationals are treated. Freedom of American missionaries to follow their calling was especially stipulated, as was the application to the island of existing treaties between Japan and the United States.

No such treaties were concluded in respect to the territories under mandate to the British Dominions (nor to the British Empire, Nauru). As the "open door" for all League members is not provided for in these "C" mandates, the United States is not, in the absence of such treaties, discriminated against in comparison with League members.

The consent of the Council of the League of Nations for any modification of the terms of the mandates is specifically provided for in the text of each mandate.

It would appear, therefore, that any rights, interests, and claims of Germany, Italy and Japan as regards the mandates regime and the status of individual mandated territories could be disposed of in the treaties of peace with them. Approval of the mandatory power concerned (unless it had been convicted of violation of the mandate) by the League of Nations (through amendment of the Covenant or by unanimous vote of the Assembly or Council), by the United States, and/or by the Principal Allied and Associated Powers would be necessary for any fundamental change in the mandates system or for any reallocation of a mandate. The agreement of the mandatory and the Council of the League would be necessary for any change in terms.

The mandates system represents the trusteeship of civilization for the welfare of dependent peoples and as almost all civilized states, through membership in the League or otherwise, have accepted this responsibility or endorsed this program, it is therefore most advisable from the broadest point of view that any fundamental change in this system should be approved by the civilized states of the world generally either through action by the Assembly of the League, by the Peace Conference, or by the new General International Organization and should not be taken by a few great powers alone.

THE EFFECT OF THE WAR ON THE MANDATED TERRITORIES

The great changes wrought by the war in the practical status and in the actual government of these territories may have a far-reaching effect on their future. The territories are divided below into five groups; the developments that may affect each group are suggested by questions asked or by statements made. Most of the questions under Group 1 are general and apply to the others as well.

1. *Six territories that are under mandate to one of the United Nations and are not occupied by the enemy: British Cameroons, British Togoland, Palestine, Southwest Africa, Tanganyika, and Western Samoa.* What steps have the mandatories taken during the war to fulfill the mandates? Did the mandatories submit annual reports to the League of Nations? Have the mandates been violated in any important respect during this period? Were any of these territories occupied by United Nations forces? What evidence is there on these points and what explanations? To what extent can the fact of war justify divergence from complete fulfillment of the mandate? What effect, if any, on the validity and continuity of the mandates system has been occasioned by the outbreak of the war and the nonfunctioning of the League of Nations during the war in so far as mandates are concerned? How will these developments affect the practical and legal status of the territories after the war ends?

2. *Two territories that are under mandate to one of the United Nations and have been partly or wholly occupied by the enemy and then reoccupied by United Nations forces: New Guinea, Nauru.* What practical and legal steps of importance were taken by the enemy during its occupation? What practical and/or legal consequences will flow from the fact of reoccupation by one or more of the United Nations other than the mandatory? To what extent did the inhabitants of the territories participate in the war? To what extent should the territories themselves, rather than the mandatories, be taxed for the cost of repairing war damage in so far as these costs cannot in fact be collected from the enemy? What assets, such as new air or naval transport facilities, have accrued to the territories as a result of the war and what status will they have?

3. *Territory under mandate to a state no longer a member of the League of Nations, now an enemy power* (*Japan*), *the terri-*

tory itself being in enemy and later United Nations occupation: the Pacific Islands under Japanese mandate. What effect, if any did the outbreak of the war have on the status of the mandate? Did Japan violate the mandate seriously before or after the outbreak of war? What evidence is there to that effect? What steps, if any, did Japan take to fulfill the mandate during the war and her continued occupation of the islands? What legal and/or practical effect will occupation of the islands by one or more of the United Nations have on the status of the territory in respect to Japan's rights, the rights of the occupying country or countries, and the members of the League of Nations? What rights under the mandate has the large Japanese population which has immigrated into the territory during the mandate regime? [7]

4. *Territory under a mandatory* (*Belgium*), *one of the United Nations, whose homeland has been occupied by the enemy, the territory being administered by the government-in-exile of the mandatory: Ruanda-Urundi.* If acts in respect to the territory were taken by the enemy or by the king of the Belgians under enemy duress, how valid would they be? Does the government-in-exile have full power to act as mandatory and will any steps be required to regularize the status of the territory after the war and the acts taken therein during the war?

5. *Three territories that have not been occupied by the enemy and are under a mandatory power* (*France*) *that was at one time one of the allied powers, later a "neutral" under enemy occupation, and still later a power "reoccupied" by and recognized as one of the United Nations: French Cameroons, French Togoland, Syria and the Lebanon.* Here again there are distinctions. The French Cameroons and Togoland were controlled during most of the war by local administrations friendly to or cooperating with the United Nations, but whether action inconsistent with the mandate was taken therein at any time and, if so, what its effect on the status of the territory may have been and may have continued to be is perhaps a question.

Treaties providing for the independence of Syria and the Leb-

[7] Huntington Gilchrist, "The Japanese Islands: Annexation or Trusteeship," *Foreign Affairs*, July, 1944.

anon under a French alliance—a status similar to that of Iraq from 1922 to 1932—were signed on November 13 and December 22, 1936, to take effect in three years. These treaties never came into force, since for political reasons they were not ratified by the French Parliament. The Permanent Mandates Commission and the Council of the League of Nations had given their blessing to this movement toward independence. Because the French Government failed to put the treaties into force and because of the consequences which not unnaturally followed, the French High Commissioner in Syria, in the summer of 1939, felt obliged to suspend the constitution of Syria, dismiss the Chamber, and directly or indirectly take over all power himself, thereby intimating that French rule in Syria would be permanent. Following the European war and the Franco-Syrian armistice in 1940, the government at Vichy held power in Syria and the Lebanon until the invasion of the country by the Free French in June, 1941. General Catroux, who headed the invasion, announced at the time on behalf of the Free French group and the British Government that "both Syria and the Lebanon henceforth will be a sovereign and independent people." On September 27 and November 26, 1941, the independence of Syria and of the Lebanon, respectively, was proclaimed by General Catroux. The United States Government gave approval to these developments but at the same time called attention to the continued existence of the mandate for these territories and to the United States treaty concerning them, which required renegotiation before full independence could be realized.

In November, 1943, serious trouble again broke out. The Lebanon Government, citing the Atlantic Charter, declared "complete independence" of France. The representative of the French Committee of National Liberation arrested the premier and his ministers, suspended the constitution and "recaptured" all power for France. This was on the ground that any such fundamental change in the situation required the approval of the French Government and the League of Nations, neither of which was in fact in a position to act at the time. The British Government intervened promptly, and General Catroux was again brought to the scene. He freed the Lebanon Government and opened negotiations which resulted in "independence" in fact for the Lebanon and Syria. Late in December he signed an agreement giving up on behalf of France all legislative and administrative functions previously exercised by the mandatory. Since January 1, 1944, the mandatory has waived the exercise of its veto power in respect to legislation in these countries and on January 3, Syria and the Lebanon took over jointly from the French the administration of the very important customs and tobacco monopolies. The mandate is still in existence legally but is to remain dormant until it can be replaced by a treaty with a recognized government of France which also has the approval of the League of Nations.[8]

What validity under the mandate have the repeated promises and proclamations of independence? What validity has the administration of the Free French and that of the French Committee of National Liberation? What steps will have to be taken to regularize the status of these territories and the developments which have taken place therein? Has the existence of the League of Nations, even though nonfunctioning, made it easier for the French to continue control of these countries and has it delayed independence for them? Should any further steps be taken before the end of the war to implement the promise of freedom and independence given to Syria and the Lebanon by French representatives with the open approval of the British and United States governments?

The solution of these problems involves the continued responsibility of the mandatory powers to the League of Nations as well as the responsibility of the League of Nations itself, under the Covenant, for the fulfillment of the mandates, or, in case of default or presumption of default, for action by the Council of the League or by the Permanent Court of International Justice.

OBLIGATIONS OF THE MANDATORY POWERS

The obligations of the mandatory powers under the mandates (and the special treaties with the United States which apply to all these territories except Nauru, New Guinea, Southwest Africa and Western Samoa) are of three general kinds: those involving

[8] See footnote on p. 155.

(1) the League of Nations—international responsibility; (2) the members of the League (and the United States) and their nationals—economic equality and freedom for missions; and (3) other obligations concerning the administration of the territories—good government and native welfare. These obligations may be grouped and summarized as follows:

1. *Obligations involving the League of Nations.*
   a. Submission of an annual report to the satisfaction of the Council of the League (duplicate to the United States).
   b. Consent of the Council of the League for any modification in the terms of the mandates and the special regime for Trans-Jordan (such modifications not to affect American rights without the consent of that government).
   c. Special arrangements to be made by the Council of the League of Nations on termination of a mandate, in particular as regards the holy places in Palestine and the financial obligations of the mandate administrations in Palestine and in Syria and the Lebanon ("A" Mandates).
   d. Deposit of the original of the mandate with the Secretary General of the League of Nations and, in certain cases, one of three originals of final reports of boundary commissions.
   e. Application to the territories of international conventions approved by the League of Nations ("A" and "B" mandates).
   f. Cooperation with the League of Nations in the execution of any common policy for the prevention of disease ("A" mandates and Tanganyika mandate).

2. *Obligations involving members of the League of Nations and their nationals (and the United States and its nationals).*
   a. Equal economic rights for nationals of all members of the League of Nations and of the United States ("A" and "B" mandates) and equal rights for archaeological research ("A" mandates).
   b. Freedom of conscience and worship and missionary activity for nationals of states members of the League and of the United States.

c. Obligation to submit to the Permanent Court of International Justice any dispute between the mandatory and another member of the League.

Obviously the continuation of the League would facilitate the fulfillment of the substance of these obligations. But if the United Nations or some other international organization should take its place, the Council of the League of Nations could, in consenting to necessary modifications of the mandates fulfill properly its own responsibility under the Covenant only if all the substance of all these points were retained in the new arrangement. The Council of the League is, however, a political body. In this connection, one should consider also what states will be members of the Council of the League at the end of the war and what action may be expected from a body so constituted, or by the Assembly of the League may have on the situation. The Council at the end of its last meeting in December, 1939, consisted of: France, Great Britain (permanent members), Belgium, Bolivia, China, Dominican Republic, Egypt, Finland, Greece, Iran, Peru, South Africa, Yugoslavia; but the periods for which most of these states were expected to serve have now come to an end.

3. *Other obligations of the mandatory powers ("B" and "C" Mandates).*[9]

a. Responsibility for maintaining peace, order, and good government in the territories.
b. Promotion of the material and moral well-being and social progress of the inhabitants.
c. Not to establish military or naval bases nor organize native military forces except for the defense of the territory.
d. Prohibition of the slave trade.
e. Prohibition of forced labor except for essential public works and services, and then only in return for adequate compensation; careful supervision of labor contracts ("B" and "C"

[9] No attempt is made here to outline the obligations of the mandatory powers for "A" mandates, as these obligations apply primarily to only one mandated territory, Palestine (the other "A" mandated territory, Syria and Lebanon, being, in fact, already independent).

mandates) and of the recruiting of labor ("B" mandates).

f. Control of the traffic in arms and ammunition.

g. Prohibition of supply of liquor to the natives ("C" mandates); strict control over the sale of liquor ("B" mandates).

h. Protection of the interests of the natives in their lands ("B" mandates).

i. Promulgation of strict regulations against usury ("B" mandates).

j. The "B" and "C" mandatories have the right to administer their mandated territories as integral portions of their own territories (or federate with adjacent British territories in the case of Tanganyika), provided that the other provisions of the mandates are not thereby infringed.

The League of Nations has supervised the fulfillment by the mandatory powers of their obligations through action of its Council, Assembly, and Permanent Mandates Commission—primarily the last. The Permanent Mandates Commission has regularly examined the annual reports of the mandatory powers with the assistance (friendly "cross-examination" would be a more accurate, if less official, word) of a representative of the mandatory power concerned in each case and has presented its observations thereon to the Council of the League of Nations. The Council has passed them to the mandatory powers with a request that the latter comply with the report of the Commission. The Commission has usually limited itself to asking for further information on points of doubt and to noting developments of interest or concern. Only occasionally has it directly criticized the activity of the mandatory or expressed an opinion as to the compatibility of action of the mandatory power with its obligations under the mandate. As a rule, the Commission and Council limited their comments to events which had taken place and did not attempt to prescribe action for the future.

Despite this limitation, the Council and the Permanent Mandates Commission did, through a twenty-year period, constantly watch over the fulfillment of the various provisions of the mandates. Moreover, they laid down many general and detailed interpretations. It is most important that the standards thus set up should be retained. First, they should be properly analyzed, codified, and indexed. This could be done at once by some official or unofficial body with the necessary competence, foresight, and budget, and would be of great value to the international authorities taking over supervision of the administration of the mandated territories. If a new commission is formed, these standards should constitute a starting point for its work; if the Permanent Mandates Commission and the League of Nations are continued, the analysis and codification will be useful as a review and tabulation of past achievements.

THE MANDATES COMMISSION DURING THE PRESENT WAR

Annual reports on the administration of certain mandatory territories since 1939 have been received at Geneva, but how many reports have been submitted to the League of Nations and to the United States Government and by what mandatories is not known. This obligation, however, remains in force and it would appear useful for the mandatory powers to carry it out and to publish their reports, except to the extent that military necessity might require modification of the content. Even in the absence of meetings of the Permanent Mandates Commission and the Council, fulfillment of the obligation would free the mandatories of any possible criticism, underline their scrupulous respect for the principle of international responsibility, and perhaps stimulate the organs of the League of Nations to take action to fulfill their obligations. It would enable public opinion to follow developments in these territories on the basis of official reports and to register its views, thus continuing one of the strongest ultimate sanctions behind the operation of the mandates system.

The Mandates Section of the Secretariat still exists in Geneva, with a Norwegian and a Portuguese member, and the work of collecting and analyzing information on developments in the territories that they are presumably carrying on should prove valuable after the war. If the League of Nations showed some continued interest in the operation of the system—for instance, through reminders from the Secretary General to the mandatory powers of the time for submission of their annual reports—League members and other states might be encouraged to recognize the special international status of the mandated territories. Mandatory powers like Australia and the British Empire might then advise the League through the Secretary General of the fact that because of the war certain provisions of its mandates had been suspended or become inoperative. The United States might similarly give notice to the League of the military occupation of parts of New Guinea and of the islands under Japanese mandate. Such acts would keep the record straight in the interests of all concerned and give proper recognition to the world trusteeship involved in the control and administration of these territories.[10]

POST-WAR DISPOSITION OF "BACKWARD" TERRITORIES

Various proposals have been put forward by private groups or individuals, especially in Great Britain and the United States, for post-war action in respect to all or certain of the so-called "backward" territories of the world. These territories may for the most part be classified in four groups:

1. *Territories under mandate* to members of the United Nations whether occupied by the enemy or not.

2. *Territories under Axis ownership or control* in the pre-war period which have been or will be taken by the Allies: Libya, Eritrea, Italian Somaliland, the Dodecanese and near-by islands, the Pacific islands under Japanese mandate, Pacific islands belonging to Japan and not claimed by non-Axis powers (Bonins).

3. *Dependencies formerly under United Nations or neutral control* which have been occupied by the enemy and which will be reoccupied by one or more of the United Nations: including Borneo, Burma, Dutch East Indies, French Indo-China, Malay States, Philippine Islands, and other islands formerly belonging to Australia, Great Britain, France, Portugal, and the United States. Formosa and other Chinese and Russian islands seized and occupied by the Japanese before the war may also be included in this group. Hongkong is perhaps in a special position here.

4. *Dependencies which have remained under the control of*

[10] See footnote on p. 155.

one of the United Nations or one of the neutral nations: including large parts of Africa controlled or protected by Belgium, France, and Great Britain; and the Caribbean Islands belonging to France, Great Britain, the Netherlands, and the United States. Strictly speaking, the war should not be expected to affect neutral "colonies" (largely those of Spain and Portugal) in this group, but they are mentioned in order to complete the picture.

Whatever might be advisable, no disposition appears in official allied quarters to do otherwise than to return dependencies previously or continuously under the control of any of the United Nations or neutral nations (Groups 3 and 4 above) to the status of national control which they held prior to the war. This seems to hold true whether or not the territories were occupied by the enemy and reoccupied by other members of the United Nations. Such status has apparently been promised to France as regards its dependencies. The United States has promised independence for the Philippine Islands in so far as this may prove practicable, even earlier than 1946—the date which had been fixed before the war. Holland has announced plans for much greater autonomy for the Dutch East Indies but would object to international supervision. Certain influential groups in Australia and New Zealand seem to favor a transfer of some of the small British islands in the Southwest Pacific to Australian and/or New Zealand administration. Formosa and other former Chinese islands should be returned to China. The disposition of Hongkong must depend on negotiations between Great Britain and China.

A progressive program was outlined in the House of Commons on July 13, 1943, by Colonel Oliver Stanley, Colonial Secretary, for the creation of regional commissions, to be composed of representatives from governments with territories in a given region or with major strategic or economic interests therein. The peoples in the territories would be associated with these commissions. They would provide for *consultation* and *collaboration,* but *administration* would remain solely the responsibility of the governing power. A system somewhat similar to this has been inaugurated in the Caribbeans for the islands under American and British control through the Anglo-American Caribbean Commission.

Under the system proposed by Colonel Stanley, the British Government apparently does not visualize *international* "trusteeship" but, rather, looks forward to "partnerships" for these territories within the British Commonwealth. Regional partnerships may eventually develop toward the creation of new British dominions —for instance in East Africa—rather than toward independence; but such a move might, by offering an example to nations less progressive in these matters, complicate the problem of raising general standards of colonial administration.

A Central International Colonial Council or Commission should be established to coordinate the work of regional organizations of the type mentioned by Colonel Stanley and to advise the General or Political Council of the League of Nations [11] or United Nations on all "colonial" questions that may require its attention. This would not include the supervision of mandated or other colonial territories placed under the direct or indirect control of the League. These duties should continue to be delegated to the Permanent Mandates Commission or some equivalent body.

This is a minimum program. It leaves a wide gulf, at least in theory, between international responsibility for the mandated territories and national responsibility for other colonial areas. The difference between these two groups is largely fortuitous and artificial. If the backward peoples in Togoland and Ruanda-Urundi need to be considered as the wards of civilization, the same in logic can be said for the backward peoples of the Gold Coast, Guam, Dahomey, the Belgian Congo, and Angola. The proper treatment of all native peoples is in fact an interest of the modern world. If the status quo is to be strengthened by the creation of a world security organization, and the intervention of other states in serious colonial situations thus made more difficult, the colonial powers should then accept some responsibility to the world organization for their treatment of the backward peoples concerned. One might conclude that this leads logically to the extension of the mandates system to all colonial areas, but the world is after all

[11] "World Organization," "League of Nations," "United Nations," "International Authority," are used interchangeably in referring to the future, unless the context clearly indicates otherwise.

a "political," not a "logical" world. Colonial nations are jealous of their independent powers, usually proud of their self-made records, and cannot easily be persuaded that international responsibility is an unmixed blessing. An unlimited extension of the mandates system to colonial areas might be generally beneficial but it would be cumbersome, would not in many cases be a real need, and cannot in fact be considered as "practical politics."

The General or Political Council of the League, acting by a two-thirds vote on the advice of its Colonial Commission, could however be authorized to take up any question of native welfare which it considered serious; to make an inquiry, including investigation on the spot; to publish a report and recommendations; and to take such other action as might be consistent with its competence.

After the war, several actions are possible in relation to the other dependent territories: Group 1, those under mandate to members of the United Nations whether occupied by the enemy or not, and Group 2, those previously under Axis control which have been or will be taken by the Allies.

Of the fourteen territories originally included within the mandate system, one (Iraq) was granted a quasi-independent status at the start and in 1932 full independence in alliance with Great Britain, a second (Syria and the Lebanon) is already recognized as independent in fact and this status will doubtless be confirmed legally shortly after the war. Thus, in two cases, the ultimate aim of the mandates system has been achieved in a comparatively short time. During the twenty-year period between the wars, independence was also obtained by Egypt but not by many other "backward" countries or territories, although definite commitments toward independence were made in the case of the Philippines. To what extent any other colonial areas were ripe for self-government during this period or could have been made so would make an interesting study.

None of the other eighteen territories in these two groups (1 and 2) appear ready for independence in the near future. Aside from participation in regional councils or commissions, there appears to be no sound proposal or special reason, short of a radical reorganization of present arrangements, for altering the status of the mandated territories in Africa and the Near East—eight in number. The evolution in Trans-Jordan has been noted above.

The remaining ten territories fall into two geographic groups: the islands in the Pacific formerly under mandate to or belonging to Japan and the Italian dependencies in Africa.

Attitudes toward the future of both of these groups show two tendencies. The late Secretary of the Navy, Frank Knox, declared that the United States should annex the islands formerly under mandate to Japan. The governments of Australia and New Zealand at the end of the last war preferred this solution for New Guinea and Western Samoa. Nauru (British Empire) has in fact been administered by Australia all along, not by Great Britain, and important influences in these two dominions would seem to favor dominion control of all the various islands in the Southwest Pacific previously under the control of the United Kingdom.

On the other hand, the Cairo Declaration of December 1, 1943, might be held to rule out annexation of the Pacific Islands by the United States. The Canberra Agreement of January 21, 1944, between Australia and New Zealand (Article 28) refers to the mandates for these dominions which are still in force. This agreement also insists (Articles 26 and 27) that there be no change "in the sovereignty or system of control of any of the islands of the Pacific" without the concurrence of these governments. This may seem a rather large order but it indicates an interesting basis for building in that area an international community of interest.

After this war, these islands will doubtless be considered of great importance to military strategy and civil aviation. Power in these respects could be given to the dominant nation in the area—to the United States for the Marshall, Caroline, and Marianas and Bonin islands, and to Australia and New Zealand for New Guinea, Western Samoa, and perhaps other British islands in the orbit of the new Canberra Agreement. Access to and joint use of bases in these islands and in other outlying regions in the Pacific and in the Atlantic Oceans should be provided for by agreements between the United Nations or a Security Committee thereof. An alternative program would give strategic control of all South Pacific islands to the United Nations, acting through a Pacific Council. Costs of fortifications and defense should be borne in any case by the powers concerned and should not be charged to the territories except as authorized by the United Nations Council for the area acting on the recommendation of the Permanent Mandates Commission.

The most important need is that the mandate principle of trusteeship and international responsibility for civil administration be continued. Direct international administration through a Pacific Council would be one possibility but there appears to be little support for such a program. Continuation of the existing mandates for New Guinea, Western Samoa, and Nauru (with possible modifications and extensions in view of rearrangements within the British Commonwealth) and the transfer of the Japanese mandate (to include the Bonins) to the United States would be the simplest solutions, with modifications as regards fortifications and defenses and with authority to return all the Japanese immigrants to Japan at the expense of the Japanese Government and to liquidate their holdings in these islands.

The only specific plan concerning the former Italian dependencies in North Africa that has received much public attention has been a movement for their return to Italy.

The administration of all or some of these African territories directly by the United Nations through a Mediterranean Council may present the best opportunity for direct international administration at the close of the war. The experiment should be tried, because a successful outcome offers solution for territorial problems of the future. If the British and French governments were willing to cooperate, joint administration of Eritrea and British, French, and Italian Somaliland under British-French mandate, with responsibility to the United Nations, would appear superficially as a practical solution. In any case, Abyssinia's outlet to the sea through Eritrea and Italian Somaliland should be thoroughly and permanently protected.

Administration, in whatever hands, should be under mandate. Fortifications and defense arrangements should be permitted, but only with the approval of the Mediterranean Council, acting under recommendation of the Permanent Mandates Commission. These fortifications might be under the administration of an "authority" other than the mandatory power. The small Italian island of Pantelleria and the others in the central Mediterranean should be ruled by the United Kingdom from Malta under mandate, as the simplest solution for this small problem. The Dodecanese should be returned to Greece.

SUGGESTED CHANGES IN THE MANDATES SYSTEM

The mandates system is likely to continue and probably to expand territorially. The experience of the past twenty-five years indicates a need to modify, interpret, and supplement the mandates themselves, or to take new steps in carrying out the system.

1. *Defense:* In the past, emphasis on this point in the "B" and "C" mandates has been negative. Military training of the natives, except for internal police and local defense of the territory, and the erection of fortifications or of military or naval bases has been prohibited, with the intention of protecting the natives from military exploitation in the interests of the mandatory power and of "neutralizing" the territories from the strategic point of view. In the islands under Japanese mandate, however, despite this prohibition, naval and air bases were established. Australia, the mandatory for New Guinea, respected this provision of the mandate and so was less able to defend the territory entrusted to it. If such provisions remain in the mandate, the chief necessity for the future is better means for their enforcement, by inspection and possibly by sanctions.

Attempts will doubtless be made to guarantee post-war world security through some collective system based largely on the police power of the "Big Three" or "Four" among the victorious United Nations. Mandated territories must be permitted to play their part in any such program. Bases should be established therein if necessary. The mandatory's positive responsibility for the defense of the territory should be made clear. "Neutralization" should be abandoned and the mandatory permitted to take such steps as it considers appropriate for defense purposes, but approved by the proper organ of the United Nations in view of the other provisions of the mandate. Specific advance approval should be given by the United Nations to the mandatory's program for training natives for defense purposes and for using funds raised from the natives for this purpose, thus recognizing the advantage of adequate defense to the territory as well as to the mandatory power, but imposing sufficient safeguards against exploitation of the natives.

2. *Economic equality:* The present provisions of the "B" mandates should be extended to the "C" mandates and to all new mandates.

3. *Investments:* Special steps to encourage the investment of outside capital (public and private) in the mandated territories should be taken by the United Nations and the mandatories by providing such guaranties as may be necessary in view of the special status of these territories. The guaranties given for the Austrian and Hungarian League of Nations Reconstruction loans of the 1920's might be considered as precedents and partial examples.

4. *Economic development:* It should be made clear that the mandatory's main economic responsibility is not to assure equality of interests for outside corporations and individuals, but the economic development of the territory in its own and its people's interest. It would be useful for the United Nations to create an Economic Development Commission to suggest a *positive* program for each territory and necessary supervision to prevent exploitation by home or foreign capital or control. Such commissions might be regional and cover colonies as well as mandated territories.

5. *Boundaries:* The United Nations should ascertain whether the boundaries of any mandated territories handicap in any important way the normal tribal life of natives living near such boundaries, for instance in West Africa. If so, subject to the prior approval of the United Nations, the boundaries should be altered to provide some special regime for the tribes concerned, or migration should be arranged if this can be done without detriment to the important interests of the natives.

6. *Self-government and independence:* As this is the ultimate

aim of the whole mandates system, a general review and summarized "progress report" should be made regularly, say at least every ten years, by the Permanent Mandates Commission.

7. *Regional cooperation:* Mandated Territories should be encouraged to join in regional cooperative administrative or consultative arrangements (as has been proposed by Colonel Stanley), provided that thereby the provisions of the mandates are in no way infringed. The Permanent Mandates Commission should be encouraged to suggest regional arrangements which it considers to the interest of mandated and neighboring territories under the control of the same nation or of different nations.

8. *Officials:* The mandatories should be encouraged to recruit their officials from other nationalities, especially from nations without colonial or mandated territories, and from any existing international civil services.

9. *Petitions:* Under present rules, an inhabitant of a mandated territory can petition the League of Nations only through the mandatory powers. This point, frequently criticized, is not of great importance, since the mandatory powers must pass on the petitions to the League and copies can be sent by the petitioner direct to Geneva. Any attempt by a mandatory power to prevent action on an important matter by failing to forward a petition is unlikely and would hardly be successful, as other methods—an outside petitioner, for instance—could be used to bring the matter before the Permanent Mandates Commission.

10. *Special reports from mandatory powers:* The Permanent Mandates Commission should be specifically empowered to obtain from any mandatory power at any time a special report on any important subject concerned with the execution of its mandates, and to propose that the mandatory power appoint a special commission to investigate any such subject. For certain inquiries on matters of interest to more than one mandatory, a mixed commission consisting of representatives of the mandatory powers concerned and of the Permanent Mandates Commission might be proposed to the Council by the Permanent Mandates Commission or by the mandatory powers.

The procedure followed in the past for dealing with the Annual Reports of the mandatory powers was slow and sometimes ineffective. The annual report of a mandatory might be received for consideration by the Mandates Commission many months after the period covered, while the comments of the latter might reach the mandatory powers through the Council only several months later. Again, some time would elapse before the mandatory powers' replies reached the Commission. These replies were often embodied in the Annual Report for the next year. This procedure should be carefully investigated for possible improvements. In any case, the mandatory powers should be expected to reply promptly and definitely to the recommendations or comments of the Permanent Mandates Commission and these replies should be placed separately on the agenda of the Commission.

11. *Visits to territories by United Nations representatives:* It is most important that in the future, representatives of the Mandates Commission should visit the various mandated territories regularly, in order to become directly acquainted with them and their problems. The Commission has felt in the past that it had no power to arrange such visits. Moreover it was divided as to the wisdom of such action, several members believing that visits would undermine the necessary authority of the mandatory powers. However, given a high standard of administration by the mandatory and discretion by the visitors, the authority of the mandatory should, if anything, be increased. If the mandatory's standards are not high, such visits should stimulate improvement. They should be made regularly by small groups of Commission members or by officials of the Secretariat at the expense of the League.

These regular visits should be distinct from investigations of special problems. In most cases where the mandatory power appoints a royal commission or similar body and a thorough job is done, the League of Nations may well refrain from making a direct inquiry on the spot. In other cases where no such arrangements are made by the mandatory power or where some international problem is involved or where a problem is acute and of the highest importance, the Permanent Mandates Commission should investigate at once on the spot, but such investigations should be specifically authorized in each case by the Political or Colonial Council on the recommendation of the Permanent Mandates Commission.

12. *Legal status of mandated territories:* It should be made clear that the mandatory power has no title to the territory, that title is held in trust by the United Nations, that the regime can be terminated only by action of the Assembly, that a mandatory power can only resign a mandate with the permission of and after release by the Council, that the Council alone has power with the agreement of the mandatory to transfer a mandate and that the Council or the Assembly, on the basis of a judgment of the Permanent Court of International Justice, has the right to terminate a mandate on the ground that the mandatory has failed to fulfill any of its important provisions.

13. *Authority of the Council and Permanent Mandates Commission:* It has been the general practice of the Permanent Mandates Commission to limit its recommendations and comment to the Annual Report under review—that is, to the past, and not to recommend or attempt to prevent action for or in the future, as this was considered beyond its authority. The Commission did often deal with the future by its comments on the past and this was usually done with great tact and diplomacy.

To obtain more assurance of effective results, the Council, acting on the advice of the Commission (and the Commission should be authorized to take the initiative here) should be empowered, whenever it considers the matter urgent and important, to issue instructions to a mandatory power regarding the fulfillment of its mandate.

14. *Voting by the Council on mandates questions:* Generally the Council should be required to act on mandates questions by a majority or two-thirds vote only. The rule in the past was unanimity. In fact the Council almost never took a vote on a mandate question, but the requirement of unanimity could not fail to influence the Permanent Mandates Commission in drawing up its reports and recommendations for action by the Council.

On matters involving the legal status of a territory, such as the transfer or termination of a mandate or changes in its terms, unanimity or near unanimity of the Council or Assembly, with the exception of the interested party, should be required, and on any judicial or quasi-judicial matter involving specifically one or more mandatory power the same rule should apply. Japan, for instance, should clearly not have been allowed to block the termination by the Council of its mandate if the Permanent Court of International Justice had found that it had fortified the Islands in violation of one of the important provisions of the mandate. The legal position, however, was not clear in the past, although the result desired might have been obtained under the "dispute" articles of the Covenant.

Despite some black spots on the record, important progress has been made in the government of backward territories especially for the welfare of dependent peoples by national administrations without international supervision. To be realistic, one might better compare progress of civilization in backward territories not with idealistic standards, but with political, economic, and social progress in the independent countries. There is this essential difference, however; in the latter the peoples are largely the masters of their own fate, whereas in backward territories, the colonial or mandatory powers have taken over responsibility for the welfare of others. This situation explains the international character of the problem and justifies the special attention given to it by an international organization.

Four main lines of future institutional development have been suggested in this article:

(1) The creation of Regional and General Colonial Commissions as cooperative, advisory, international bodies.
(2) Recognition of the principle of trusteeship in the administration of all backward territories and of the right of the United Nations in accordance with agreed rules and procedure to deal with any serious situations which may arise.
(3) Continuation, extension, and improvement of the mandates system of the League of Nations.

(4) Possible creation of direct international administration, especially for certain former dependent territories of the Axis powers.

The dependent territories of the world constitute the best testing ground for new steps in international cooperation and administration. The problems of race, language, and religion and of rivalries and hatreds inherited from centuries of conflicts and wars are less deep-seated or real in these areas than in Central and Eastern Europe. Boundaries are of comparatively recent date and, from the native point of view, for the most part artificial. Vested economic interests, too, are small here compared with those in Europe or America. Finally, the trusteeship of the more advanced nations for the native peoples in these areas is generally recognized, leaving a freer field for international action.

The more immediate need is for a proper fruition of the program already in existence—the mandates system. First, as far as practicable, steps should be taken to bring some life to this regime now and to prepare for its complete rejuvenation after the war. The Acting Secretary General of the League of Nations could remind mandatory powers to submit annual reports; mandatory powers and others concerned with military operations in mandatory territories could recognize the special status of these territories; the Mandates Section of the Secretariat could become active in codification and analysis of the work of the Mandates Commission during the past twenty-five years, in preparation of data on developments in the territories during the war years, and in maintaining liaison so far as practicable with members of the Commission, the International Labor Organization, the Economic and Financial Organizations of the League of Nations, the United Nations Relief and Rehabilitation Administration, etc. If the Secretariat is carrying on some or all of these activities the facts should be made known.

Second, the United Nations should bring about a transition from the somewhat deferential attitude of the past toward the mandatory powers to a firmer, more positive handling of mandates questions. Some authorities have taken pains to point out the need for the Permanent Mandates Commission to "cooperate" with the mandatory powers, as there was no other way by which in practice to get results. This policy was doubtless to some extent necessary, in view of the political temper of the 1920's and 1930's, of the fact that the League is not a super-government, and of the attitude of France and Great Britain. Ultimately, however, perhaps inevitably, this policy of delay and compromise called "cooperation" with the great powers, led to failure in the League's main aim of keeping the peace.

The League's record in the field of mandates is not one of clear-cut success or failure. A few critics of the system maintain that it amounted to little more than veiled annexation, but it seems to be generally agreed that, in addition to such direct results as the Permanent Mandates Commission has achieved in specific cases, the unspectacular operation of this international system and its public procedure has in given cases indirectly helped toward fulfillment of its purposes. One commentator, for instance, pointed out in regard to the Syrian rebellion of 1925 that,

> With the publicity attendant upon the work of the Commission serving to intensify the public demand for fulfillment of the spirit of the mandate, France has not cared to force Syrian Nationalists to renounce the chief principles for which they fought. Military defeat was not accompanied by moral defeat.[12]

A more tangible but deeper gain is the effect of establishing this system and of its twenty-year functioning upon the general attitude of the world toward the problem of all dependent peoples and the standards which should govern their administration. The International Labor Office in its report on "Social Developments in Dependent Territories" (Proof; Montreal, March, 1944) well summarizes this point (page 2):

> The ethical basis of colonial administration was, however, deeply affected by the principle of trusteeship. The place of the mandates system in history is assured as having strengthened a sense of the responsibility of colonial Powers for the progress of dependent peoples.

[12] Elizabeth P. MacCallum, *The Nationalist Crusade in Syria* (New York, Foreign Policy Association, 1928), p. 248.

Quincy Wright, in his monumental work *Mandates under the League of Nations*, surveys the achievements of Mandatory Administration in all its aspects, and, despite the recognition of various shortcomings and limitations in the record, draws the following conclusions:

While the period of its operation has been short and the available data incomplete, it seems fair to say that the mandates system has proved a practical method for administering backward areas, more satisfactory than others that have been tried from the standpoint of the natives and from the standpoint of the world in general. Whether or not it has been as advantageous to the administering state as have the traditional systems of colonies, protectorates, and spheres of interest, at least none of the mandatory powers has offered to resign.[13]

Many concrete cases showing successful action by the Permanent Mandates Commission could be cited; also others in regard to which the comments of the Commission had no effect on the policy of the mandatory. One keen, fair-minded, searching analyst, J. A. Decker, for instance, concluded:

Despite the limitations of its position, the Permanent Mandates Commission has shown a very active interest in almost all phases of the labor problems in the mandated territories located in the Pacific area, although it must be admitted that it has exercised only negligible influence in shaping or moderating the policies of these administrations.[14]

The results of the mandates system have been appreciable but they may well be greater. The legal basis for more complete success already exists. The mandates provide that the mandatories "shall make to the Council of the League of Nations an annual report to the satisfaction of the Council." The mandatory powers are not acting here as sovereigns but as trustees reporting to the recognized supervisory body. The Permanent Mandates Commission, however, although adviser in this field to the League Council, has not, in its desire to "cooperate" with the mandatories, usually

[13] Quincy Wright, *Mandates under the League of Nations* (Chicago, University of Chicago Press, 1930), p. 581.

[14] J. A. Decker, *Labor Problems in the Pacific Mandates* (New York, Oxford University Press, 1941), p. 221. Institute of Pacific Relations, International Research Series.

insisted on a *complete* fulfillment of this provision of the mandates. Sometimes the Commission has side-stepped a collision with the mandatory, at other times it has allowed its own recommendations which the mandatory did not carry out to gradually disappear from view. In other cases, however, the Commission has set forth its views frankly and firmly. It has naturally had to keep in mind both the political character of the Council and the possible advisability of dropping insistence on some points in order to achieve success on others of greater importance.

In view of the strength of the legal position of the Permanent Mandates Commission and the background of confidence and prestige already achieved by it, it is suggested that the Commission and the Council could afford and should in the future adopt a more courageous attitude toward the fulfillment of their responsibility, expecting from the mandatory powers at least as much cooperation as they are given. Some practical recommendations for action in this direction have been made earlier in this chapter.

Whether the present mandates system can be regenerated and fortified, whether regional and general colonial commissions can be set up, and what success they may have, will primarily depend upon the virility of the international authority of the future. A revived League of Nations would start with some legal and practical advantages. But whatever the political and administrative machinery may be, behind it must exist a genuine desire on the part of the governments to make that machinery work.

General de Gaulle and his associates in the various Free French groups and committees outside metropolitan France indicated to the Acting Secretary General at various times in 1941 and 1943 their recognition of the responsibility of France to the League of Nations in respect of fundamental changes in the status of Syria and Lebanon. (Report on the work of the League 1942 and 1943 by the Acting Secretary General.) Especially striking is this sentence from the telegram sent on April 19, 1943, by General de Gaulle to the Secretary General of the League: "It is in this spirit that you have kept informed of the measures taken in virtue and within the sphere of the mandate entrusted to France in the territories of the Cameroons and of the States of the Levant."

WORLD ECONOMICS

BY HENRY F. GRADY

MODERN WARFARE resembles the military actions of earlier periods in little else than in name. Then, a long war often brought heavier taxes and perhaps a breakdown in the system of transport, but in general its direct impact on society was relatively slight and was confined to small sections of the population. Today, "total" war, mobilizing all the vast resources of modern industry for war purposes, shapes the life of every member of the community.

The more far-reaching the economic organization for war, the greater are the changes required to convert the economy back to the tasks of peace. At the close of hostilities we shall be confronted by a world in which the structure of production and exchange will be distorted almost beyond recognition. In all nations, the strains upon international balances of payments will be severe.

It must also be emphasized, however, that the regulatory mechanisms of international economic organization, centered upon the money and commodity markets in London, were not casualties of the present war, but of the great depression which preceded it by a decade. Economic reconstruction must be thought of, therefore, not as eventual return to pre-war conditions of instability but rather as a transition to a new international economic system, which will ensure, as far as possible, high and steady levels of employment within national economies, and broad and smoothly flowing streams of trade and investment among nations. In these circumstances, an international organization to implement economic arrangements becomes more necessary than ever.

HENRY F. GRADY is chairman of the Economic Committee of the League of Nations. He was United States Trade Commissioner to London and Europe in 1919–20; vice-chairman of the United States Tariff Commission, 1937–39; Assistant Secretary of State, 1939–40; and in 1943 was appointed vice-president in charge of the Economic Section of the Allied Control Commission for Italy. Mr. Grady, born in San Francisco, is an eminent American in the field of trade and economics, and has taught, lectured and written widely on these subjects. He is president of the American President Lines in San Francisco.

INTERNATIONAL ACTION IN THE POST-WAR PERIOD

Two main types of international action in the economic field will be required. On the one hand, many governments will need help in tackling their problems of national reconstruction. On the other hand, the attempt must be made to construct a framework of international organization which will facilitate the flow of goods and capital among nations.

Reconstruction loans will be needed, but, as the experience of the 1920's showed, reconstruction by lending requires careful handling, and should be kept to a minimum, for such loans are liable to lead to a further financial crisis when the flow of new capital ceases.

Timely and expert technical assistance and advice will be even more acutely needed, on feeding, rehousing, resettlement, on handling new financial and monetary problems, overhauling antiquated tax systems, and reorganizing national banking and currency systems, wrecked by the Nazi financial shock troops.

Remembrance of the dreary depression years of the interwar period have led the peoples of industrial nations to demand that in the post-war period their governments accept the responsibility for preventing the recurrence of protracted mass unemployment. "Full employment" involves both the immediate task of finding civilian employment for demobilized servicemen and workers in war industries, and the longer-range task of maintaining productive employment at a consistently high level.[1] But the lesson of experience after 1918 is that to concentrate exclusively upon the task of demobilizing the war economy is to invite disaster. As has been very clearly demonstrated in a recent League of Nations study, "the major problem of the transition from war to peace economy . . . proved itself to be not one of getting demobilized men and machines re-employed, but of the cyclical effects of the perhaps unavoidably bumpy nature of post-war pent-up de-

[1] International Labor Organization, International Labor Conference. Twenty-sixth Session. Report III, "The Organization of Employment in the Transition from War to Peace" (Montreal, International Labor Office, 1944), p. V.

mand." [2] The conclusion is inescapable that if economic demobilization is to have any chance of success, it must be carried out within the framework of a long-run policy designed to maintain a high and steady level of economic activity and employment.

Although many of these measures will require international action, they all relate primarily to the reconstruction of national economic systems. Very quickly, however, another set of problems will appear. The danger of monetary inflation will be both greater and more widespread than it was after 1918. The occupied countries will find themselves faced with an almost complete scarcity of goods and with greatly swollen currency issues, backed only by worthless credits in Berlin. Their ability to pay for the materials they require urgently from abroad will depend upon their opportunity to sell their goods in foreign countries and upon the existence of a mechanism by which the payments can be transferred from one country to another.

The first and most urgent need therefore is for an international monetary mechanism which will make available a volume of international short-term credit, sufficient to allow a large volume of trade to flow among countries and to exercise a stabilizing influence on the value of national currencies in terms of one another —in other words, on the foreign exchange rates. It must be so organized as to allow for some degree of flexibility in national monetary policies, at the same time maintaining stable international exchange relationships.

But the economic problems of the post-war world will be "real," and no monetary manipulation will solve them. International monetary reorganization must be backed up by a smoothly functioning system of international trade organized on a multilateral, nondiscriminatory basis. To bring this into being, national barriers to imports, such as tariffs, must be substantially lowered, and discriminatory systems of quota allocation, exchange control, and preferential treatment must, as far as possible, be removed. Furthermore, red tape in customs procedure, onerous food inspection and regulation, and other administrative impediments to

[2] *Economic Fluctuations in the United States and the United Kingdom, 1918–1922* (League of Nations publication 1942.II.A.7).

legitimate international commerce, which are in fact invisible protectionism, should be reduced to a minimum. It may also be necessary, in the disordered condition of the transition period, to set up an internationally administered stabilizing agency in the commodity markets, which, while aiming at the coordination of national price and production policies, would hold buffer stocks, buying temporary surpluses which threatened to disorganize the market and liquidating them when demand conditions improved.

In the nineteenth century a free flow of international investment was an essential condition for expanding trade. By means of a steady and broadening stream of capital, originating mainly in Great Britain, the direct effects of the Industrial Revolution were transmitted overseas, and the modern world of specialized production developed. The mechanism which directed that flow of funds, with the connected system of international trade, broke down in the "great depression." If the post-war period is to see extensive economic development, especially in countries hitherto industrially backward, new institutional arrangements must be devised and must be so designed as to retain the desirable features of past forms of international lending and to eliminate their more unwelcome aspects.

EXPERIENCE ACCUMULATED BY THE ECONOMIC AND FINANCIAL ORGANIZATION OF THE LEAGUE OF NATIONS

The Economic and Financial Organization of the League of Nations was created to deal with the difficult problems of reconstruction after the first World War. At first expressly provisional and temporary, it quickly became an established mechanism for international cooperation in the economic field.

The activity of the Economic Intelligence Service in collecting and analyzing economic and statistical information, grew out of the preparation of the documentation for the Brussels Conference, convened by the League Council in 1920 "on the subject of the world-wide financial and exchange crisis." Gradually the scope of the work was widened, progress was made in rendering national statistics comparable from country to country,[3] and at

[3] The International Convention Relating to Economic Statistics, 1928, is in force in 26 countries.

the outbreak of the present war, regular publications[4] including a wide range of demographic, economic, financial, and social statistics for the various countries of the world had been appearing. Other volumes were devoted to the analysis of particular questions.[5] *Balances of Payments*, for instance, set out the debtor and creditor relations of more than thirty countries with the rest of the world, while *Money and Banking* gave both a survey of recent monetary history and the accounts of central and commercial banks in well over forty countries of the world. The results of the various studies of the Economic Intelligence Service were gathered together and placed in their proper perspective in the *World Economic Survey*, a historical analysis of the main economic developments of the year. These regular publications were supplemented from time to time by special studies on topics of particular current importance, so that the Organization provided, in a very real sense, a world center of economic information.

Since the outbreak of war, these services of current information and the work of analyzing and recording have been maintained, as far as possible, so that the basic material may be readily available when hostilities cease and the urgent problems of the transition to peacetime conditions must be faced.

Besides a permanent staff of economists whose theoretical training was supplemented by an intimate knowledge of the practical problems facing governments, the Organization included a wide range of temporary and permanent committees engaged on programs of work entrusted to them by the League Assembly or Council. Despite the difficulties imposed by war conditions, the activity of several of these, notably the Economic and Financial Committees, the Fiscal Committee, and the Delegation on Economic Depressions, has been continued and oriented to an examination of the successes and failures of the past. These studies will be invaluable to those responsible for formulating and executing policies to cope with the vast economic problems of the post-war period. The first part of the Delegation's report, published in

[4] *Monthly Bulletin of Statistics; Statistical Yearbook; International Trade Statistics: International Trade in Certain Raw Materials and Foodstuffs.*

[5] *World Production and Prices; Review of World Trade; Balances of Payments; Money and Banking; Survey of National Nutrition Policies.*

1943 under the title of *The Transition from War to Peace Economy*, has been aptly termed "much the most detailed piece of sound thinking that has so far been published on a matter which will affect the lives and prosperity of millions."

PROBLEMS OF NATIONAL RECONSTRUCTION

In the years following the armistice, when the United Nations are confronted with the task of rebuilding shattered national economies, the experience acquired by the League, both in the period of financial reconstruction after the first World War and in the troubled years since the "great depression," will be especially valuable.

Financial Reconstruction. The economic and financial difficulties of the early twenties were particularly severe in Central Europe. By the spring of 1921, the plight of Austria was desperate, and the four major ex-Allied governments appealed to the League to propose a general scheme of reconstruction. This was worked out by the Financial Committee, and in 1923 an international loan was raised under League auspices and was guaranteed in varying proportions by eight European nations. Its success was immediate and spectacular. The depreciation of the currency was halted, refugee funds flowed back into the country, the budget was soon brought into balance, and a solid foundation was laid for economic recovery. This achievement brought similar requests from other governments, and in the first post-war decade, nine international loans and reconstruction schemes were carried through under League direction. So successful was the work of the Financial Committee that, both in the first post-war decade and after the depression, various governments asked the League of Nations for aid and advice on their banking and currency problems.[6] The principles and methods used in the League Reconstruction plans were summarized in a special study published by the League Secretariat in 1930.[7] At a joint session held in December, 1943, the

[6] Technical advice was given to Austria, Hungary, Greece, Bulgaria, Roumania, Estonia, and the Free City of Danzig.

[7] *Principles and Methods of Financial Reconstruction Work Undertaken under the Auspices of the League of Nations* (League of Nations publication 1926.II.30).

Economic and Financial committees decided to prepare a critical analysis of the work of financial reconstruction undertaken by the League after the first World War, a study which should be of exceptional value to those charged with similar problems after this war.

Technical Aid and Advice. The Organization has accumulated, over the years, much information which will be useful both to governments engaged in programs of national reconstruction and to international bodies which may be set up to deal with particular problems that are international in scope. It has recently published, for example, studies on the organization of relief and rehabilitation after 1918,[8] emphasizing the need for immediate, concerted action, and on the place of relief aid in the general work of reconstruction. Working relations have already been established with the United Nations Relief and Rehabilitation Administration. At the first session of that body a resolution was adopted, inviting representatives of the League of Nations technical organizations to "attend as observers and to participate in the meetings of the Council, its committees and sub-committees, and in the meetings of the regional committees and technical standing committees." In addition, the Director General of UNRRA is to avail himself of these organizations as the nature of the work and other circumstances make appropriate.

Ever since the middle twenties the Health Organization of the League of Nations has been engaged in studies of the state of nutrition in different countries. Since these had shown that the problem concerned economists as well as physiologists and public health officers, a mixed committee of agricultural, economic, and health experts was appointed to report on national programs designed to improve food conditions and to recommend methods by which this work could be improved.[9] The importance of the League's work in this field may be gauged by the fact that the dis-

[8] *Relief Deliveries and Relief Loans*, 1919–1923 (League of Nations publication 1943.II.A.1); *Europe's Overseas Needs 1919–1920, and How They Were Met* (League of Nations publication 1943.II.A.6).

[9] The Economic Intelligence Service planned to issue regularly a *Survey of National Nutrition Policies*. The first volume was published at the end of 1938 (League of Nations publication 1938.II.A.25).

cussion of future international nutrition policy at the Hot Springs Conference on Food and Agriculture in 1943 was based upon the findings and recommendations of the Mixed Committee's Final Report.[10]

It would be easy to mention other phases of national reconstruction in which the work of the Economic and Financial Organization will be significant. The work done on problems of urban and rural housing will be of real assistance in the formulation of policies both for the rebuilding of devastated areas and for the long-run maintenance of employment. The recent volume on the growth potential of European populations [11] will be important both to those who will formulate future policies of international migration and resettlement, and to national governments in mapping out programs to provide employment for their people. Much of the documentation [12] prepared for the European Conference on Rural Life, as well as the recent comprehensive study on *Agricultural Production in Continental Europe during the 1914–18 War and the Reconstruction Period* and the work done on the problem of agricultural credits will be invaluable in the preparation of plans for agricultural reconstruction in Europe, and for the resettlement of displaced persons. The principles, worked out by the Fiscal Committee, that should govern taxation in countries at different stages of economic development could serve as a guide to national governments in nations where tax reforms are necessary after the war.

The main task confronting national governments at the close of the present war will be to provide productive employment and high living standards for their people. It will be impossible to

[10] *The Relation of Nutrition to Health, Agriculture and Economic Policy* (League of Nations publication 1937.II.A.10).

[11] The Future Population of Europe and the Soviet Union (League of Nations Publication 1944.II. A. 2). Since the outbreak of war the work of the League Committee on population problems has been taken up by the Office of Population Research of Princeton University, under the general editorship of the Director of the Economic, Financial and Transit Department of the League.

[12] The scientific documentation for this conference, which was to have been held in 1939 but was postponed indefinitely by the war, was prepared by the International Institute of Agriculture, the International Labor Office, and the International Institute of Intellectual Cooperation, as well as the Economic and Financial and the Health Organizations of the League.

secure these unless means are devised for "preventing or mitigating economic depressions." For several years the Economic Intelligence Service has been engaged on a program of research into the nature and causes of economic fluctuations,[13] and on different occasions before the war the Economic and Financial Committees issued recommendations in particular situations. Little progress was made, however, in coordinating national recovery policies, and the situation was aggravated by the fact that certain great powers chose to pursue policies of economic self-sufficiency. The work of the Delegation on Economic Depressions was well advanced by the fall of 1939, but with the outbreak of war it became necessary to consider the problem of economic security in a wholly new context. Members' attention was therefore turned to an examination of the methods by which a smooth transition from war to peace conditions might be effected, and the first part of the Delegation's report and recommendations, entitled *The Transition from War to Peace Economy*, was issued in 1943.[14] Work on the second part, the longer-range, but no less vital, problem of maintaining high and steady levels of economic activity and employment, is now in progress. It is perhaps in this field that international economic cooperation after the war will be both most urgently needed and most difficult to secure.[15]

INTERNATIONAL ECONOMIC COOPERATION

The League of Nations Economic and Financial Organization was created to deal with the emergency problems of the post-armistice years. Soon, however, it became the established mechanism for international economic cooperation in a wide range of

[13] *Economic Fluctuations in the United States and the United Kingdom, 1918–1922* (League of Nations publication 1943.II.A.7).

[14] Publications directly relating to the problem include: *The Course and Phases of the World Economic Depression* (League of Nations publication 1931.II.A.21); *Prosperity and Depression: a Theoretical Analysis of Cyclical Movements* (League of Nations publication 1939.II.A.4[1]); *The Statistical Testing of Business Cycle Theory*, Vol. I, "A Method and Its Application to Investment Activity" (League of Nations publication 1938.II.A.23); Vol. II, "Business Cycles in the United States of America, 1919–1932" (League of Nations publication 1939.II.A.16); *Economic Fluctuations in the United States and the United Kingdom, 1918–1922* (League of Nations publication 1942.II.A.7).

[15] *The Transition from War to Peace Economy* (League of Nations publication 1943.II.A.3).

subjects on which action could be usefully undertaken only by joint effort. Sometimes that action succeeded, either wholly or in part; more often than not it ultimately failed. But in all cases issues were clarified, and experience was gained from which the future can benefit.

Monetary Organization. Official discussions have already begun with a view to establishing future mechanisms of international currency stabilization. Especially since the breakdown of the world currency system in the early thirties and the spread of bilateral arrangements for settling international payments, the Organization has been concerned with international monetary problems. Inquiries into the experience of numerous countries with clearing agreements and exchange control were initiated in the middle thirties, and the reports issued [16] provided a thorough analysis of possible methods by which national governments might relax these controls which were hampering world trade, and achieve a smooth transition from controlled to free economies. Although this work could do little to check the trend towards autarky which grew stronger as the threat of war increased, its importance for the current discussions should not be lost sight of. Study of these problems continues, and a comprehensive volume on the monetary experience of the interwar period will be published in the near future.

Commercial Policy. It is perhaps in the task of reorganizing international trade after the war that the work and experience of the Economic and Financial Organization will be most rewarding. Article 23e of the Covenant laid down that the members of the League "will make provision to secure and maintain . . . equitable treatment for the commerce of all Members of the League." In the immediate post-war period, the opinions of national governments on problems of trade and commercial policy were sharply divided, and the Economic Committee, which was mainly responsible for work in this field, confined its attention to the less controversial matters on which agreement and progress was most likely to be achieved. Among these were the simplification of customs formalities, the elimination of methods of unfair com-

[16] League of Nations publication 1935.II.B.6 and 1938.II.A.10.

petition between traders, commercial arbitration, the assimilation of statistical terminology and methods, and the assimilation of national legislation on bills of exchange, promissory notes, and checks. On all of these questions, international conventions were secured, which were later ratified by a long list of countries.

The Brussels Conference had urged that governments should remove the "artificial restrictions," mainly prohibitions and restrictions on imports and exports, which had been imposed during the war and which continued to hamper trade. Accordingly, an attempt was made to secure the abolition of these by collective agreement. At the World Economic Conference of 1927 a convention was adopted, but the position taken by some nations in making ratification of it contingent on ratifications by others rendered progress difficult. It did finally come into force in 1930, but the severity of the "great depression," and the change in outlook toward concerted action in matters of commercial policy which it brought, had led all to denounce it by 1934. The Conference also suggested that measures be taken—by unilateral action on the part of individual states, by bilateral action through the conclusion of commercial treaties, and by multilateral action through the League—to reduce obstacles to trade. Little progress was made, however, and after 1929, trade restrictions increased sharply. But although import duties were raised on many products, tariffs were no longer the main instruments of trade regulation. Faced by increasing strains on their balances of payments or by mounting unemployment registers, governments imposed new and more effective weapons of protectionism, notably quotas and exchange control.

Efforts were made to secure tariff reductions on selected groups of products, but to no avail. The idea of a "tariff truce" was proposed in 1930 at the diplomatic Conference with a View to Concerted Action, but no agreement could be reached even on this. Hopes were raised in 1932, when the Lausanne Conference, which ended reparation payments, proposed that the League of Nations call an International Monetary and Economic Conference. The Conference, held in London in the following year, proved, however, to be not only the most ambitious, but also the last and least successful attempt to restore a system of multilateral trade and payments. On the crucial question of monetary policy the leading powers could not agree, and it soon became evident that, failing an agreement on currency stabilization, no effective action could be taken in regard to trade policy.

The depression marks a dividing line in the economic work of the League. Before the world crisis, the approach of the Economic and Financial Organization to trade problems had been multilateral, and it had sought gradually to build up a body of international legislation on these and other economic matters. With the onset of the depression, its work changed in two ways. In so far as the method of procedure by international convention was retained, it was narrowed down so that, instead of seeking multilateral conventions, the Organization now prepared model conventions on certain subjects, which countries might use in their bilateral negotiations. Most-favored-nation treatment was codified, for example, and a standard customs nomenclature was drawn up, which is now used by many countries.

At the same time a more fundamental change was taking place in the methods used. National governments were constantly called upon to solve new and embarrassing problems at home, and it was natural that they should turn to the League for information and advice. To an increasing degree the work of the Economic and Financial Organization took the form of inquiries into individual economic problems of widespread importance, to the collection of material and the drafting of reports and recommendations which might help governments to deal with these matters in their own countries. Most of this work—which covered a wide range of topics, including clearing agreements, exchange control and quota restrictions, business cycles, taxation, nutrition, housing, and rural life—has already been mentioned.[17] But in almost every case where concerted action by governments was recommended, nothing was done.

It must be emphasized at this point that the failure of attempts to reopen the channels of international trade did not lie with the Organization. Just as in the political negotiations of the League,

[17] See Footnote 8, supra.

the real cause of failure lay in the lack of a general willingness on the part of the great powers to take the initiative in pursuing policies designed to expand trade. This is the crucial lesson that must be learned from the League experience.

Since the outbreak of war an extensive new program of studies in international trade and commercial policy has been undertaken.[18] Better than any other work, the *Network of World Trade* shows how modern civilization is dependent on a world economy functioning through a system of multilateral trade, and how the present war and its economic consequences are likely to change the pre-war pattern. It is perhaps the most eloquent argument for the restoration of multilateralism in international trade relations. *Commercial Policy in the Inter-War Period* attempts to draw lessons from the successes and failures of international action aimed at the reduction of trade barriers. It shows, among other things, how the lack of joint action for achieving an orderly peace economy increases the difficulty of getting subsequently adopted a commercial policy designed to expand rather than restrict trade, how first political and then economic insecurity prevented the acceptance by countries of liberal trading policies. By the same token, it demonstrates that a smooth transition to peace economy, and the achievement of political and economic security, are essential prerequisites to expanding multilateral trade. Studies such as these show the unique contribution which the Organization can make in analyzing economic developments and making recommendations for future policy.

Economic Development. From the outset the Financial Committee has been concerned in various ways with the problem of international investment. Besides its extensive experience with financial reconstruction in Europe after 1918, it worked to remove burdensome double taxation, which frequently acts as a hindrance

[18] The following volumes have already been published: *Europe's Trade* (League of Nations publication 1941.II.A.1); *The Network of World Trade* (League of Nations publication 1942.II.A.3); *Commercial Policy in the Interwar Period; International Proposals and National Policies* (League of Nations publication 1942.II.A.6); *Quantitative Trade Controls; Their Causes and Nature* (League of Nations publications 1943.II.A.5); *Trade Relations between Free-Market and Controlled Economies* (League of Nations publications 1943.II.A.4).

to foreign investment.[19] This work is now being carried on by the Fiscal Committee, which is also studying the whole problem of the relation of taxation to the promotion of private international investment.

During the great depression, numerous defaults occurred on international loans issued by governments and other public bodies, and disputes sometimes arose as a result of ambiguities in the contracts. In 1936, therefore, a special committee of experts was organized to examine the whole subject of international loan contracts. Their report,[20] containing recommendations regarding the drafting of contracts, currency clauses, the designation and functions of agents responsible for the service of loans, the representation of bondholders, the law applicable to contracts, the drafting of arbitration clauses, and the setting up of an arbitral tribunal to decide cases concerning the interpretation of contracts, will be of great value if the attempt is made to revive private international long-term lending after the war.

Among the longer-range economic needs of the post-war period the industrialization of economically backward areas ranks high. In the past the process of economic development was brought about by private international investments, but the outward flow of capital from the industrial countries dried up in the depression years and has since shown little signs of reviving. It is probable that if international investment again becomes important, newer forms, among them direct investment, will be used. Much more information and additional analysis of this whole problem is urgently required, and among the projected studies of post-war problems, the Economic and Financial Committees of the League have included one on the industrialization of undeveloped countries and its repercussions on the older states.

THE FUTURE

The Economic and Financial Organization of the League of Nations has a background of experience and a competency of

[19] "Double Taxation," by Mitchell Carroll.
[20] League of Nations publication 1939.II.A.10.

personnel which would give it a decided advantage over any new organization that might be set up to do the work it has been doing. The League has prestige in connection with its work in the technical fields, even though it may have none for its work in the political field. The failures of the Economic and Financial Organization in the interwar period were not the result of insufficient knowledge or ability: it could facilitate international agreement and issue recommendations on specific economic problems referred to it, but its role was purely advisory, and it had no power to enforce decisions. Some problems were never referred to it, while the prospect of agreement on others was so remote that they never advanced beyond the stage of study and informal discussion. The technical solution of the major economic problems —such as tariffs and other obstacles to trade—on which it was mainly engaged, depended ultimately on political decisions. If no agreement was reached, or if the recommendations of the Organization were not followed, reasons of national policy rather than defects of organization or technique were to blame. If economic cooperation is to be effective in the future, national sovereignty must be limited over large areas of economic policy.

The outlines of future world economic organization are already beginning to appear. Organization of institutions in the fields of monetary stabilization and foreign lending is under discussion. While it is not yet clear how far international cooperation will go in the economic field, how the work of these specific institutions will be coordinated, or how their decisions will be implemented, it is obvious that any future international arrangements should include the functions which the Economic and Financial Organization of the League of Nations has endeavored to discharge in the past. It would be a great tragedy if the expert knowledge and wide experience accumulated by that Organization were not utilized.

INTERNATIONAL DOUBLE TAXATION

BY MITCHELL B. CARROLL

RELIEF from international double taxation presents two problems, (1) that of accommodating the tax systems of two countries so that income taxable in both because of conflicting principles of taxation will not in effect be taxed more than once, and (2) that of providing for cooperation between the interested tax administrations so as to assure the proper application of the provisions for relief from double taxation and at the same time prevent taxpayers from utilizing the relief measures in order to evade taxes in one country or the other, or both.

Residents of one country who sell goods or invest money in another country have to bear the burden of taxation in both places, if the country where the individual or company is construed to be "resident" imposes its income tax on the basis of income from all sources and the other country taxes all income which it attributes to sources within its territory.

Fearing that income derived abroad by residents was not being reported for taxation at home or that income flowing abroad was escaping taxes due at home, some governments have resorted to various unilateral measures to prevent fiscal evasion. These tended to penalize the honest taxpayers and increase the burdens on international commerce. The necessity for coordinated action by gov-

---

MITCHELL B. CARROLL attended the meeting of experts on international double taxation in London in 1927 and the general meeting of governmental experts on the same subject at Geneva in 1928. He attended the first meeting of the Fiscal Committee of the League in 1928. From 1930 to 1933 he was director for the League of Nations of a survey of tax systems in thirty-five countries throughout the world. In 1934 he was appointed the American member of the Fiscal Committee and was elected chairman in 1939. He has been chief of section in the United States Department of Commerce and special attorney to the Treasury Department. He is chairman of the Double Taxation Committee of the American Bar Association, vice-chairman of the Tax Committee of the Inter-American Bar Association, and is now serving as chairman of the League of Nations Joint Committee on Foreign Investments. He is practicing in New York City.

ernments became evident at the close of the first World War, when the cumulation of the high rates of two countries often exceeded the income which flowed from sources in the one to persons resident in the other.

The International Financial Conference held in Brussels in 1920 took cognizance of the importance of the problem and referred it to the League of Nations for study. The League first appointed a committee of four world-known economists to examine the problem, and their report was submitted to a technical committee composed of heads of the tax administrations of a number of European countries. This committee elaborated draft conventions for preventing double taxation in the field of income and death taxes and for mutual assistance in the assessment and collection of taxes. These model conventions were revised and were supplemented by two additional models on income taxes at a general meeting of governmental experts on double taxation, representing twenty-eight countries, held at Geneva in 1928; this meeting also recommended that the work be continued through a permanent fiscal committee, which met the following year and has continued its activities ever since. Consequently, there has been over the past twenty years a continuous evolving of principles and rules for the prevention of international double taxation and fiscal evasion in the form of model bilateral conventions as well as recommendations to governments on technical aspects of the taxation problem as a whole.

MODEL CONVENTIONS TO AVOID DOUBLE TAXATION

The most significant conclusions reached in the course of this work are embodied in the conventions of 1928 on income taxes and death duties, the model convention of 1935 on the allocation of business profits for tax purposes, and the model conventions of the Regional Tax Conference held under the auspices of the Fiscal Committee in Mexico in 1943. The texts of 1943 constitute a revision of the earlier draft conventions in the light of the major trends shown in the general conventions adopted by governments on the bases of the earlier models before the outbreak of the present war and take into account the particular interests of states in the Western Hemisphere. Hence, they constitute an up-to-date synthesis of the past work of the committee on international tax relations and are likely to be of value to countries in other parts of the world in post-war negotiations of tax treaties.

DIRECT EFFECT OF LEAGUE WORK ON TREATY NEGOTIATIONS AND LEGISLATION

Since their first meetings, the tax experts gathered under the auspices of the League have had a noteworthy influence on the movement towards elimination of tax barriers to international intercourse and towards cooperation between national tax authorities.

When the League work on prevention of double taxation began, there existed only a few international agreements on tax matters, most of them restricted in scope. Since then, the measures embodying the principles advocated have been reflected in an increasing number of treaties and national laws which, at the outbreak of the second World War, included some sixty general agreements for the prevention of double taxation of income and many special agreements and provisions of internal legislation.

While progress was made through the conclusion of bilateral treaties, the network of such agreements between European states embodying essentially the same principles and terminology had in substance the effect of a vast multilateral treaty.

ACTIVITIES IN THE WESTERN HEMISPHERE

As most of the problems of double taxation arose between the highly developed European countries, practically all the meetings had taken place in Geneva and they had been attended by very few experts from Latin America. However, at the instance of a Mexican delegate, the Assembly of the League had charged the Fiscal Committee with the preparation of a report on the principles which should underlie the taxation of income and property, with particular regard to countries which were in the process of developing a tax system. A report pertaining to income taxation was being completed just as war began in 1939. Subsequently, the minister of finance of Mexico invited the committee to consider this report at a meeting to be held in the capital of his country in June, 1940.

High officials or experts from seven countries (Argentina, Brazil, Peru, Venezuela, Canada, Mexico, and the United States) participated in the preparation of the recommendations based on this report, which are still under consideration in connection with the committee's studies on post-war problems.

When war spread to the Western Hemisphere, the committee's work was inevitably impeded, but it was resumed again at a second meeting as guests of the Mexican minister of finance in July, 1943—a meeting which was almost twice the size of the previous one. (The new countries represented included Chile, Uruguay, Bolivia, Ecuador, Colombia, Cuba, and Guatemala.)

This meeting not only formulated the previously mentioned model convention for preventing the double taxation of income but also one in the field of death taxes, which was reflected in the recent treaty on the subject signed on June 8, 1944, by Canada and the United States. The model tax conventions were supplemented by model conventions on administrative and judicial assistance in the application of tax treaties. The meeting also prepared a preliminary report on post-war fiscal policy.

The fact that governments have seen fit to participate in these meetings even during the war shows the importance they attribute to keeping alive the pioneer work of the League committee in the face of mounting burdens under tax systems that are developing much too rapidly under the pressure for revenues to meet the emergency. The committee has been striving to keep abreast of developments, so that after hostilities cease it will be prepared to contribute its part to the general program of reconstruction in Europe as well as in the Western Hemisphere.

ADVANTAGE OF COMMITTEE'S PROCEDURE

The technique of consultation among experts for working out conventions and for analyzing the tax situation as a whole has undoubtedly facilitated formal negotiations between governments on the subject of double taxation and fiscal evasion.

The experts who attended the committee meetings in the secretariat of the League often met afterwards at some restaurant overlooking Lac Leman to explore informally the possibilities of reaching an agreement between their respective governments. Very frequently these talks led to formal negotiations which resulted in treaties. The experience of the United States is significant. The Americans who since 1927 had actively participated in the League work on model conventions were assigned in 1930 to meet with a French official who had been a colleague in the pioneer work at Geneva, for the purpose of negotiating the first convention to prevent double taxation between France and the United States. Similarly, attendance at Geneva was a prelude to the negotiation of the treaty concluded by the United States with Sweden in 1939.

The meetings at Geneva and then at Mexico City in 1940 afforded a background for the negotiation of the tax convention between the United States and Canada in 1941, and the officials who represented the respective governments in these negotiations subsequently participated in their private capacity as experts in the elaboration of the model conventions at the Mexico meeting in July, 1943. Thus, the benefit of their practical experience was passed on to the officials of other governments, and, as a result, certain governments have undertaken conversations to explore the possibility of conventions along similar lines, but taking into account the particular features of their respective tax systems. It is hoped the conclusion of bilateral treaties on the basis of model conventions drafted at Mexico City will lead to the bringing into effect of essentially the same principles of taxation for international business and investments throughout the Western Hemisphere and, eventually, the rest of the world.

REASONS FOR CONTINUATION OF THE FISCAL COMMITTEE

The achievements of the Fiscal Committee show the benefits which countries can derive through common studies, unofficial discussions, and personal contacts between national tax administrators within an international organization. The continued activity of the committee, even through the depression and the war, shows that such a means to cope with fiscal problems is needed to complete any machinery for international cooperation on financial, economic and social matters.

Indeed, improvement of national tax systems and practices from the point of view of efficiency, equity, and economic soundness, adaptation of taxation to general economic and social policies, removal of direct and indirect tax impediments to trade are matters of collective interest for the people of all nations. On all these matters, the competent national authorities should be afforded the opportunity to join their efforts in order to harmonize their policies, assist one another in matters of administration, pool the results of their experience, and study together problems of common concern. To continue the work initiated by the Fiscal Committee, there should be, within the post-war economic and financial organization, a similar permanent body of tax experts entrusted with the following main functions:

Consultation: Periodical meetings, general or regional, should enable tax administrators to discuss in common problems where international exchange of views might be of value and to establish direct contacts with one another.

Advice and assistance to governments and international agencies: Such a body would be in a particularly favorable position to give competent and impartial advice on matters of fiscal policy and administration to national and international authorities and to arrange for technical help to particular countries.

Information and research: Such a body could fill the common need of tax administrations to be kept informed of developments abroad in the fields of legislation, administration and research, through periodical and special publications.

The Inter-American Bar Association recognized the significance of the work of the Fiscal Committee of the League of Nations by adopting, at its meeting held in Rio de Janeiro in August, 1943, the resolution of its committee on taxation, which reads as follows:

The Committee recommends:
(1)That the Committee on Taxation of the Inter-American Bar Association study the means of making uniform the income tax legislation in the various countries, with a view to avoiding international

double and extraterritorial taxation, taking into account the resolutions of the Fiscal Committee of the League of Nations at its meeting held in Mexico in July, 1943, and recognizing, as a general principle, the prior rights of the country of origin of the income to tax the said income.

With the present tendency of taxes to increase, both in amount and complexity, and of levies to overlap on the same income or property, there is a growing need for an international group of experts to study the situation and make recommendations. The continuation of the Fiscal Committee as a part of the League of Nations, or of any institution which may take its place, recommends itself because the committee's work, which has been so effective in the past, will be all the more vital to the restoration of trade and capital movements in the coming period of reconstruction.

STANDARDIZING WORLD STATISTICS

BY E. DANA DURAND

UP TO the present war, the most important agency in the world in the field of statistics was the League of Nations, including the International Labor Office. This aspect of League activity rendered two valuable services in statistics: first, preparing comparative compilations of the major data collected by individual countries, and second, taking the lead in improving statistical work in the various countries as to scope, quality, and international comparability. Both these services covered all the major fields of demographic, economic and social statistics (except for agricultural, which were covered by the International Institute of Agriculture at Rome). Leadership was in the hands of highly competent experts in the Secretariat of the League and of the Labor Office, but much creditable work was also done by various international committees set up under the League. Some of these committees covered more general subjects but paid great attention to collating statistics and improving statistical methods in their fields, and one, the Committee of Statistical Experts, devoted itself exclusively to statistical matters.

The Secretariat of the League compiled and analyzed comparative statistics of the various countries and issued numerous reports, some of periodical and some of occasional character. Through its many contacts all over the world, the Secretariat was able to obtain original data more completely and more promptly than any individual government could have done, to say nothing of any individual citizen. The cooperative service thus rendered saved expense and effort to governments and private statisticians, while the quality of the data was in general superior to anything an in-

---

E. DANA DURAND has been for nearly ten years a member of the United States Tariff Commission. He is a statistician and economist, born and educated in the Middle West. He has been the director of the United States Census Office, and a member of the Department of Commerce, and has acted in many other national and international capacities. He is a member of the League of Nations Committee of Statistical Experts.

dividual agency could have secured. The Secretariat's methods of arrangement and interpretation also greatly increased the usefulness of the material.

Equally important with this data collation was the League's task of improving methods of statistical work within the countries themselves. Here one can scarcely claim that as satisfactory results were secured. The effort encountered many obstacles—indifference, lack of competent national experts, lack of adequate government funds to support satisfactory work, a tendency to adhere to established tradition, partially justified, in some cases, by the need to retain comparability of present with past national statistics. However, many countries did show a cooperative spirit and a great deal was accomplished. Statistical activities were improved and a greater measure of international comparability was reached.

The present writer is particularly familiar with the activities of the League in the field of economic statistics. In this field, League initiative brought about an International Conference on Economic Statistics, which was called in Geneva in 1928; it covered all branches of economic statistics except those relating to agriculture and to labor, which were under other jurisdictions. Signatories to the Convention which was drawn up there agreed to collect regularly certain classes of economic statistics and to employ specified methods which would promote comparability. Occupations, production in all fields except agriculture, general measures of economic activity, prices, and international trade were the principal subjects covered. The Convention, including the annexes, entered into great detail as to scope and methods of compilation.

Among the provisions of the International Convention was the establishment of a Committee of Technical Statistical Experts to interpret the Convention, to work out standards along certain specified lines, and in general to seek improvement in world economic statistics. This Committee was appointed by the Council of the League of Nations, sitting together with one delegate chosen by each state not a member of the League but signatory to the statistical convention. Members of the Committee were selected for their qualifications as experts, not merely as delegates from their respective countries. The Committee usually had about ten members, and at no time was there more than one member from the same country. It met at somewhat irregular intervals but on the average about once a year. It took numerous subjects under consideration, some in great detail; on a number of matters it completed its labors and issued valuable reports and recommendations.

One result of the work of the Commitee of Technical Statistical Experts was *The Minimum List of Commodities for International Trade Statistics.*[1] This list specifies some four hundred commodities, arranged in logical groups, of which each country signatory to the Convention would make use in publishing its trade statistics. Up to 1929, although many countries had published supplemental trade tables according to a much shorter and less logical list known as the "Brussels Nomenclature," the extreme diversity of commodity names throughout the world had made comparability of trade statistics almost impossible. Following the publication of the Minimum List numerous countries, including the United States, which had not adhered to the Convention on Economic Statistics, undertook to compile their statistics according to the new list, usually not substituting it for their own nomenclature, but providing supplemental tables based upon it, as an aid to international comparisons.

The leading United Nations, and no doubt also the leading Axis powers, have found it necessary to collect more detailed economic statistics during the war period than ever before. The plans which many countries are making for the assurance of full employment in the post-war period will call for more adequate statistical information than was available before the war. It is to be hoped that means will be worked out for international cooperation in these larger statistical tasks.

Like many of its other activities, the League's work in improving statistical methods has been interrupted by the war. However, through its temporary offices at Princeton, New Jersey, and at Montreal, Canada, some publication of comparative international statistics has continued, despite the fact that the belligerent coun-

[1] League of Nations publication 1939.II.A.21.

tries, as well as some of the others, have for obvious reasons been withholding statistical information on many subjects.

As soon as practicable after peace comes, some measure of international cooperation in the field of statistics should be restored. Even if broader efforts to organize a continued peace and to improve international economic relations should not be fully successful, the compilation of comparative statistics and efforts to improve the quality of national statistics could be continued and would be greatly needed.

Presumably, most of the countries which adhered to the International Convention on Economic Statistics will consider it still in force when the war is over. Although the principal Axis countries either did not adhere to it or withdrew their adherence some time before the war, some of these countries, once we have outlived post-war disorganization, are likely to conform again to the Convention and to the recommendations previously published by the Committee of Statistical Experts. Unless, however, something resembling the League of Nations is reestablished, no agency will exist for appointing experts to an international group, and the Committee of Statistical Experts as heretofore constituted would presumably disappear. It is possible, however, that the signatory countries to the 1929 Convention and those which may hereafter declare adherence could agree among themselves on some method of selecting an expert committee to continue this international task.

DANGEROUS DRUGS

BY HERBERT L. MAY

IN INTERNATIONAL PARLANCE the terms "dangerous drugs" and "narcotic drugs" refer to opium and its derivatives (morphine, heroin, codeine, dionine, and many others less well-known), cocaine (derived from the leaf of the coca shrub), and some substances derived from the Indian hemp plant (such as marihuana, hashish, etc.).

During and toward the end of a war, and in the post-war period, addiction to dangerous drugs tends to increase. This is a fact noted and recorded by scientific observers since the second half of the nineteenth century. During and after the American Civil War addiction to opiates became so widespread among the soldiers on both sides that it became notorious as the "army disease," and the same result followed the Crimean, the Franco-Prussian, and the World War of 1914–1918, when the use of morphine, heroin, and cocaine spread through many countries of Europe and in the United States. Unfortunately it is possible that our present unprecedented conflict may bring in its train a drug problem as widespread as the war itself.

This problem is aggravated by the activities of the illicit traffickers. At the close of a war there are surplus stocks of drugs, and unless the most rigid control over them is exercised by the military and civil authorities, there is grave danger of "leakage" into the illicit traffic, fed by an increased demand from the greater number of addicts.

"So great a blessing and so great a curse to mankind," Doctor H. H. Kane of New York, called opium and its derivatives in

---

HERBERT L. MAY, vice-president of the Permanent Central Opium Board and acting chairman of the Drug Supervisory Body, both affiliated with the League of Nations, has been a member of these organizations since their inception in 1928 and 1933, respectively. He was born in Philadelphia, practiced law in New York City, and was for some time a business executor in Pittsburgh. In the first World War he was Assistant Food Administrator for Western Pennsylvania, and has served on a number of state and city commissions. He is an American authority on the international control of dangerous drugs.

1880. Within these two extremes is locked the whole problem of narcotics. If it were only a blessing, surely there would be no problem. If it were only a curse, its solution might be much easier.

Morphine, for instance, is unique for relieving pain, but beginning as a justifiable necessity for deadening suffering, it may become, for some individuals, a deadly habit from which they cannot escape. Although this does sometimes happen in the case of soldiers injured in patriotic service, evidence seems to show that only a small percentage of sick and wounded in time of war form the habit solely because they have been treated for some time with narcotic drugs. It is not usual that such treatment has ill effects on well-balanced, well-integrated persons. A stronger urge to drug addiction comes in certain persons from their inability to face and bear life as it is, and a consequent tendency under war conditions to seek in drugs an escape from anguish and uncertainty and from a reality, already difficult, which war has rendered more nearly intolerable.

Such neurotics are at all times, war or no war, potential drug victims. Others may acquire the habit through the influence of other addicts or through curiosity and search for new sensations. But whatever the reasons, once an individual has become an addict, his desperate craving to increase his daily dosage creates a drug market out of all proportion to other economic demands. In exchange for drugs, he will give anything he has, even to the extent of starving to death rather than spend his remaining money on food instead of his drug.

And so a campaign against the abuse of drugs started, in the early years of this century, first as isolated national efforts to limit production and use to medical and scientific needs only, and then—as it became clear that to control a world evil, world cooperation was necessary—on an international scale. The first step was the summoning of a conference at Shanghai in 1909, and this cleared the way for the first international opium convention at The Hague in 1912. Unfortunately, the first World War interrupted these efforts, but, nevertheless, rapid advances were made after 1918.

The peace treaties opened the way by bringing the Hague Convention of 1912 automatically into force, and by inserting into the Covenant of the League of Nations Article 23, which provided that "Subject to and in accordance with the provisions of international conventions existing or hereafter to be agreed upon, the Members of the League . . . (c) will entrust the League with the general supervision over the execution of agreements with regard to . . . the traffic in opium and other dangerous drugs." Since that time a considerable body of international law regulating traffic in drugs has been built up, and international administrative organs exist to which are entrusted the application of this law. This law and these organs, still functioning even in war time, stand available either for continued use by the League or by a new international organization, when the world faces the problem of dangerous drugs after the war.

The legal basis for the international administration now functioning in the field of "narcotic drugs," frequently called "opium and other dangerous drugs," consists of four treaties and two agreements:

(A) General drug conventions
 1. The Hague Convention of 1912
 2. The Geneva Convention of 1925
 3. The Limitation Convention of 1931

(B) Suppression of illicit traffic
 1. The Convention for the Suppression of the Illicit Traffic of 1936

(C) Opium smoking agreements
 1. The Geneva Agreement of 1925
 2. The Bangkok Agreement of 1931

All these are in force. Some sixty-seven sovereign states are parties to one or more of them. Only Argentina and Ethiopia are not party to any of these international instruments.

The Hague Convention of 1912 embodies the general principle of control and limitation of dangerous drugs; its provisions refer in the main to the supervision of the national field, and it did not set up any machinery for international supervision.

The Geneva Convention of 1925 is characterized by the adoption of certain stringent measures of national and international control for narcotic substances except prepared opium for smoking. The most far-reaching innovations of the Geneva Convention were, firstly, the adoption of what is called the "import and export certificate system" to control effectively the trade in drugs; and, secondly, the creation of an international accounting system through a special agency—the Permanent Central Opium Board—invested with certain wide powers over-riding, under conditions specified in the Convention, national sovereignty.

The Limitation Convention of 1931 is the first international convention which directly limits manufacture. The quantity of drugs to be manufactured is determined by a special organ—the Drug Supervisory Body—created by this Convention. In the light of estimates supplied by governments, the Supervisory Body determines this quantity, and when such estimates are not supplied by the governments, they are established by the Supervisory Body itself. The sum total of these estimates fixes the total legitimate consumption of the world and lays down the limits for legitimate manufacture. The estimate system in addition effects a limitation of the international trade and of the supplies available to each country or territory. The restriction of national sovereignty is increased under this Convention.

In *the Geneva and Bangkok Agreements of 1925 and 1931*, respectively, a number of measures have been adopted with the object of reducing gradually and suppressing ultimately opium smoking in certain Far Eastern countries and territories.

The Convention for the Suppression of the Illicit Traffic of 1936 (which came into force on October 26, 1939, after the outbreak of the war) aims directly at preventing and punishing illicit operations in narcotic substances; it provides for severe penalties and facilitates extradition of traffickers. Its object is to coordinate the criminal laws of the various countries, to facilitate the cooperation of national police authorities, and so prevent drug traffickers from escaping their due punishment. This Convention contains provisions which are considered as an innovation in international criminal law.

The first international body in this field created to supervise the application of the Hague Convention and of all drug treaties to be concluded in future was the *Advisory Committee on Traffic in Opium and Other Dangerous Drugs.* The Committee was appointed by the Council of the League in 1921 on the basis of a resolution of the first Assembly of the League in December, 1920, to help the members of the League discharge their responsibilities under the Covenant and the Hague Convention. The Advisory Committee is the policy-suggesting body and is also concerned with the general supervision of the application of the existing conventions.

Through the information collected by the Advisory Committee, the extent of the abuse of dangerous drugs was quickly revealed and the ground was prepared for the Geneva (1925) and the Limitation (1931) Conventions. The last great task performed by the Advisory Committee before the outbreak of the present war was the draft for the Convention for the Limitation of Opium Production, which was submitted to all governments.

Under the 1925 Convention the *Permanent Central Opium Board* was created. It is a body with full technical independence in carrying out its duties and was designed for administrative and quasi-judicial functions. The Board is vested with the duty of examining detailed statistics furnished by governments and of watching over the international trade in drugs. It has powers to ask for explanations from governments and to recommend restrictive action (general embargo on exports under the Geneva Convention) or to take such restrictive action itself (embargo under the Limitation Convention). These powers of the Board extend to every country in the world. The Board is therefore an organ of international supervision with a definite competence.

Under the Limitation Convention of 1931, the *Supervisory Body* was instituted. This international organ is responsible for determining in advance each year, on the basis of estimates furnished by the governments, the quantity of drugs required for medical and scientific needs. In case a country, party or non-party to the Convention, does not furnish its estimates, the Supervisory Body has the right to frame estimates for that country; these estimates have the same legal binding force as estimates furnished by a government. The Supervisory Body has the right to demand, if it thinks fit, further information or details from a government with regard to the latter's estimates. Under certain conditions the Supervisory Body is entitled to amend this estimate in accordance with the information obtained, with the assent of the government concerned.

The Supervisory Body is also required to draw up each year a statement consisting of the estimates furnished by the governments and all those framed by the Supervisory Body itself. This statement is a plan for the world's drug industry and trade for the coming year. This statement is not merely a guide to the industry and trade; it constitutes on the date of its communication to the governments a statement of obligation binding upon the governments and the basis for the Permanent Central Board to judge whether the governments have fulfilled their obligations.

Twenty-three years of effort have resulted in the following achievements:

1. Sixty-seven countries, parties to one or more different international drug conventions and agreements, are now under obligation to enact and apply national legislation satisfying the provisions of international treaties and to operate administrative systems based on internationally uniform principles.

2. The total medical world requirements in drugs are now known, and the quantities of these drugs manufactured legitimately by some sixty licensed factories have been brought down to the level of the world's medical needs.

3. A clear dividing line between the authorized trade and the illicit traffic has thus been drawn, and the previous free passage of legitimately manufactured narcotics directly into the illicit traffic has been stopped; the leakages which may still occur have been reduced to a police problem.

4. A world system of estimates and statistics based on national returns forms the foundation of an international system of accounts under which are recorded all legitimate operations connected with the trade in drugs.

5. All the channels of distribution, national as well as international, are supervised.

6. This work has been continued even in the midst and in spite

of a world conflict in which almost all the parties to the Conventions are involved. A considerable degree of success has been achieved in this field. For the five years from 1925–1929, before the Geneva and the Limitation Conventions started to operate, at least 100 tons of narcotics, which included an annual average of about 16 tons of morphine on a conservative official estimate of the League of Nations, had passed into the illicit traffic from *licensed* factories. This was possible because the average yearly manufacture of morphine during that period was between 44 and 45 tons, whereas, as was later discovered, legitimate medical requirements in the same period averaged about 29 tons per year. Since 1930 the authorized factories have stabilized their manufacture of drugs at the level of the world's legitimate needs, and during the period 1931 to 1935 not more than an average of 29 tons of morphine per year was manufactured in the whole world. So much for the manufacture. Now, to illustrate how the international trade was brought under control, it will be sufficient to mention that in 1926 the total volume of this trade (only legitimate trade, crossing national borders) in morphine, heroin, and cocaine amounted to 23.1 tons; in 1937 this volume had shrunk to 2.3 tons or 10 percent of the 1926 volume—part of this shrinkage being due, doubtless, to the fact that a number of countries at that later date manufactured their own requirements.

7. In pursuance of the general objectives of the Hague Convention of 1912 and the Agreement of February 11, 1925, the policy of total prohibition of opium smoking and of the abolition of opium monopolies in the Far East has been adopted by the British (November 10, 1943) and the Netherlands (October 1, 1943) governments. The other governments maintaining monopolies will doubtless adopt the same policy.

Before the war broke out in 1939 the Opium Advisory Committee submitted to all governments a draft convention on the limitation of opium production. When a new convention accomplishing this object is adopted, it will be a decisive step on the road of progress marked by the preceding treaties. The legal and administrative structure would then be completed, and narcotic substances would be submitted to a stringent control extending from the production of the raw materials to the ultimate use of the drugs for the benefit of the sick. This new convention would carry with it a further restriction of the freedom of action of states in matters of opium, and international control would be greatly strengthened.

There are some other important problems which will have to be solved. These are:

1. The total suppression of opium smoking and of addiction to other non-manufactured narcotic substances (for example, raw opium and preparations of the resin of Indian hemp such as marihuana, hashish).

2. The problem of drug addiction.

3. The limitation of the production of coca leaves.

4. A further important task would be the simplification of the present machinery of control and the consolidation or codification of all international treaties in this particular field in order to eliminate inconsistencies, close gaps, avoid overlapping, and simplify the procedure. As matters stand now from the point of view of three conventions only (the 1912, 1925, and 1931), the states of the world are divisible into: (a) States which have ratified all three conventions; (b) States which have ratified only one convention (three categories of states); (c) States which have ratified two conventions (again three categories of states); (d) States which have ratified none of the conventions.

Thus for the purposes of these three conventions alone, there are now not less than eight different categories of states. It is obvious that this tends to burden the application of the Conventions and to make their operation more complex.

The international drug control extends over the whole field of the drug industry and includes: agricultural production, international trade, drug manufacture, internal distribution and consumption, medical and public health aspects, government administration, customs, police, and the judiciary. Within the framework of the League of Nations the drug question has been dealt with by specialized bodies and administrative authorities, both international and national, working in close collaboration with authorities and experts in affiliated fields of activity. The existence of a special international drug administration has contributed essentially to the success so far achieved.

The most important task, however, which will in all likelihood face the League of Nations, the International Control Organs, and their staffs in the not too distant future will be the campaign in close collaboration with national authorities against an epidemic of drug addiction after this war. A strengthened staff of League experts may have to assist national authorities in the task of reestablishing national controls in some countries now under enemy occupation; simultaneously all measures necessary to reestablishing the international control to its full pre-war scope will have to be taken.

In any future world organization place must be made for international drug administration. The special treaties on which international collaboration and supervision of narcotic substances are based are, in many ways, closely connected with the League of Nations and with various League bodies and authorities having general or specific tasks through provisions of these treaties.

As the reasons and particular conditions which made it necessary to create a special and separate international drug service are not likely to change radically in the post-war period, it is essential that the effectiveness of the present drug control should be preserved.

The League of Nations plays an important role in the international drug administration as built up through the conventions concluded under its auspices. If the League should not survive, there would be complications. For example, the Advisory Committee is a League body, the Permanent Central Opium Board and the Supervisory Body are treaty organizations. The conventions provide, however, that the members of the Board should be elected by the Council of the League and representatives of the United States and Germany; that the Board should report annually to the Council; that its Secretary and staff should be appointed by the Secretary General on the nomination of the Board and subject to the approval of the Council; that the members of the Supervisory Body should be chosen by four organizations two of which are League committees; furthermore, its staff is part of the League

Secretariat. Besides, both the Board and the Supervisory Body are financed through the budget of the League, with contributions, however, from some non-members. The Health Committee of the League has important functions under the Conventions, and the Secretary General has duties to perform as the official channel of communications between the parties to the Conventions on certain questions. Finally, the secretariat of the Advisory Committee forms part of the League Secretariat.

If the League of Nations should not survive, there seem to be two possibilities: that it will be replaced by another world organization with another name or that no general world organization will be created to replace it. Obviously, the simplest solution for drug control would be for the League to survive. Otherwise new arrangements would have to be concluded among more than sixty countries, parties to one or more of the Conventions. If a new world organization should be created, one could imagine that both the League, before its formal dissolution, and the new world organization would pass resolutions transferring the duties under the Conventions from the League and League bodies and authorities, to corresponding organs of the new organization.

If there should be no new world organization, there is no doubt that a special international organization would have to be created to take over the League functions specified in the Conventions. In such case it would be necessary to revise all the drug Conventions and Agreements concluded under the auspices of the League of Nations to adapt them to the new circumstances. It would seem almost as easy to conclude a new over-all drug convention combining and simplifying the existing ones and at the same time providing for further progress. It should be pointed out, however, that the negotiation and ratification of new conventions is a very long procedure, and that there would be confusion unless all states parties to the old conventions became parties to the new convention.

In the meantime, however, the control must not weaken, because, as the League's Opium Advisory Committee put it, the dangerous drugs could be compared to "water under tremendous hydraulic pressure; it feels and saps its way steadily, irresistibly to every furthest point of the system to which the pressure reaches. It searches automatically and continuously for any flaw, any imperfection, any method of breaking down the iron barrier which surrounds it, it is forever striving to overcome its bonds and to become free." However, it must be realized that, though no one country can alone solve the problem of drug addiction but must needs have the cooperation of all other countries, the international control functions mainly "post factum"; that is, it checks on the performance of obligations; it acts, sometimes with "embargos," when these obligations have not been fulfilled; it can advise national administrations to take appropriate action and can publish its findings. Although it cannot directly control or physically enter a sovereign state without the state's consent, it can and does give information upon which a state may base action. In some instances it indeed can prescribe action ("embargoes"). But in the last analysis the protection of the peoples of the world against drug addiction is primarily the responsibility of national administrations and such civil and military authorities of occupying powers as may temporarily replace them.

In conclusion, it is clear that, beginning with the convening in 1909 by President Theodore Roosevelt of the first international conference at Shanghai (largely on the initiative of Dr. Hamilton Wright and Bishop Brent) up to the present time, the United States has been in the forefront of efforts aimed at national and international control of the traffic in dangerous drugs. Successive administrations, no matter what their political complexion, have proposed and adopted progressive national and international legislation, have loyally cooperated with and participated in League and quasi-League advisory and control organizations, and have even had a representative sit with the Council of the League when it acted as an electoral body to elect members of the Permanent Central Opium Board. The Department of State approved of the setting up in Washington, in 1940, of branch offices of the Board and the Drug Supervisory Body when the war made difficult the continuance of their functioning from Geneva, and the Secretary of State has made favorable public statements on the accomplishments in this field by the organizations that are part of or affiliated with the League.

INTERNATIONAL HEALTH WORK

BY FRANK G. BOUDREAU, M.D.

IN TOTAL WAR, disease and health of soldier and civilian alike are potent weapons which may turn the balance to victory or defeat. Hence, the prevalence of infectious diseases; the rise and fall of epidemics; the kinds and amounts of food available; the state of nutrition of the people; the conditions of housing; the adequacy of clothing; the scarcity or abundance of drugs, serums, and vaccines, of antiseptics and disinfectants, of soap and insect powder—information on each of these subjects is restricted by countries at war and just as eagerly collected by every military intelligence service. Disease and health of civilians and armed forces have always been great assets or liabilities, but in modern war they have become more potent than ever, because the speed and volume of transportation have multiplied the possibilities of spreading disease, and modern science has given us new means of controlling epidemics and of promoting health. Typhus fever is the classic example of an infectious disease which rises to its greatest heights in the conditions of scarcity and confusion occasioned by war. "It is hardly debatable," states Zinsser, "that the power of Napoleon was broken by disease (mainly typhus) more effectively than by military opposition or even by Trafalgar." [1]

The Crusaders found in disease a much more powerful enemy than in the Saracens, and scurvy was as potent as the infections. However, it is not necessary to go back to the Crusades or to Napoleon to find grim evidence of the destructiveness of typhus fever and scurvy, for both operated on the military and civilian fronts during the last war and could we but lift the veil of censorship, both would be found among armed forces and civilians alike in the present war, ready to take full advantage of the disorder and confusion occasioned by defeat.

[1] Hans Zinsser, *Rats, Lice, and History* (London, Rutledge, 1935), p. 164.

POST-WAR HEALTH CONDITIONS

Infectious and deficiency diseases will be the most immediate and acute post-war problems in the European and Far Eastern countries which have been occupied by the enemy. The stage has been set for epidemics of typhus fever, dysentery, cholera, and many other infections, such as bubonic plague, smallpox, relapsing fever, diphtheria, and typhoid fever, may at any time assume epidemic proportions. In the Mediterranean and Pacific areas malaria is already recognized as a powerful enemy of our armed forces and may in the long run become one of the most serious post-war disease problems.

Nutritional deficiency diseases will be second in immediate concern only to epidemics of infectious diseases, and their ultimate consequences may be of even greater significance.

Housing and clothing will be of immediate and pressing importance. Overcrowded, poorly heated, unsanitary housing predisposes to disease; insufficient or unsuitable clothing fails to protect the body from exposure to heat and cold or to maintain cleanliness and to prevent the lousiness which is the handmaiden of typhus and relapsing fevers.

Populations of countries liberated from the enemy will suffer from the lack of medical care. There will be a scarcity of doctors and nurses, of food and drugs, of hospital accommodations, of dressings and soap, and of antiseptics.

All this we know from history. We have but to look back to the last war and its aftermath to appreciate the character of the problems which will face the liberated countries and the United Nations Relief and Rehabilitation Administration when the Axis forces have been driven out. But history gives us no yardstick with which to forecast the dimensions of these problems. After the last war, in proportion to the magnitude of the disruption and destruction, epidemics were greater than ever before. One might therefore expect disease prevalence and epidemics to be as much greater after this war as this war has been vaster and more destructive than the first World War.

There is, however, a new factor to be considered—the recent

rapid advances in medicine and public health, which make it possible to prevent and treat many of the most important infectious and deficiency diseases far more effectively than in 1920. The almost miraculous results of the sulphonamides and penicillin are known to everyone who reads a newspaper. Lousiness, the plague of the trenches and military fronts, can be more readily controlled than ever before by new agents and methods which may ultimately mean the death blow to typhus fever; and great advances have been made in the individual prophylaxis and treatment of the disease itself.

Granted an effective civil administration to control movements of population and to provide for basic human needs, science may reduce the peril of post-war epidemics to a shadow of its former dimensions. But it is possible that military collapse of the Axis may throw occupied and enemy countries into such confusion that there will be little chance to use such advances effectively.

All will agree that in the light of history and the absence of positive knowledge concerning the future, plans must be made to deal promptly and effectively with infectious diseases likely to become epidemic, to provide food and nutrients for those suffering from nutritional deficiencies, to restore and purify water supplies, and to reestablish national and local health administrations as rapidly as possible. Many other health problems must be solved, but these are the most pressing and the most acute.

NEEDED POST-WAR HEALTH MEASURES

In order to solve these problems effectively the following measures are necessary:

1. National health administrations must be prepared to act together just as closely as the Allied armies in North Africa and Sicily. There must be combined chiefs of health just as there are combined chiefs of army staffs. Epidemics are not limited by political frontiers, and without closely coordinated action by the different health administrations the danger of a "break through" is great.

2. There must be a complete and effective system of epidemiological intelligence, receiving from the different countries accurate reports on the prevalence of disease and warning all health forces of the size, direction of march, and position of the enemy. Such a system

must work accurately and rapidly, for failure to recognize a focus of typhus or to warn of its presence in time may lead to disaster. Specialists in diagnosis should be available, the most rapid means of transport must be used to hospitalize patients, and wireless, cable, and telegraph employed to warn of impending danger. Rapid and complete means of communication are just as essential to the health services in epidemic prevention as the Signal Corps is to the Army.

3. Epidemics cannot be prevented unless doctors, hospitals, and laboratories are available in the right places at the proper time. In the confusion following collapse and defeat, doctors, hospitals, and laboratories may not be sufficiently numerous in areas where the health problems are likely to be most acute. Hence reserves of doctors, mobile hospitals, and laboratories must be kept on call.

4. Drugs, serums, vaccines, antiseptics, disinfectants, and means of destroying lice on human bodies and in clothing and bedding must be stock-piled. Drugs must be labeled in terms which doctors from the different countries will understand. Units and dosage of serums and vaccines must be standardized internationally so that differences in notation and unitage in products from different countries may not lead to confusion.

5. Nutritional deficiency diseases, malnutrition, and hunger cannot be overcome effectively merely by providing supplies of food. Deficiency diseases and malnutrition, like infections, must be sought out, their exact nature identified, and appropriate treatment (in this case nutrients in food or more concentrated form) provided. In order to restore the hungry to health it is necessary to give them a balanced diet, and to do so requires a study of the foods locally available as well as prevailing food habits. There must be some agreement as to dietary standards for different age groups and occupations. Measures of this kind cannot be improvised; they must rest on organization, study, and experience.

6. Vast numbers of war prisoners and of civilians in enemy industrial plants or concentration camps, as well as millions who have been evacuated from their homes, will require relief and repatriation. The problems of transport, shelter, and clothing will have to be solved rapidly, economically, and with due regard to the health and welfare of these displaced persons.

7. In order to cope with these and many other health problems, effective health services—national, state, and local—must be reconstituted or established anew. In certain Far Eastern countries or regions emergency health services must be improvised, while in some European countries existing health services need only appropriate assistance and support to permit them to take up anew the responsibility of disease prevention and health promotion.

EXPERIENCE ACCUMULATED BY THE HEALTH ORGANIZATION OF THE LEAGUE OF NATIONS

The Health Organization of the League of Nations has accumulated a vast experience in dealing with health problems like those described above, and it has built up a great coordinated system of epidemiological intelligence, which, before the war, stretched around the world and to every quarter of the globe. The pathways still remain although the traffic has greatly diminished, and it will be much easier to renew the traffic along established paths than to hew out new pathways. This applies equally to almost every activity of the League's Health Organization, which represents the result of years of hard work and difficult pioneering endeavor.

Certain activities and experiences of the Health Organization bear with particular force upon situations which are expected to arise when hostilities cease.

Epidemic Disease Control

The following is a description of epidemic conditions immediately after the first World War.

> Of the many difficult problems which confronted the newly established League . . . none was more difficult than this problem of disease. The war had destroyed or disorganized the machinery of prevention in many countries. New countries with new frontiers had been established. The movements of refugees and troops, carrying with them the seeds of epidemics, sowed a crop of pestilence in many hitherto immune countries. The harvest was not long in coming, and soon Europe found itself overrun with epidemics of typhus and relapsing fever, cholera, and smallpox, which not only ravaged Eastern Europe but threatened also to overwhelm the West.
>
> Immediate action was forced upon the League. There was no time to set up elaborate machinery. The defences of the new countries must be strengthened immediately if Western Europe was to be saved from the ravages of disease. So an Epidemic Commission was organized, consisting of a few experienced public health officers. . . . At the suggestion of the League the Government of Poland called the now historic conference of Warsaw (1922) . . . to secure united action by the various health administrations against the common enemy. . . . New principles of international cooperation were established; new freedom of communication between national health

services became the accepted order. A number of bilateral sanitary conventions were negotiated, most of them containing a clause providing for recourse to the Health Organization of the League in case of differences arising in regard to their interpretation or application.[2]

Shortly afterwards the Epidemic Commission, forerunner of the League's Health Organization, was called upon to deal with epidemics of smallpox, cholera, and typhoid which had been introduced into Greece by hordes of refugees from Asia Minor after the conclusion of the war with Turkey in 1922. The Epidemic Commission organized columns of physicians, nurses, and students who brought these diseases quickly under control by vaccinating more than half a million refugees against them.

Here we have the combined chiefs of health services, and the mobile reserves of doctors, nurses, and students. In Poland and elsewhere on the Eastern border of Europe, mobile hospitals were used and other facilities improvised to isolate and treat the sick. A most important means of prevention was a sanitary barrier (*cordon sanitaire*) through which refugees were obliged to pass to get to their homes. This enabled medical inspectors to locate and treat those who were ill and to disinfest (destroy lice on) the bodies, clothing, and bedding of the refugees.

But it was also necessary to set up a system of epidemiological intelligence whereby all persons with certain diseases would be reported, and all health agencies in near-by areas notified of their existence. The Warsaw Conference in 1922 opened the way by making possible the communication of such information directly between the national health services and between these services and the Health Organization of the League. Before that time all such communications had passed through the respective foreign offices with delays that may be imagined. This result of the Warsaw Conference helped to make possible the development of the world-wide system of epidemiological intelligence which was established by the League. Begun soon after the first World War, it grew steadily until it covered areas holding 80 percent of the world's population, and was adapted to the special needs of regions

[2] F. G. Boudreau, "International Health Work," *Proceedings of the Academy of Political Science*, XII (1926), 381–82.

like the Far East. The Health Organization of the League and its eastern bureau at Singapore were written into the International Sanitary Convention (1926) and were thus legally authorized by international law to perform the duties of collecting reports of certain diseases and of making the appropriate notifications. Before Japan took over Malaya the Singapore bureau was receiving from more than 180 ports in the Far East daily and weekly reports on the occurrence and spread of the chief epidemic diseases. These reports came in by cable, wireless, and the mails. Summaries of the reports were broadcast daily and weekly by twelve wireless stations, so that port health officers, national health services, ships at sea, and planes in flight could pick them up. An equally effective but less rapid system was established in other parts of the world where in peacetime the need was less urgent. In addition Geneva was in close touch with the Pan American Sanitary Bureau, the regional health bureau at Alexandria, and the Austral-Pacific Bureau in Melbourne, the latter an offshoot of the Singapore bureau. That bureau is no longer functioning, and many governments are withholding their reports from Geneva because of the war. But the routes have become established so that it will be easier to start traffic rolling over them again than to build new routes.

Biological Standardization

Serums, vaccines, and certain vitamins and drugs cannot be measured merely by weight owing to variations in their composition (that is, the potency of similar amounts). To ensure their proper use, it is necessary to measure their effect on laboratory animals and this effect is expressed in units. Such units are apt to differ markedly from country to country, so that a doctor using diphtheria antitoxin manufactured in another country may be misled. Such instances actually happened after the last war, and this led the Health Organization to embark on the international standardization of such biologicals. When war broke out some twenty-seven of the biological preparations commonly used in medicine had been standardized by groups of scientists from different countries working under the auspices of the League.[3] After

[3] In 1943 the list included 15 curative or protective sera, 9 hormones, 5 vitamins, and 5 other drugs, a total of 34 preparations commonly used in medicine.

agreement had been reached by the scientists concerned on the definition of a standard unit and on the means of assaying it, the safe keeping of the international standard was entrusted to a national laboratory, acting on behalf of the League of Nations. The various governments would then send samples of their national standards to the designated laboratory, where the sample was compared with the international standard, and they would also receive samples of the international standard for comparison in their own laboratories with the national standard preparations. The three national laboratories commonly entrusted by the League with this work were the Serum Institute in Copenhagen, the Medical Research Institute in Hampstead (England), and the National Health Institute in Washington, D.C., each specializing in particular preparations. Many of these international standards have been written into the United States Pharmacopeia. The importance of such standardization is illustrated by the case of a man with diabetes who is obliged to travel from country to country. Because of the League's work in this field he can be assured that the insulin he needs will be equally effective wherever he goes, and his doctors know that the dosage he is supposed to use will not differ from one country to another.

This work of biological standardization has been slowed down but not brought to a stop by the war. The moment the enemy is defeated, the system will be ready to operate normally again.

Nutrition

When the outbreak of war brought many of its activities to a halt, the League had developed a system of national nutrition committees covering twenty-two of the most advanced countries and twenty-six British dependencies. These committees were concerned with the formulation of national nutritional policies based on dietary studies and the appraisal of the state of nutrition. One of the principal recommendations of the United Nations Conference on Food and Agriculture at Hot Springs was that such National Nutritional Organizations should be set up in every country, and the projected Permanent Organization for Food and Agriculture was advised to make use of the national nutrition committees which already exist. In addition the League had set up a table of dietary standards through a committee of physiologists, physicians, and biochemists which met under its auspices. These dietary standards were widely accepted; they provided for the first time in history an internationally recognized frame of reference for dietary studies and requirements. Building on this work of the League of Nations, the Food and Nutrition Board of the National Research Council in this country has adopted new dietary standards or allowances which take account of advances in the science of nutrition since the League standards were formulated in 1936. The League and International Labor Office have published many other studies on the subject of nutrition; among them, *Workers' Nutrition and Social Policy*,[4] *Guiding Principles for Studies on the Nutrition of Populations*,[5] *Food Consumption and Dietary Surveys in the Americas*,[6] and, most notable of all, the *Final Report of the Mixed Committee of the League of Nations on the Relation of Nutrition to Health, Agriculture, and Economic Policy*.[7] It is readily apparent that the work of the League in the field of nutrition, together with its widespread system of national nutrition committees, can be of the greatest value to the United Nations Relief and Rehabilitation Administration and the projected United Nations Permanent Organization for Food and Agriculture.

Technical Committees

The League had also set up many international committees of experts in different fields of health and medicine. The Committee on the Hygiene of Housing brought together the latest informa-

[4] International Labor Office. *Workers' Nutrition and Social Policy*. Studies and Reports, Series B (Social and Economic Conditions), No. 23. Geneva, 1936.

[5] E. J. Bigwood, *Guiding Principles for Studies on the Nutrition of Populations*. Health Committee, Technical Commission on Nutrition. League of Nations Publication (1939.III.1).

[6] Robert Morse Woodbury, *Food Consumption and Dietary Surveys in the Americas; Results, Methods*. Report presented by the International Labor Office to the Eleventh Pan American Sanitary Conference held in Rio de Janeiro, September 7–18, 1942. Montreal, International Labor Office, 1942.

[7] League of Nations, *Final Report of the Mixed Committee of the League of Nations on the Relation of Nutrition to Health, Agriculture, and Economic Policy*. League of Nations Publication (1937.II.A.10).

tion on economical and effective methods of constructing healthful housing. Under League stimulation similar committees were set up in different countries. The studies and reports of the American Committee which works under the auspices of the American Public Health Association have been freely used and greatly appreciated by our national and local housing agencies. When United Nations Relief and Rehabilitation Administration confronts the problem of providing shelter for refugees and other displaced persons, it can with profit utilize the experience of the League and the advice and cooperation of League and national housing committees.

The League's Malaria Commission performed notable service not only in advising governments on methods of controlling malaria, but in training malariologists (hundreds were trained at special courses and in field work organized under League auspices in London, Paris, Hamburg, Rome, Singapore, Spain, and Yugoslavia), in testing the value of different antimalarial preparations, and in studying and classifying the anopheline vectors of malaria in different regions and countries. These and other technical committees still exist; they are composed of the leading experts in the different countries, accustomed to working together and with an international outlook found among scientific men who have broadened the scope of their work to include problems in countries other than their own.

Organization or Reestablishment of National Health Services

But it will be when the United Nations are confronted with the task of organizing or reorganizing the national health services of one or more countries that they will find the benefit of League experience most rewarding. For it was in this field that the Health Organization achieved its greatest triumphs, and if war had not intervened, it is along this road that the League would have traveled to far greater successes. The beginnings of this work were modest: a request from Yugoslavia for a study of malaria in one of its districts and similar requests in other fields from other countries. But the work grew rapidly, until the Health Organization was requested by the government of Greece in 1928 and the Republic of China in 1929 to assist in the reorganization of their entire public health systems. Full accounts of the results of this cooperation will be found in official League documents and in many private publications.[8]

It is enough to say here that methods were worked out and techniques perfected which brought to bear on the problems of Greece and China through the League the expert knowledge and long experience of the health services in the most advanced countries. The government of China valued the results of this cooperation so highly that it embarked on a far more ambitious program of cooperation with the League for the purpose of improving much of its economic and financial structure. Long after Japan invaded China many experts appointed by the League were still working with their Chinese associates.

The lessons learned by the League in this field of work will be most useful not only to United Nations Relief and Rehabilitation Administration but to the Permanent Organization for Food and Agriculture when it undertakes to assist governments in reorganizing the production and distribution of food for the purpose of improving national nutrition; and to the future over-all General International Organization when that agency finds that it must act on behalf of the advanced countries to raise the level of living of the poorer members of the community of nations.

Work of the Health Organization in Wartime

The Health Organization of the League of Nations still exists. Its sadly diminished staff in Geneva is still receiving epidemiological reports from a number of countries; is still publishing the *Weekly Epidemiological Report*, and undertaking certain studies, such as that on food rationing in various countries. The Serum Institute in Copenhagen and the National Institute of Medical Research in England still preserve the international samples of

[8] F. G. Boudreau, "Health and World Organization," in *World Organization;* symposium of the Institute on World Organization. Based on the Proceedings of the Institute's Sessions at American University, September, 1941 (Washington, American Council on Public Affairs, 1942). F. G. Boudreau, "International Aspects of Disease Control," in New York Academy of Medicine, *Preventive Medicine in Modern Practice* (New York, Harper, 1942). F. G. Boudreau, "International Health Organization," Chapter 1-A, *Nelson's Encyclopedia,* 1941.

serums and other biological preparations and still pursue the work of standardizing new preparations. The Health Committee of the League, which last met after war was declared, is still in being, as are many technical committees in the field of health and medicine. Recent information on the work of the Health Organization in wartime may be found in the official reports on the Work of the League submitted by the Acting Secretary General to the Council and the Members of the League.

In 1943, for example, the Health Organization continued to develop its work on subjects of current interest and importance. Its strategic position in Europe enabled it to keep in touch with national health administrations which felt the need for information on the trends of disease abroad. A series of notes was prepared and published on the prevalence, trend, and probable course of the principal communicable diseases occurring on the continent of Europe: typhus fever, cerebrospinal meningitis, typhoid fever, scarlet fever, smallpox, and acute poliomyelitis. A particularly detailed report on typhus fever was published in the Bulletin of the Health Organization in January, 1943. The Organization is now preparing a comprehensive survey with regard to "the vitality of the European populations, the increased incidence of diseases favoured by malnutrition, and the present prevalence of epidemics and their possible extension."

It is felt that the facts published will serve both to allay exaggerated fears, based on erroneous premises, and to help national health administrations and international organizations dealing with medical relief to concentrate their means to combat those diseases which constitute the most real and most immediate menace to public health.[9]

In addition to its work on epidemic diseases the Health Organization has made a careful study on food scarcity, nutrition, and health on the continent of Europe. Since it receives medical journals and statistical returns from most European countries, it is in a strategic position to study the trend of morbidity and mortality in relation to food shortages. A preliminary study was published in 1942 and a more comprehensive one is now in preparation. This

[9] League of Nations, *Report on the Work of the League of Nations, 1942–1943.* League of Nations Publication (C.25.M.25.1943), p. 54.

should assist UNRRA to settle conflicting priority claims for food, medicines, and other forms of relief. For this purpose members of the Health Organization have been in touch with OFRRO in Washington, the Allied Postwar Requirements Organization in London, Lend-Lease in Washington, and the International Red Cross in Geneva.

This by no means exhausts the health work being carried on by the League in these war years. A Health Information Service has been maintained at Geneva, which in a little over a year collected and summarized masses of technical documents to meet nearly one hundred requests.

A comprehensive glossary in twenty-four languages bearing on the significance of terms used in connection with communicable diseases was compiled last year for the Red Cross.

International biological standardization was maintained and extended, a standard and international unit of heparin (used in war surgery) being set up, and researches undertaken with respect to other new drugs. Preparations for an international pharmacopeia have been carried on, and members of the Malaria Commission have been asked to advise on the possibilities of mass treatment with the synthetic preparations used in place of quinine now that supplies from Java, the main producing country, have been shut off.

Most notable among the current activities of the Health Organization is the establishment in Washington, D. C., on May 15, 1944, of a Research Unit of the League's Health Section to assist and advise UNRRA in its work of disease prevention in the countries now occupied by the enemy. This Unit was set up at the request of UNRRA and is now at work preparing reports and interpretations concerning the march of epidemic disease in occupied Europe.

THE INTERNATIONAL HEALTH WORK OF THE FUTURE

The logic of events will undoubtedly drive the United and Associated Nations to some form of collaboration in matters of health, beyond that already projected for United Nations Relief and Rehabilitation Administration and the Food Organization. It is to be hoped that existing international and regional health organizations will be merged into a single coordinated agency with greater scope and more positive authority than that possessed by any of the former organizations. The knowledge and experience of every existing organization will be needed to cope with immediate post-war health problems. Once conditions have become stabilized, vast new opportunities will open out and vast new fields of work will be—I might have said, have already been—uncovered by the march of science. If suitable international and regional health agencies are thus developed, the work of preventing the spread of the major epidemic diseases will not occupy them long, for in a peaceful, well-organized community of nations, with a rising standard of living, such diseases come quickly under control. The work of the Permanent Organization for Food and Agriculture, if at all successful, will result in a great improvement of the health of the underprivileged throughout the world. How great that improvement may be can be estimated by the remarkable differences in morbidity and mortality existing between the different social and economic classes in a given country.[10] The new international health organization, if a new one be established, will work closely with the Permanent Organization for Food and Agriculture, unless it is to become a mere appendage of the latter. Once the major epidemic diseases are brought under control, such lesser ones as typhoid fever will need to be tackled. Malaria and tuberculosis will continue to plague mankind for some generations unless the improvement in the world-wide level of living is unexpectedly rapid. Problems of housing and clothing, of climate and disease, of physical education, and bodily and mental fitness, will require new studies and investigations, the development of new methods and novel techniques.

The experience of the Health Organization of the League of

[10] F. G. Boudreau, *New Frontiers of Preventive Medicine*. Reprinted from Transactions of the International Society of Medical Health Officers Institute, Kansas City, Mo., October 24, 1938. F. G. Boudreau, *Our Nation's Health; an International Problem*. Reprint of one section of a Handbook for Discussion Leaders, Carnegie Endowment for International Peace, Division of Intercourse and Education, February, 1940. F. G. Boudreau, *Social and Economic Implications of Freedom from Want of Food*. Reprinted from Proceedings of the American Philosophical Society, 1943, Vol. 87, No. 2.

Nations provides a foundation on which the international health work of the future may rise to greater heights than ever before. The United Nations Relief and Rehabilitation Administration and the Organization for Food and Agriculture—will powerfully supplement the work of any such organization in the future. The great strength of the Health Organization of the League lies in the fact that it is an integral part of an over-all political, economic, and social international structure. It is plain that no international health organization could function half as effectively on its own. It is equally plain that any future over-all international agency needs a health organization, measuring up to the new opportunities provided by the advance of science and greater national recognition of the need for fuller cooperation among nations in health matters. There is no real reason why the Health Organization of the League, with expanded powers and increased assets and facilities should not be the international health agency of the future. This solution would greatly simplify the task of the statesmen who must provide for the health needs of the postwar world and would also enable the present Health Organization to continue its work and take advantage of the new opportunities without the delays and inconveniences of an unnecessary break with the past.

REFUGEES

BY JAMES G. MCDONALD

AN OBJECTIVE SURVEY and a critical estimate of the League of Nations' two decades of work on behalf of refugees [1] is an essential preliminary to sound planning for international cooperative assistance to the vastly larger numbers of refugees who will be in dire need when this war is over. The League successes in this field are due to leadership by a few far-sighted and courageous men; its failures, to obstruction by timid and short-sighted governments whose representatives have, more often than not, determined refugee policies at Geneva. Hence, the lessons to be drawn from the League's experiences are both affirmative and negative. They point encouragingly to tried procedures but they also give warning that only generous and comprehensive international solutions will suffice to prevent human tragedies on a scale unprecedented in world history.

Consistently, the League of Nations has limited its refugee responsibilities. Though the forms under which the League has extended protection to refugees differ, the main principles laid down expressly or tacitly on Dr. Nansen's appointment in 1921 have not seriously varied:

JAMES G. MCDONALD, a native of Ohio and formerly a professor of history and political science, was appointed by the League of Nations High Commissioner for Refugees (Jewish and Others) Coming from Germany. He served from 1933 through 1935 in this capacity, where he acquired the first-hand experience of which he writes. From 1919 to 1933 Mr. McDonald was chairman and is now honorary chairman of the Foreign Policy Association. He has been an editorial writer on the *New York Times;* he is now chairman of the President's Advisory Committee on Political Refugees and advisor on post-war relations to the Blue Network.

---

[1] It was suggested that this chapter be entitled "Displaced Persons." Although the term "displaced persons" is more current and more broadly descriptive than the word "refugees," it would be inaccurate and misleading. For nearly twenty years the accepted League word was "refugees." "Displaced persons" came into vogue only about the time the League ceased, because of the war, to be the central agency for activities on behalf of refugees, and the term would therefore be an anachronism.

a. The League has accepted responsibility for political and legal protection of certain classes of refugees; at no time has official encouragement been given to suggestions for the extension of League protection to all classes of refugees.

b. League intervention is on a temporary basis.

c. League funds may be used for the administrative expenses of the Central Office and in some cases for local offices.

d. League organizations are expected to co-ordinate efforts made for relief and settlement, but they may not spend League funds for those purposes.[2]

The League has never accepted responsibility for refugees as a whole; always it has restricted its assistance to certain specific categories. These have included all or portions of the following:

1. More than a million from Russian territories after the Bolshevik Revolution and the resulting civil wars.[3]

2. Several hundred thousands of Armenians, and much smaller numbers of Assyrians, Assyro-Chaldeans and other non-Moslem groups "displaced in or from the late Ottoman Empire."[4]

3. More than 200,000 Bulgarians repatriated to their homeland.[5]

4. Nearly 600,000 Turks repatriated from the Balkans to Turkey.[6]

5. Approximately 1,500,000 Greeks returned from Asia Minor and elsewhere to their homeland.[7]

The League insisted on limiting its refugee responsibilities also in terms of time; nearly invariably the decisions of the Council and the Assembly incorporated expressly the idea that the particular responsibility assumed was for a definite period, at the end of which the League would be free of further obligation. It is noteworthy, however, that the best authority on this subject holds that the League has "never denied permanent responsibility for legal protection" of refugees under its charge.[8]

[2] Sir John Hope Simpson, *The Refugee Problem; Report of a Survey* (London, Oxford University Press, 1939), p. 192. This study "issued under the auspices of the Royal Institute of International Affairs" is the most comprehensive and authoritative yet made on this subject. Its sound scholarship and rigid objectivity cannot be praised too highly, and the volume has served as an invaluable guide to this paper.

[3] *Ibid.*, p. 82.

[4] *Ibid.*, pp. 36–37 and pp. 47 ff.

[5] *Ibid.*, pp. 24–26.

[6] *Ibid.*, p. 2.

[7] Charles B. Eddy, *Greece and the Greek Refugees*, p. 52; also, pp. 348–52.

[8] Simpson, *op. cit.*, p. 194. Despite Sir John's profound knowledge of the League's refugee record, I must make a reservation about the League's attitude on this point when I was serving as High Commissioner. I know of nothing either in the written record of the League's decisions or in the unofficial and verbal expressions of views to support the conclusion that in the case of refugees from

The third major self-imposed limitation on the League's work on behalf of refugees is its explicit denial of responsibility for either relief or settlement. With rare exceptions, and these usually in cases involving very small amounts of money, League funds have been used solely for administrative expenses. Almost never in principle and rarely in practice has the League gone beyond its rule not to engage in direct "operations." In sharp contrast to its acceptance of responsibility for political and juridical protection of certain categories of refugees, the League has insisted that its task in the humanitarian field is limited to administrative efforts to stimulate and coordinate governmental and private activities in feeding, clothing, transporting, and finding new homes for refugees.

Though the League has firmly refused to vote money for the relief and settlement of refugees (the exceptions have been so rare as to prove the rule) it has consistently recognized the necessity of international effort to achieve these ends. Often the League representatives in the field—even the greatest of them, Dr. Fridtjof Nansen, scientist and explorer—have been embarrassed and hampered by the insistence of Geneva on the principle that all funds for other than administrative purposes must be sought outside the League. Repeated efforts were made to change this League policy in the Council and the Assembly, usually by representatives of the Scandinavian countries, who were more alert than most members to the broader and tragic implications of the refugee problem—but these attempts failed.[9] There were minor exceptions when the League authorized small sums for relief or settlement but these were usually coupled with a reaffirmation of the

---

Germany, the League from December, 1933, to the end of December, 1936 (e.g., the period I was in office) continued to claim or to exercise any right of legal protection of the refugees within the competence of the Governing Body of our High Commission. Possibly it might be contended that this was an interim period during which the League did not consider that it was in charge of German refugees, and does not, therefore, invalidate Sir John's general statement. Or perhaps Sir John meant that the League by promoting the drafting and the ratification of international conventions to give refugees continuing legal protection recognized its "permanent responsibility."

[9] An often cited example of one of several of Dr. Nansen's vain appeals for League Funds to aid in relief or settlement is contained in *Report to the Council*. C.124 M.74.1922, p. 1.

rule against such League assistance.[10] As a result, League of Nations high commissioners have of necessity often been more occupied in stimulating private charity—frequently generous in its gifts—and in appealing for aid from governments—usually niggardly in their responses—than in carrying out their assigned task of international administration.

The application of these four basic principles of the League's refugee activities can perhaps be best illustrated by brief but frank résumés of the workings, both successful and otherwise, of four of the different refugee agencies used by or sponsored by the League. These are the Nansen Organization, the International Labor Office, high commissioners other than Dr. Nansen, and *ad hoc* committees or commissions. Some of the League efforts can then be contrasted and compared with the two chief recent intergovernmental efforts on behalf of refugees being made outside the League. These are the Intergovernmental Committee and the United Nations Relief and Rehabilitation Administration (UNRRA). Finally one can suggest tentatively a few conclusions for the consideration of those who at the end of this war will have the arduous responsibility of improving upon the League and other techniques in dealing with refugees or displaced persons.

DR. NANSEN AND THE NANSEN ORGANIZATION

For nearly a decade, beginning in 1921, the League's refugee work was the length and shadow of one man, Dr. Fridtjof Nansen. From his successful leadership in the repatriation of some 400,000 prisoners of war shortly after the conflict closed, he continued throughout the twenties to be the inspiration and director of most of the League efforts on behalf of refugees. His death in May, 1930, was literally an irreparable loss.[11] Since then no one

[10] For example, the Fourth Committee of the Sixth Assembly in favoring the grant of 200,000 Swiss francs (approximately $40,000) for the settlement of Saar refugees in Paraguay and of 86,000 pounds towards the settlement of the Assyrians of Iraq, specifically reaffirm "the principle that the League does not accept any responsibility for the settlement and relief of refugees." (*Report of Sixth Committee to the Assembly*. A.73.1936, XII, 5.)

[11] Nor did Lord Robert Cecil exaggerate when he wrote, Dr. Nansen "has left no successor." Viscount Cecil, *A Great Experiment*, (New York, Oxford University Press, 1941), p. 132.

has been able to replace him because no one has had the personal prestige or the influence to exercise the dynamic leadership essential to break down bureaucratic red tape and shortsighted governmental nationalism, the nearly impassable barriers to effective international action. But our deserved tribute to Dr. Nansen's unique personality, his utter devotion and his almost fanatical zeal should not blind us to the fact that he more often felt frustrated than satisfied with the results of his many and varied refugee endeavors. Not even he could win more than partial success against the blindness of those in authority who would not or could not see that the nations' handling of the refugee problem was one of the touchstones of the League's success or failure as an international institution.

Dr. Nansen's own estimate of the League's work during his period of leadership given in the article "Refugees," still retained, as a tribute to this unique leader, in the latest editions of the *Encyclopedia Britannica*, was in part as follows:

> The other personal and economic problems which have been raised by the refugee movements above described have been dealt with partly by individual Governments and partly by the League of Nations. To take Russians first, many Governments throughout Europe accorded them particular privileges and gave them much State help, estimated at £2,000,000 per annum—in particular Yugoslavia, Czechoslovakia and Bulgaria deserve mention. The League of Nations and the International Labour Office also played a considerable part through the action of the delegations established in Constantinople and in the Baltic States, Rumania, China, Bulgaria, Greece, Serbia, Germany, Poland, France and other countries, in breaking up the most disastrous congestions of refugees in places where no employment could be found, for example, in Constantinople and Greece, in placing some hundreds of thousands in employment in no fewer than 50 different countries; in securing for the refugees in many countries legal protection, freedom of movement in search of employment and a new form of so-called "League of Nations Passport" [It soon became universally known as the "Nansen Passport"] which has secured the recognition of over 50 Governments, under which they were enabled to travel from one country to another; and even in securing for a small number who desired it, repatriation to their native land. Under the auspices and with the help of these League offices, large movements of Russian refugees were carried out to France, where some thousands

have been settled as tenant farmers and in industry, to the United States, to Canada, to South America and to other countries where employment could be found.

For the Greek refugees the League has done still more. Through its machinery a loan of £12,000,000 for their settlement in agricultural and other employment was obtained, and under the international control of a League commission this settlement has been carried out with remarkable success. On June 12, 1926, the Council of the League of Nations announced their intention of recommending a loan of £2,250,000 to the Bulgarian Government to assist the settlement of the Bulgar refugees. [It was over-subscribed.] The conditions for administration and security were similar to those laid down in the case of the Greek refugee loan.

For the Armenians the same passport privileges and legal protection were obtained through the machinery of the League as had previously been obtained for the Russians. Their dispersal from places where they were concentrated in too great numbers, for example, from Greece, was also assisted by the agents of the League. This assistance took the form of an appeal for funds for the establishment of a national home in the Caucasus, and of the creation of co-operation with the mandatory Power and the International Labour Office of a series of agricultural colonies and urban settlements in Syria to relieve the congestion of the refugee camps in Beirut, Alexandretta and Aleppo.

The effect of this League of Nations action is likely to be cumulative, and considerable as are its short period results in mitigating the sufferings of the refugees and in helping to solve the economic problems caused to the Governments concerned, its long period results are likely to be more important still. . . . It is, therefore, possible to say that, as the result of the generosity of a number of Governments and of their enlightened co-operation through the machinery of the League, the ultimate results of the refugee movements will be better than even the most optimistic could have ventured to expect.

Perhaps Dr. Nansen's rather optimistic estimate of the long-range results of the League's refugee activities would have been more nearly realized had fate permitted him to continue his aggressive leadership. His death in the early summer of 1930 was followed by a period of uncertainty and study before the Eleventh Assembly set up an autonomous International Relief Office commonly known as the Nansen Office. It became operative in 1931 under the authority of the League in accordance with Article 24 of the Covenant but was instructed to conclude its "humanitarian" work within a ten year period.[12] Simultaneously with the creation of the Nansen Office, the Assembly decided that the political and legal protection of refugees was to continue to be entrusted to the regular organs of the League, that is, primarily to the Secretariat.

In making these decisions on refugees, the Assembly reaffirmed two of the League's basic principles that these are temporary problems, the final solution of which can be expedited by mandatory terminal dates imposed by League fiat, and that only the political protection and the legal defense of refugees are proper subjects for the League's direct responsibility. Thus, the humanitarian work, even when only a matter of administering or coordinating the efforts of private bodies or of governments, was relegated to non-League or to autonomous bodies.

Soon it became manifest that the distinction between political and legal protection by the League and humanitarian work by the Nansen Office was more theoretical than real, and that in fact the Nansen Office alone had local representatives in the chief centers where intervention in individual refugee cases was needed. Hence, in order that the juridical protection of refugees might be continued, after the dissolution of the Nansen Office, the League provided through the Convention of October 28, 1933, for the issuance of Nansen identity certificates by the governments signing the Convention. Through the same medium were to be secured the rights of residence and employment and other benefits for Russians, Armenians, and assimilated refugees then under the protection of the Nansen Office.[13]

After the Plebiscite in the Saar Valley in 1935, more than 6,000

[12] But the next Assembly, that of 1931, fixed the liquidation date of the Nansen Office as December 31, 1938.

[13] The League Arrangements of 1926, which provided, through the creation of the Nansen stamp, funds for the humanitarian work, and the Arrangements of 1928, which assured legal protection, were not binding obligations upon the signatory states and would not have been effective following the liquidation of the Nansen Office, fixed for the end of 1938. Hence, the Convention of 1933 was important, for it was binding even after 1938 upon the states which ratified it. Unfortunately only eight countries, Belgium, France, Bulgaria, Egypt, Norway, Denmark, Italy, Czechoslovakia, and the United Kingdom (Great Britain) have completed ratification; and four of these, Belgium, France, Bulgaria, and Italy have added substantial reservations.

former residents of that region became refugees in France. This new group was added by decision of the League to those already under the protection of the Nansen Office, and a recommendation was made to the governments that Nansen identity certificates be issued to them.

In 1936 Judge M. Michael Hansson of Norway was appointed president of the Nansen Office and carried the activities forward with energy and distinction until the close of the Office in 1938. He greatly simplified the work and finances of the Office, reorganized its nine representative offices in different European countries, and achieved a realistic accounting of the refugees who remained unsettled. At the close of his work in 1938, Judge Hansson reported that 600,000 refugees—Russians, Armenians, Assyrians, Assyrian-Chaldeans, Turks, and Saarlanders—remained under the care of the Office.[14] The depression years from 1931–1938 had not eased the task of settling refugees, and it was significant that, twenty years after the end of the first World War, this substantial number of people remained in an unsettled state. They were destined later to join the stream of refugees from Central Europe and the war refugees of the western European countries who fled southward into France in advance of the German armies in the spring of 1940.

THE INTERNATIONAL LABOR OFFICE AND REFUGEES

Before the Nansen Office was set up in 1931, the League tried the experiment of utilizing the International Labor Office as a refugee agency. On the advice of Dr. Nansen, then High Com-

[14] One reason there were so many refugees under Judge Hansson's care in 1938 was that citizenship is very difficult to acquire in the western European countries in which many had taken refuge. They therefore did not have the rights of citizens to permanent residence, work, and other privileges such as education and public relief. Furthermore, they were either stateless persons or, as was the case with many of the Germans, they had no protection from their government. The League organizations spent much effort on the task of trying to assure them these privileges as individuals and fix their civil status and to provide an agency which could represent them before public authorities. The same situation will exist after this war and will need a solution as long as there remain in different European countries large numbers of people who cannot become citizens of those countries but who cannot find a permanent home elsewhere. The treaties of 1933 and of 1928 may form models for agreements between the governments in making the after-war settlements.

missioner, and with the approval of Albert Thomas, director of the I.L.O., the Assembly voted, September 25, 1924, to transfer from the Secretariat of the League to the I.L.O., the handling of technical problems of employment, settlement, and migration. These activities were to be known as the Refugee Service. The Governing Body of the I.L.O., though faced with an accomplished fact, showed no enthusiasm for this new assignment and coupled two limitations with its rather grudging acceptance. Neither of these was unexpected because the Council and the Assembly had during previous years fixed both of them as basic League policies—non-use of League funds for relief or settlement and a time limit on League humanitarian responsibility.[15]

This arrangement effected a formal rather than a fundamental change in the League's handling of refugee problems. The I.L.O. was to complete what had been done in the humanitarian field, but the League itself retained responsibility for the handling of political questions. The staff of Dr. Nansen, including Major T. F. Johnson, its head, was transferred from the League Secretariat to the I.L.O., January 1, 1925. Despite the continued efforts of Major Johnson and his associates, under the general guidance of Dr. Nansen, the work assigned to the Refugee Service was not and, in view of the prevailing attitudes of governments, could not have been completed quickly.

In 1929, the Governing Body of the I.L.O. moved to free itself of refugee responsibility. They argued that the High Commissioner was especially competent to deal with the remaining problems of colonization and that the existing divisions of responsibility—as between the High Commissioner and the Refugee Service and between the League and the I.L.O.—impeded the work. It was in partial response to this appeal that the League, the next year, following the death of Dr. Nansen, authorized the creation of the Nansen Office. On the Governing Body of this autonomous

[15] The Governing Body of the I.L.O. stressed this time limit by declaring that the work should be wound up "as soon as possible." On the insistence of the director, however, the I.L.O. agreed that the words "as soon as possible" were to be interpreted as calling for the completion of the work already under way at the earliest practicable moment. See *Report of the Director*, C.359M.120.1925.

[4] See the paper on the League work with refugees, p. 208.

organization, the I.L.O. was to name one of the eleven members. Thus did the I.L.O. reduce its refugee responsibilities.[16]

In a closely related field, however, the International Labor Office has performed an invaluable function. In its world-wide research on labor conditions and the forces making for migration, the I.L.O. has also surveyed and reported on the movements of peoples, including refugees and other displaced persons from one area to another. The I.L.O. publications are therefore indispensable to the student of these problems.[17]

HIGH COMMISSIONERS FOLLOWING DR. NANSEN

The coming into power of the Nazi party in Germany early in 1933 marked the dispersal of new refugees over Western and Middle Europe, and after the beginning of the present world war, the movement gained such momentum that it ultimately developed "into an unprecedented pattern of dislocated groups and populations." Those in the Reich who refused to accept the Nazi totalitarian doctrines and those who were classified according to the Nuremberg Laws as non-Aryan were progressively deprived of opportunities to continue their work. Members of the learned and artistic professions, scientists, writers, artists, and labor leaders were first driven from their official positions and later from those in the universities and from the publishing and many other businesses. Many of them were arrested and confined in concentration camps, then robbed of their property and deprived of their citizenship. Naturally, as many as could fled from Germany, to try to establish new homes elsewhere.

[16] Attention should be called to the I.L.O.'s effort to organize migration generally in the after-war period. The I.L.O. theory is that migration cannot be organized for refugees alone but that the refugees must be included in a general plan for migration. The I.L.O. believes that there must be set up migration departments, particularly in countries of immigration, which will determine what kind of immigration they want and how the people can be settled, that the role of the I.L.O. is to coordinate efforts of governments in countries of migration and of immigration, try to find places where people can go, and perhaps be of use in easing immigration laws.

[17] The I.L.O. publications include the *International Labor Review* (a monthly); the *I.L.O. Yearbook*, a survey of social and economic movements and labor legislation; and occasional studies and reports.

During the first months of this enforced migration, the countries neighboring Germany—Austria, Hungary, Poland, Czechoslovakia, Switzerland, Belgium, the Netherlands, and France—generously permitted the refugees to flee across their borders. The usual immigration restrictions were waived in the expectation that most of the refugees, after temporary residence, would go overseas to permanent homes. Happily, almost half of the Jewish refugees who left Germany in the early days of the Nazi perescution were able to gain admission to Palestine.

In October, 1933, the writer was appointed by the Council of the League of Nations as High Commissioner for Refugees (Jewish and Other) Coming from Germany. The mandate of the High Commissioner was to "negotiate and direct" the "international collaboration" necessary to solve the "economic financial and social problem" of the refugees. On October 27 certain states were invited by the Council to appoint representatives on the Governing Body of the High Commission.[18]

Early in December the Commission was formally organized and held its first meeting, in Lausanne.

Back of this choice of Lausanne rather than Geneva for the initial session of the Commission and for the seat of the High Commissioner's office lies the story which explains one of the chief weaknesses of the Commission and its executive throughout their more than two years of work. At a first conference between the High Commissioner and the Secretary General, Monsieur Joseph Avenol (a cautious and bureaucratic official), the latter emphasized the Assembly's decision that the High Commission was to be separate from the League and that the High Commissioner would report to the Governing Body of the High Commission and not to the Council of the League. He made clear, too, that the 25,000 Swiss francs which the Council was making available to the High Commission for organizing purposes was only a loan and was to be repaid within twelve months. And, as if to leave no doubt that the League was disowning its child, Monsieur Avenol

[18] Fourteen states accepted. These were: the United States, Great Britain, France, Holland, Switzerland, Italy, Czechoslovakia, Poland, Denmark, the Netherlands, Belgium, Norway, Sweden, and Uruguay.

said firmly that it would be very unwise for the Commission to establish itself in Geneva.[19]

Several reasons explain the Assembly's decision to separate the new organization from the League. One was, of course, the League's fundamental principle that the care of refugees is not a continuing League responsibility. But this consideration alone does not explain why the Assembly was unwilling that the High Commission should be autonomous, as was the Nansen Office, with a similar right and duty to report to the Assembly. The decisive reason for the completeness of the separation was the League's desire to appease Germany, then a member of the League, in return for the German delegates' willingness to abstain from a negative vote when the final decision was taken in the Assembly. On this point, it is significant that the German representatives called special attention to the fact that the Assembly's action was so worded as not in any way to indicate criticism of internal policies of the German Government.[20]

Another interesting organizational question is this: Why was the responsibility for the German refugees turned over to a new and separate organization instead of to the Nansen Office? One factor was the preference of the large private Jewish organizations. Already they were bearing the burden of the care for the Jewish refugees from Germany—a responsibility which they have continued to bear generously—and they naturally objected to being associated with an organization, such as the Nansen Office, which had hanging over it the sentence of dissolution (the end of 1938). But the decisive factor was, more probably, the attitude of Germany, which objected to any connection between the League and the organization appointed to deal with German refugees.

Under the devoted and enlightened leadership of Viscount Cecil of Chelwood, the British representative, who remained chairman throughout, the High Commission labored for more than two years to carry out the League's mandate. During that

[19] Until the Swiss Government agreed to Lausanne, it looked for a time as if the High Commission might remain homeless.

[20] Yet within a few weeks, October 14, Germany announced its intention to withdraw from the League.

period, largely through the efforts of the great private organizations, mostly Jewish, somewhat more than sixty thousand of the eighty thousand refugees who had fled from Germany were helped to establish themselves in new homes.

By the spring and summer of 1935, Lord Cecil [21] and the writer had become convinced that the High Commission was not doing enough and under the circumstances could not do enough to justify continuance in office. The Commission's separation from the League was a grave but not necessarily a fatal weakness. Another and even more serious weakness was the unwillingness of governments, including most of those represented on the High Commission, to act together, either through the League or otherwise, to bring any pressure to bear upon Germany to cease creating refugees.

At the last meeting on October 16, 1935, of the Permanent Committee of the Governing Body of the High Commission, at which the Commissioner's intention to resign was fully discussed, action was taken to liquidate the Office of High Commissioner at the end of January, 1936, or sooner, if before that date the Council of the League had made other provisions for the coordination of the activities on behalf of the refugees coming from Germany. It was the expectation of the Permanent Committee that the Committee of Experts provided for by the Assembly of 1935, to study the reorganization of the activities on behalf of the "German" and of the "Nansen" refugees, would complete its investigations in time to present a plan for consideration, and it was hoped for action, by the Council at its meeting in January, 1936. It had been the sense of the Governing Body that the work of assistance in the countries of refuge could be better carried forward by an organization directly under the authority of the League.[22]

The Council of the League of Nations thereupon in January, 1936, established the office under its authority and Sir Neill Malcolm was appointed High Commissioner for Refugees Coming from Germany. League action on behalf of refugees was restricted

[21] See Cecil, *A Great Experiment*, pp. 252–54.

[22] James G. McDonald, Letter of Resignation, December, 1935. C.13.M.12.1936. XII. Annex. (Ser. L.o.N. P. 1936. XII B.2)

to those who had already left their country of origin and to negotiations with the governments with respect to their legal status and to employment and settlement. Responsibility for the relief of refugees was again left to the private agencies.

Through the Convention of February, 1938, drawn up under the League auspices, there were made available to refugees from Germany identity certificates similar to those provided for the Nansen refugees by the Convention of 1933. In May, 1938, refugees from Austria were included within the competence of the High Commissioner and within the provisions of the Convention of 1938.

In accordance with decisions taken in earlier years by the League of Nations, the Nansen International Office for Refugees (Russians, Armenians, Assyrians, Assyrian-Chaldeans, Turks, and Saarlanders) and the High Commissioner for Refugees Coming from Germany (Germans and Austrians) concluded their activities in December, 1938. Logically, there was no reason for distinguishing between the different groups of refugees. It was also obvious that the League could not cease its activities on behalf of refugees at a time when their number was increasing rapidly. Consequently the Assembly of the League in 1938 constituted a new High Commissioner of the League of Nations to deal with refugees hitherto handled by the Nansen International Office for Refugees and the Office of the High Commissioner for Refugees Coming from Germany. Sir Herbert Emerson was appointed High Commissioner and established his office in London.

His duties were rigidly set forth in the resolutions establishing his office: to provide for the political and legal protection of refugees; to superintend the enforcement and the application of the provisions of the Conventions of October 28, 1933, and February 10, 1938, regarding legal status of refugees; to facilitate coordination of humanitarian assistance; and to assist government and private organizations in their efforts to promote emigration and permanent settlement. In February, 1939, Sir Herbert Emerson was elected also director of the Inter-governmental Committee, whose organization is described below, and thus was able to combine the work of both organizations in one office.

OUTSIDE THE LEAGUE: I. THE INTERGOVERNMENTAL COMMITTEE

The German *Anschluss* with Austria in March, 1938, added new thousands to the stream of central European refugees, who were already taxing the capacities of the countries of temporary refuge of Western Europe. In an effort to substitute planned migration for the chaotic dispersion of refugees which was proving disturbing to the peace and comfort of other countries, President Franklin D. Roosevelt, apparently without previous consultation with the League of Nations or the High Commissioner for Refugees from Germany, summoned thirty-two governments to the Evian Conference of July, 1938. Mr. Myron Taylor represented the United States.

Reports received at Evian indicated that some 125,000 refugees had already left Germany and Austria and that 700,000 additional persons were under the necessity of departing, because of their racial origins or their religious and political beliefs. Neighboring countries reported that they could not absorb more refugees unless they were relieved of those already accepted. Only one offer to receive refugees for permanent settlement was received at Evian. Countries of immigration with their large cities already full of unemployed were fearful that the refugees from central Europe would add to their urban populations and bring with them the political conflicts of which they were the victims. The Dominican Republic, in contrast to the action of other governments, offered to accept 100,000 for settlement in agriculture. Though this figure of 100,000 could hardly be taken seriously, the Dominican offer was nonetheless the one tangible proof of governmental generosity.

The governments at Evian adjourned to a second meeting in London in August, 1938, and there, in large part because of the leadership of Myron Taylor, the United States representative, they organized the Intergovernmental Committee, with Lord Winterton, the representative of the British Government, as chairman. The first action of the Intergovernmental Committee was to explore with Germany the possibilities of orderly emigration of the refugees, with sufficient capital in their possession to contribute to the costs of resettlement. The negotiations came to naught as the German proposals proved unacceptable to the government members of the Intergovernmental Committee and to the refugees themselves.

Thereafter commissions of experts were sent to explore the feasibility of the settlement of refugees in northern and southern Rhodesia, British Guiana, the Dominican Republic, and Mindanao in the Philippines. Costs of settlement in Africa proved high but the settlement of experimental groups of 500 families were recommended in the other areas. The outbreak of the war in September, 1939, resulted in the cancellation of plans to settle refugees in British Guiana and the Philippines, but the Dominican project proceeded under the auspices of the Dominican Republic Settlement Association, a private corporation organized in New York, which entered into a contract with the Dominican Government. Over 500 refugees were received in the Sosua settlement in the Dominican Republic before difficulties of transportation prevented the transfer of additional numbers.[23]

OUTSIDE THE LEAGUE: II. UNITED NATIONS RELIEF AND REHABILITATION ADMINISTRATION (*UNRRA*)

The first session of the Council of UNRRA, held in Atlantic City from November 10 to December 1, 1943, defined more clearly than had been done theretofore the scope of the functions of this ambitious international cooperative enterprise. The relief and repatriation of displaced persons is only one of several tasks which UNRRA has set for itself.

At the Council meeting there were considerable differences of opinion concerning the categories of displaced persons whose care and return to their previous homes should be the responsibility of UNRRA. It was finally determined that UNRRA

> Should assist not only the repatriation of citizens of the various United Nations to their countries of origin, but also the return of United Nations nationals and of stateless persons "who have been driven as a

[23] Only eleven countries have ratified the 1938 Convention: Belgium, France, Bulgaria, Italy, Egypt, Norway, Denmark, Czechoslovakia, the United Kingdom, the Netherlands, and Spain. Several of these signatories have made reservations about the application of the Convention to all or certain of their protectorates or colonies.

result of the war from their places of settled residence in countries of which they are not nationals, to those places." This provision would empower UNRRA, for example, to arrange for the return to Burma, the Malay States or the Philippines, of Chinese residing in these areas before the war, instead of repatriating them automatically to China; and also to return stateless Jews, Russians and so on to countries other than those of their origin in which they may have been residing before the Nazi invasion. UNRRA is to work in the closest possible co-operation with the Intergovernmental Committee on Refugees, and it will be the function of this Committee to find places, over the long run, for such persons as fall within its competence and as cannot or do not desire to be repatriated either to their countries of origin or of former residence. It was also decided that UNRRA should not have any responsibility for the repatriation of prisoners of war who have served in the armies of the United Nations "unless requested by the member government concerned to undertake such responsibility in respect of any particular group." [24]

UNRRA's operations are to be financed by large appropriations from governments. It is estimated that there will be a common fund of from two billion to two billion five hundred million dollars for a contemplated two-year period. Thus UNRRA was at once placed financially in a wholly different category from the Intergovernmental Committee and from the various League agencies which are or have been concerned with refugees—the several High Commissions and Commissioners, the Nansen Office and the earlier Refugee Service. None of these agencies had adequate government or League funds and some of them had no government or League funds at all.[25]

TODAY'S PROBLEMS

A competent authority, after a searching investigation, estimates that "more than thirty million of the inhabitants of Europe

[24] Vera Micheles Dean, *UNRRA;—a Step toward Reconstruction.* Foreign Policy Reports, January 1, 1944, Vol. XIX; No. 20.

[25] Some of these agencies were forced, therefore, as was the High Commission for German Refugees during the time I was the executive, to rely solely on the generosity of private organizations, mostly Jewish, not only for the funds for relief and settlement of refugees but also for the money to pay the administrative expenses of our office. The unstinting support of the Jewish organizations, especially the American Joint Distribution Committee, was beyond praise; but the JDC's funds and those of the other private bodies were of necessity so

have been transplanted or torn from their homes since the beginning of the war . . . [This] does not include the millions of Germans and Italian refugees who since 1943 have fled or been evacuated from heavily bombed cities in increasing numbers." [26] And that estimate, of course, does not include the additional millions who may have to leave their homes on the continent before the war is ended. On the other side of the world, it is conservatively estimated that since the war in China began in 1937, approximately thirty million Chinese have fled before the Japanese armies in two substantial movements from the coast areas to agricultural hinterland; one from central China and the southeast to the southwest and the other from the northeast to the northwest.[27]

Even if we assume that most of the millions of displaced Chinese are beyond international aid and that a large portion of the displaced Europeans will, in the event of allied victory, be able through their own strength to return to their old home, there will remain a residue of perhaps as many as twenty millions whose return to normal life will depend upon international cooperative effort.

Now it should be plain to the most limited vision that there can be no hope of solving today's and tomorrow's problems of refugees and displaced persons except through the grant of large funds by the interested governments. And all governments are vitally interested not only from the humanitarian point of view but also because there can be no restoration of economic well-being throughout the world until the millions of homeless have been reabsorbed in creative life in their homelands or in other countries. UNRRA'S initial assumption that only generous government funds will be adequate to needs, and the success it may have in securing such funds from governments, are the best promise that its ambitious plans will be effective.

[26] Eugene M. Kulischer, *The Displacement of Population in Europe* (Montreal, 1943), p. 163. Mr. Kulischer's volume is one of the latest in the I.L.O.'s series of excellent special studies.

[27] This estimate and some of the other material in this chapter are from my article on refugees prepared for the forthcoming edition of the *Encyclopedia Britannica.*

No longer is it possible to maintain the earlier fiction that relief and settlement can be left to the private agencies. These organizations, Jewish and others, will continue to welcome opportunities to play their proper roles, but these are of necessity limited. Only governments, acting through appropriate official international agencies, will be able to cope with the appalling tasks that will continue to be imposed upon the world by the war.

Nor should it be forgotten that there still remains the very serious problem of finding countries which will be willing to open their doors to refugees. Until permanent homes are made, many refugees who do not, or will not be permitted to, return to their former homes will constitute a serious situation in the countries in which they happen to be found. Some of these are stateless, others are Germans who will not want to return to Germany. Some German refugees who formerly lived in France, Holland, or Belgium may be barred from returning to their original homes by government action. These people are mostly stateless at this time.

Another difficulty which is often overlooked is the very large expenditure required to settle refugee families on the land or in cities. Sometimes this is as much as $5,000 per family, rarely is it less than half that amount. Hence, some of the potential countries of immigration may be unwilling to receive refugees unless funds from the outside are provided to help settle these newcomers. Funds in the required amounts can only come from other governments.

The League experience in dealing with relatively small numbers of refugees demonstrates the impossibility of fixing in advance a definite terminal date for the conclusion of relief and settlement activities. It is to be hoped that those responsible for UNRRA and other current and post-war efforts on behalf of displaced persons will not permit themselves to be maneuvered into promising to conclude their work by a specific time.

THE REAL SOLUTION

The only real solution for the problems of refugees and displaced persons is to eliminate the causes which force these innocent victims from their homes. That these causes must be eliminated is the deepest conviction gained during the writer's experiences with German refugees. Hence, it is without apology that the following extracts of appeal and warning to the League of Nations and to the countries in and out of the League nearly nine years ago, are quoted from the writer's letter of resignation, December 27, 1935, to the Secretary General of the League.[28]

In the period of over two years since the establishment of the office, conditions in Germany which create refugees have developed so catastrophically that a reconsideration by the League of Nations of the entire situation is essential. . . .

Apart from all questions of principle and of religious persecution, one portentous fact confronts the community of states. More than half a million persons, against whom no charge can be made except that they are not what the National Socialists choose to regard as "Nordic," are being crushed. They cannot escape oppression by any act of their own free-will, for what has been called "the membership of non-Aryan race" cannot be changed or kept in abeyance. . . .

The task of saving these victims calls for renewed efforts of the philanthropic bodies. The private organizations, Jewish and Christian, may be expected to do their part if the Governments, acting through the League, make possible a solution. But in the new circumstances it will not be enough to continue the activities on behalf of those who flee from the Reich. Efforts must be made to remove or mitigate the causes which create German refugees. This could not have been any part of the work of the High Commissioner's office; nor, presumably, can it be a function of the body to which the League may decide to entrust future administrative activities on behalf of the refugees. It is a political function, which properly belongs to the League itself. . . .

The developments since 1933, and in particular those following the Nuremberg legislation, call for fresh collective action in regard to the problem created by persecution in Germany. The moral authority of the League of Nations and of States Members of the League must be directed towards a determined appeal to the German Government in the name of humanity and of the principles of the public law of Europe. They must ask for a modification of policies which constitute a source of unrest and perplexity in the world, a challenge to the conscience of mankind, and a menace to the legitimate interest of the States affected by the immigration of German refugees. . . .

The efforts of the private organizations and of any League organi-

[28] Letter of Resignation. C.13.M.12.1936. XII. Annex.

zation for refugees can only mitigate a problem of growing gravity and complexity. In the present economic conditions of the world, the European States, and even those overseas, have only a limited power of absorption of refugees. The problem must be tackled at its source if disaster is to be avoided.

This is the function of the League, which is essentially an association of states for the consideration of matters of common concern. The Covenant empowers the Council and the Assembly to deal with any matter within the sphere of activity of the League or affecting the peace of the world. The effort of the League to ensure respect for human personality, when not grounded on express provisions of the Covenant or international treaties, has a sure foundation in the fact that the protection of the individual from racial and religious intolerance is a vital condition of international peace and security. . . .

I feel bound to conclude this letter on a personal note. Prior to my appointment as High Commissioner for Refugees Coming from Germany, and in particular during the fourteen years following the War, I gave in my former office frequent and tangible proof of my concern that justice be done to the German people. But convinced as I am that desperate suffering in the countries adjacent to Germany, and an even more terrible human calamity within the German frontiers, are inevitable unless present tendencies in the Reich are checked or reversed, I cannot remain silent. I am convinced that it is the duty of the High Commissioner for German Refugees, in tendering his resignation, to express an opinion on the essential elements of the task with which the Council of the League entrusted him. When domestic policies threaten the demoralization and exile of hundreds of thousands of human beings, considerations of diplomatic correctness must yield to those of common humanity. I should be recreant if I did not call attention to the actual situation, and plead that world opinion, acting through the League and its Member-States and other countries, move to avert the existing and impending tragedies.[29]

[29] The above major conclusions drawn from the League's refugee experiences should be compared and checked with the excellent article "Postwar Problems of Refugees," by Sir Herbert Emerson, *Foreign Affairs* (January, 1943), pp. 211–20. Sir Herbert, as the present League High Commissioner and the executive for the Intergovernmental Committee, speaks with special authority.

SOCIAL PROBLEMS[1]

BY ELSA CASTENDYCK

YEARS BEFORE the establishment of the League of Nations as an international agency for studying the social problems of modern society, many countries had already recognized the fact that these questions are international in character, solvable only by international effort. Gradually, too, social science has begun to realize that these problems are closely interwoven with the economic and labor issues of the world. For instance, traffic in women and children involves the transportation of its victims from one country to another. It also tends to grow worse under bad economic conditions and subsequent unemployment, as do other problems that the League has been considering such as child welfare conditions and the plight of indigent foreigners. Since war usually aggravates social and economic ills, both the victorious and the vanquished countries after the present conflict are likely to face complicated social problems of great gravity. The whole problem of prostitution, including such aspects as preventive action, traffic in women, regulation, rehabilitation of prostitutes, measures against venereal disease, will be aggravated by the destitution to which an enormous number of women and children will have been reduced. Not only this increase in prostitution but also the breaking up of families from such causes as the disappearance of parents and the removal of children without their parents from

---

ELSA CASTENDYCK has been for many years connected with the Children's Bureau of the Department of Labor in Washington, where she is now Director of Research in the Social Service Division. She was a member of the Advisory Committee on Social Questions of the League of Nations, and attended the meetings of this international committee in Geneva until the War.

[1] The Social and humanitarian work of the League covered a wide field, including health (see pp. 193–207), the suppression of illicit opium traffic (see pp. 182–92), slavery and forced labor, relief from famine and disease, assistance to and settlement of refugees, et cetera. For a detailed description of the League's early work in this field see the volume *Ten Years of World Cooperation* published by the Secretariat of the League in 1930. This chapter is restricted to the work of the Social Section.

familiar to unfamiliar regions and the uprooting and migration of families, will have increased the number of young persons in moral danger. The need for renewed emphasis on spiritual re-education of youth will confront the world.

The war will not only have intensified old problems and created new ones; it will also have interrupted years of social progress begun at the turn of the century and accelerated by the work of the League of Nations. Among these are the activities of the Social Questions Section and the Advisory Committee on Social Questions of the League, which have for more than twenty years been dealing with certain special aspects of social problems, namely, the legal and moral protection of women and children, assistance to indigent foreigners, and the suppression of obscene publications. Some parts of the work had reached a very advanced stage when war broke out in 1939. For example, the final report on preventive action against prostitution was ready for printing; a thorough study, in conjunction with the Health Committee, of the social and medical aspects of venereal disease had been proposed; a draft convention had been drawn up for the suppression of prostitution; good progress had been made on the improvement of the social position of the unmarried mother and her child. A significant reorientation of the social work of the League had been begun, substituting prevention for the out-of-date curative approach, and linking its studies and activities with the larger stream of social thinking and planning of the modern world. Social welfare was envisaged no longer as an isolated concept but as a problem inseparably bound up with other forces and developments in the world. This new approach would have opened the way for the League to fulfill in this field a function as important as that of the health section or the economic and financial sections.

Although certain plans have had to be suspended during the war, the Social Questions Section of the League has nevertheless continued to function. It has collected documentary material for future use, published summaries of social activities based on current reports from member nations, maintained the Child Welfare Information Center in Geneva, and so far as possible continued to supply information for which requests, even in wartime, have continued to come from governments and private organizations.

Countries wishing to initiate or to continue active work on their social problems after the war, will need some international center of information, some international agency for inquiring into facts and possible solutions and for cooperating with world agencies in related fields of social importance. It would be a tragic waste of time and effort not to make use of the accumulated information and experience of the Social Questions Section of the League.

The activities of the Social Questions Section and the Advisory Committee on Social Questions of the League of Nations were concerned chiefly with the suppression of the traffic in women and children and of obscene publications, promotion of child welfare, and assistance to indigent foreigners.

The responsibilities of the League involved supervising the execution of agreements and conventions, calling international conferences, drafting international instruments for submission to the various countries, making inquiries into the nature and extent of certain social problems, assembling facts, laws, annual reports, and other information on social questions and child welfare activities in various countries, disseminating this information to states, organizations, and individuals, and maintaining the Child Welfare Information Center.

TRAFFIC IN WOMEN AND CHILDREN

The League was entrusted under Article 23 (c) of the Covenant, "with general supervision over the execution of agreements with regard to traffic in women and children." It became responsible for devising methods to control and prevent traffic, for conducting extensive studies to determine the nature and scope of the problem, and for providing the countries of the world with facilities for an exchange of information on the subject.

The first step taken by the League was to secure the members' ratification of already existing agreements—the International Agreement for the Suppression of White Slave Traffic of 1904 and the International Convention for the Suppression of White Slave Traffic of 1910.[2]

[2] The misleading term "white-slave traffic," for a matter involving all races, has gradually been superseded by the more exact "traffic in women and children."

The International Agreement of 1904, signed by thirteen countries and acceded to by the United States, represented at the time a great step forward. Each contracting government agreed to establish a central authority for combating traffic in women and children, to coordinate and exchange information with the offices of other countries, to keep watch at railway stations and ports for persons involved in the traffic, to repatriate foreign prostitutes, and to supervise employment agencies. Since that time practically all the countries of the world have created such offices.

The International Convention of 1910 went further and formed the basis for subsequent international legislation in this field. It provided for the punishment of persons "procuring, enticing, or leading away for immoral purposes" girls under the age of twenty, even with their consent and even though the separate acts which constituted the whole offense might have been committed in different countries. It covered the same offense toward women over twenty "when there is fraud, violence, and any measure of compulsion." The governments agreed to pass laws enforcing these provisions and providing extradition for offenders. A more effective method of exchanging information on laws and methods of enforcement among countries was also provided.

The United States, while citing constitutional objections—involving state's rights—to becoming a signatory, expressed official sympathy with the purpose of this treaty.

But legal protection and administrative measures within the nations—the aim of both of these international instruments—proved inadequate, and the League of Nations called its first International Conference on Traffic in Women and Children, which met in 1921. This conference resulted in the convention of 1921, which marked an advance over previous agreements in its emphasis on early discovery and prosecution of offenders. The age of protection to minors of either sex was raised, conviction was no longer made a condition for extradition, new methods were found for the protection of women and child emigrants, arrangements were made to supervise employment agencies, and a more adequate system for the exchange of information was established. Many nations expressed acceptance by ratification, accession, or adhesion, and the United States, though not a member of the League, was invited to appoint a member to serve on the newly created Advisory Committee on Traffic in Women and Children. Grace Abbott, then chief of the United States Children's Bureau, was appointed by the Secretary of State with the approval of the President, to represent the United States on the Committee in an unofficial and consultative capacity. Subsequently other Americans have been members of the Advisory Committee. Julia C. Lathrop served for some years as an assessor.

An early task of the experts appointed by the League was to ascertain the nature and extent of the traffic and how far the facts warranted further international study. For this purpose the League undertook a number of inquiries. In 1924–26 field representatives studied conditions in a number of countries of Europe and North and South America. Their report had such far-reaching repercussions that in 1930 the inquiry was extended to the Far East—the first comprehensive study ever made on the traffic in women and children in that area. An exhaustive report submitted to the Council of the League and published in 1934, aroused world-wide interest and resulted in the regional conference held in Bandoeng, Java, in February, 1937.

One of the chief purposes of this Conference was to find ways of promoting collaboration and the exchange of information between the police and other responsible authorities in different countries. Other aspects discussed were the protection of migrants against such traffic, the possibility of abolishing licensed or tolerated brothels, closer collaboration between police and other authorities with private organizations, the possibility of employing a larger number of women in official positions relating to the traffic, and the danger to women refugees of Russian origin in the East.

Among its important recommendations the Conference proposed that a bureau, or regional office, of the Social Questions Section of the League of Nations should be set up in the East, to receive and to circulate reports from participating countries, to suggest measures for facilitating the collection and distribution of information, and generally to promote collaboration between the participating countries. This bureau was to make annual reports on its work to the League of Nations.

The establishment of such a regional office and the further development of constructive measures dealing with organized prostitution were interrupted by world events in 1939. The need, however, for such a regional office and such a program as that outlined in the conclusions and recommendations of the Bandoeng Conference will be even greater after the war.

International machinery to prevent traffic in women and children was completed by a draft convention for the Suppression of the Exploitation of the Prostitution of Others (Souteneurs), drawn up by the Social Questions Committee and taken under consideration by the League in 1938. This convention filled gaps left by former agreements, providing, among other things, protection against "procuration for profit" for persons of full age and of either sex, even though they consented to be transported and did not cross national frontiers. Although the League decided that it was not the time for a diplomatic conference to consider the draft convention, so many countries expressed interest in the proposals submitted to them that the Social Questions Committee suggested that in the meantime the nations themselves might put into force any provisions that could be carried out without formal international ratification.

It must not be overlooked that modern social students regard traffic in women and children as a reflex of the shortcomings of the social organization of states. As social security is gradually extended and "freedom from want" becomes a matter of state concern and state action, this traffic will gradually diminish.

OBSCENE PUBLICATIONS

Closely linked to prostitution is the problem of obscene publications, which the Social Questions Section has always considered a corollary of traffic in women and children. Earlier national and international attempts to deal with this question had been ineffective until 1923 when an international conference was held in Geneva under League auspices. This resulted in a convention concerning the traffic in obscene literature, which is now almost universally accepted by the nations of the world. At present, the problem has virtually disappeared because of war conditions and vigilant censorship.

CHILD WELFARE

Some constructive results have been achieved in the field of child welfare, although no international convention for child protection was concluded under the League. Under the Social Questions Section, the Child Welfare Information Center was established, where reports and information on activities in both League member and non-member countries are assembled and summarized. Special investigations were undertaken and studies published on the treatment of young offenders, on provisions for children born out of wedlock, on placement of children in families, and on the social effects of the cinema on child welfare. A study was carried through in cooperation with the Mixed Committee on Nutrition [3] on the minimum food allowances essential for child health. Wherever the work of other sections of the League touched the child's welfare, the Social Questions Section worked in collaboration.

Preliminary study was started on the welfare of the unmarried mother and her child, the training of persons engaged in social work and in the field of health, the organization and administration of youth-protective services, family desertion, and the Chinese practice known as "Mui Tsai," whereby little girls are placed in families where they often become virtual slaves.

Information on child welfare was collected and distributed, and annual reports were published, based on facts sent to the Center by governments all over the world, concerning legislative and administrative measures already adopted or under consideration. Requested information has been furnished to governments, organizations, and private individuals.

[3] The Mixed Committee of the League of Nations on the Relation of Nutrition to Health, Agriculture, and Economic Policy (League of Nations publications. 1937.II.A.10), which prepared a well known report.

To the extent possible all this work has been continued during the war. Although fewer governments are sending in reports, the documentary material collected during this period will ultimately be of unique value.

TREATMENT OF INDIGENT FOREIGNERS

The treatment of indigent foreigners and especially of indigent children in a country other than their own is a question to which the League through its Social Questions Section has given continuous consideration since 1931, when it appointed a temporary Committee of Experts to examine the precarious condition of indigent foreigners in most countries and to consider the question of assistance and of the execution of maintenance obligations abroad. Although forty-two countries replied to the Committee's first two draft conventions, submitted to member and non-member states, results did not seem to justify convening a diplomatic conference at that time. The Council of the League then asked the Committee to propose practical measures on an international scale for bettering the situation.

At the Committee's last session in 1938, a third draft convention was drawn up, constituting a compromise. Since the previously proposed multilateral convention seemed unlikely to be an effective international instrument, the Committee recommended that the Council submit its third draft to the nations as a model, for use as a basis for multilateral and bilateral treaties which the nations might decide to arrange among themselves. Many practical recommendations were also offered embodying important basic principles.

Although an international convention would be the most effective way of dealing with the problem of indigent foreigners, the Council accepted the compromise recommendations of the Committee and submitted them to the various states, requesting that at the end of three years (which would have been 1941) they inform the Council as to the extent to which this draft convention had been embodied in treaties. A few states subsequently concluded bilateral conventions concerning assistance and repatriation, but the disturbed conditions during the years just before the war probably account for the hesitation of many countries to undertake new international obligations.

After the war the League or some other international organization will have to consider both the social and the legal problems of refugees,[4] including the question of displaced persons, for this will be a long-term situation on which information will have to be gathered and problems disposed of for an indefinite period.

PROPOSED REVIEW OF SOCIAL QUESTIONS

The war prevented the realization of a plan for a periodical, *Review of Social Questions*, which would have given an account of the accomplishments and plans of the League of Nations, serving both to stimulate interest and to pool the experience of different countries. Under the guidance of a competent staff, such an international periodical would be of great value.

The League rendered an important service to the social welfare of the world by acting as a forum for leaders from different countries with widely diverse opinions. Association and exchange of ideas on League Committees enabled such leaders to reconcile at least some points of view, to find certain subjects in common for further study and action, and gradually to develop techniques for dealing with these subjects. To countries seeking to rebuild their social systems after the war, this assembled body of information will be vitally important.

When peace comes, there will be millions of orphaned children, hosts of displaced people and depressed racial minorities. There will be health and nutritional problems growing out of food shortages and the interruption of the usual medical services. The organization of rehabilitation and educational services will require great skill and broad knowledge and understanding. In the vast and complicated international situation that will await us there must be considered in the field of social welfare, as in other fields, both the immediate and the long-term needs. First, what international services are needed immediately and are likely to continue to be needed in the indefinite period before a stable order has been achieved? Even at this moment, social problems involv-

limited as to finance only a fraction of the services desperately needed.

ing certain nations of Europe and the Americas are being approached by cooperative action. Inter-American child welfare services are now functioning, bringing the organizations of North and South America into closer relationship. The work of the United Nations Relief and Rehabilitation Administration is under way. Although the task of providing financial, material, and personal assistance across international boundaries in time of war is anything but simple, ways can and should be found. Another immediate question is the care of European refugees, including unaccompanied children, some in the European countries but many in the United States and Canada.

For effective international service in the promotion of child welfare three types of action would seem to be indicated: To establish advisory services to aid nations in solving their post-war problems, to place increased emphasis on the promotional and educational aspects of social welfare, and to provide assistance and grants-in-aid to areas of special need and areas for which special international responsibility has been assumed, such as countries depleted by war, mandated territories, and protectorates. Grants-in-aid, being based on the principle of mutual responsibility, should be kept free of all implications of charity.

All these prospects point to the urgent need for an international body with a staff of experts, broadly experienced in the administration of public welfare, competent to provide consultative services and guidance for reestablishing welfare organizations throughout the world. Research will be vitally needed, but the job to be done requires primarily leadership and administrative experience in the field. Certain temporary needs will be met by the United Nations Relief and Rehabilitation Administration, but the continuing need for years to come demands a permanent international organization for social welfare, closely cooperating with international agencies in the related fields of economics, labor, and health. Only through such a partnership can the nations carry out the promises embodied in the Atlantic Charter.

An appraisal of the League's work in social welfare has been made by a great American, Grace Abbott, first American representative on the League's Advisory Committee of Experts on

Traffic in Women and Children, and former chief of the Children's Bureau, U.S. Department of Labor.

The important and very useful task which the League can perform in the social welfare field has been established by these years of somewhat timid experimentation.

There are two ways of looking at any undertaking. First, what has been accomplished, and second, what might have been accomplished or what remains to be done. The League's committees in the social welfare field can point to accomplishments. Cooperation has been developed, and reports of value have been made. What is far more important, however, is that a foundation has been laid for what should be a world center for research, consultation and education as soon as the nations are ready to build upon it.[5]

[5] "Social Welfare by Cooperation," p. 55 in *Windows on the World,* published for distribution at the League of Nations Pavilion, New York World's Fair, 1939.

THE LEAGUE OF MINDS

BY MALCOLM W. DAVIS

A GERMAN SCHOLAR, at the meeting of the International Studies Conference in Madrid during May, 1936, referred to himself as a representative of "National Socialist science." His meaningless phrase showed in sharp relief what tasks needed to be taken up between peoples in the effort for mutual understanding. This was a gathering of educated and informed men and women, committed to impartial inquiry into political and social subjects. Yet his remark revealed the lack of any common basis of approach. It would have made as much sense if others had spoken of "Corporative Fascist physics" or "Soviet Communist chemistry" or "Constitutional Monarchist mathematics" or "Democratic Liberal logic." Obstructing the reasonable search for truth, a struggle of wills was going on in which words were used often for national and individual ends rather than for disinterested analysis; and this struggle exerted a great influence in precipitating the present war.

Above and beyond the bodily combat, the fighting issues have been joined most passionately and persistently on the plane of ideas. When the hard physical strife succeeds in victory, there must remain a rigorous spiritual triumph to be won. An uneasy armistice can be imposed by mastery and power, but a reliable peace needs to be kept in the end by consent and accord. This requires more than the effective force of governments joining in mutual policies for security and trade. It calls for a meeting of minds among nations, for popular sentiment and support.

MALCOLM W. DAVIS, international relations specialist, is New England born and served in the United States Government Information Service in Russia in World War I. He was director of the Geneva Research Center, and associate director of the European Center of the Carnegie Endowment in Paris, American member of the Executive Committee of the League Committee on Intellectual Cooperation, and chairman of the International Studies Conference. During the first year and a quarter of this war he represented the American Red Cross at Geneva, acting as associate secretary-general of the League of Red Cross Societies. In addition to his international activities, he is engaged in a United States Government service for the duration and has conducted a seminar in the School of International Administration, directed by Columbia University.

Undoubtedly this was true at the end of the first World War. Yet among the manifold provisions of the League Covenant there was none for cultural and intellectual interchange. Its articles dealt with the economic, legal, military, political, and social subjects that were at the time uppermost in the minds of men. Also in the early days there was hostility to attempts for furthering collaboration in scholarly and scientific work. Actually, however, such opposition served only to emphasize the importance of this movement. Diplomats at once objected that such matters lay in the exclusive domain of each country, to be regulated by its system, and they specially urged this view in regard to programs of education, implying that any initiative amounted to interference with liberty of teaching and thought. This attitude was buttressed by the fearful independence of new nations and by the fierce jealousy of older powers. Advocates of better comprehension and exchange of ideas had to yield to suspicions of a superstate. Nevertheless, from the first Assembly onwards they made progress.

Leaders in the movement at the beginning had come chiefly from the continental countries of Europe. It was a Belgian delegate at the Paris Peace Conference who took the initiative in asking the Commission on the Covenant of the League to provide for an International Committee on Intellectual Relations. Repulsed there, the Belgian representatives resumed the task in the first Assembly of the League in 1920, where Senator Henri La Fontaine advocated arrangements for cooperation among intellectual workers. Austria, France, Greece, Italy, Poland, Rumania, Spain, and Switzerland rallied to this suggestion, aided and encouraged by representatives from Latin American states which had long maintained relationships with the artistic and literary and scholarly world of Western Europe and most closely with France, Italy, Portugal, and Spain. Their proposals looking to the improvement of such contacts were furthered indirectly by League programs which were being set under way for the association of experts and the establishment of services in economic and financial and social spheres of technical work. These supplied precedents for plans in the field of cultural activities.

A practical step was taken with the recommendation by the

League Assembly on December 18, 1920, that the Council should associate itself with endeavors to form an organization of intellectual work. In the course of the year ideas were developed in Council discussions and in reports by the Secretary General. Then on September 2, 1921, M. Léon Bourgeois, the French representative, submitted a report on Organization of Intellectual Work, urging improved and fuller exchanges of documents in all branches of knowledge and calling upon the League to fortify its ideals through the intellectual life uniting the nations and to favor educational enterprises and research study as important influences on opinion among peoples. The Council adopted the report and transmitted it to the Assembly. There Professor Gilbert Murray for South Africa reemphasized its recommendations. On September 21 the Assembly approved the report in a resolution authorizing the Council to appoint a Committee charged "to examine international questions regarding intellectual cooperation." In consequence the Council then decided to form the International Committee on Intellectual Cooperation, whose members it later appointed, as a consultant body.

The original Committee comprised twelve persons, with M. Henri Bergson, the French philosopher, as chairman, and a membership including Mme Marie Curie, Professor Albert Einstein, Dr. Robert Millikan, Professor Gilbert Murray, Gonzague de Reynold, and Senator Ruffini. Its first meeting was held in August, 1922, and its first report to the Council in September, 1922, outlined its plans of procedure and recognized its relationship and responsibility to the League in conformity with the Assembly's action. Within the next year, growing interest in its possibilities led the Assembly to request an increase in its membership and the introduction of a method of rotation in its system. The Committee eventually consisted of nineteen members, under the chairmanship of Professor Murray, and it also appointed an executive committee to see that its program progressed satisfactorily in the period between annual sessions.

At the start, the sums provided were so limited that the Committee had to appeal to governments for help. Then the French

Government proposed to the Committee in July, 1924, the establishment of an Institute of Intellectual Cooperation, for which it indicated that a building would be made available in Paris as well as a contribution of funds toward its support. After considering the question whether an Institute should be located elsewhere than at Geneva, the headquarters of the League, the Committee reported the proposal in September, 1924, to the Council; and it in turn accepted the offer subject to the Assembly's approval. This was given on the 23d by a resolution which directed the Committee to define the duties and powers of the Institute and to determine its relations with institutions of an intellectual character. The Assembly further empowered the Council to conclude the necessary agreements with the French Government for the operation of an Institute under the Committee's administration. The arrangements were made in the course of the following year, and in January, 1926, the Institute began its activities in Paris as an autonomous agency, not placed under supervision by the Secretary General but controlled directly by the Committee on Intellectual Cooperation, as its governing body, sitting for this purpose with a French statesman, Edouard Herriot, as chairman. The Institute secretariat, together with a section of the League Secretariat at Geneva, especially organized to serve the Committee, constituted the executive staff of the International Organization for Intellectual Cooperation.

In September, 1926, the Assembly formally recognized by special resolution the existence of this organization for technical work with the same status as other League institutions. So the first phase of the struggle was won, against the handicaps of inadequate means and personnel as well as resistance, and the system was under way which, until the present war disrupted it, developed an expanding program steadily throughout the world.

At the outset, the Committee and its Institute had to emphasize enterprises of a limited nature, such as improvement of relations between universities, interchange of methods and publications among libraries and institutes of art and archaeology, work on a uniform terminology in the sciences, instruction in schools about the objectives of the League and principles of international collaboration, and encouragement of exchanges already existing among academies and conferences of learned societies.

Beyond this, the International Committee adopted the essential and far-sighted plan of fostering the formation in the different countries of national committees, comprising representatives of various branches of knowledge. Each of these, acting in accordance with the conditions and customs of its land, was designed to serve as an intermediary between the International Committee of the League and, so far as possible, persons and organizations of leading importance in the intellectual field. The Catholic Union of International Studies and the Interparliamentary Union likewise appointed Intellectual Cooperation Committees which were affiliated with the International Organization. Moreover, the International Committee wisely concluded that it should supplement cooperating bodies already existing throughout the world and not try to subordinate or supplant them. So it proffered its organization services and the Institute facilities to these groups and came more and more to serve as the corresponding center for some of the chief international scholarly and scientific associations. The Committee acted also through the Institute as the correlating agency for the national committees, of which there came to be more than forty throughout the world, and for their general congresses of delegates, held at Geneva in 1928 and at Paris in 1937, to review the results of the program promoted by the Organization and to develop ideas and proposals.

Special conferences, such as one on higher education at Paris in 1937, were another achievement of the Organization, as were general meetings on matters including the protection of works of art and historical monuments, collaboration between libraries and museums, and the improvement of relationships and research in the sciences. The Organization also formed a number of committees of experts on conventions for official ratification by states, dealing with copyright, with radio transmissions and their use, and with the distribution of educational films.

Likewise the International Committee developed a variety of special committees concerned with the different divisions of intellectual interest. Among these was the Committee on Arts and Letters, which carried on an active plan of conferences and correspondence between members and issued a series of publications; the Committee on Literary Exchanges with Latin America; the Advisory Committee on League of Nations Teaching; the Committee on Higher Education; and the Committee on the Natural Sciences. On American initiative, under the leadership of Dr. James T. Shotwell, who had replaced Dr. Millikan as American member of the International Committee, there was under way a project for a Committee on the Social Sciences. These activities were extended through the Institute, which had in its turn services and sections for museums, for university information and educational documentation, for the arts and literature and the sciences, and for folklore (corresponding with the Folk Arts Center in the United States among others). So the Intellectual Organization was broadening its activities to deal with many interests in the life of peoples.

Moreover, since it was at the disposal of governments whose nations took part in its work whether League members or not, the Organization was sometimes utilized to carry through, with the approval of the Assembly, special tasks of technical work. Such was the duty assigned in 1931 of drafting a convention to regulate the use of broadcasting in the interests of peace. Another was the declaration on the teaching of history prepared by the Committee on Intellectual Cooperation and adopted by the Assembly for presentation to governments. The International Labor Office, under the directorship of Albert Thomas in 1931, asked the Institute to conduct an inquiry into popular libraries and arts in relation to the leisure of workers. Finally, the most significant request from a government came likewise in 1931 when China took the initiative for an international educational mission, which made a report and recommendations as to plans for reorganizing the Chinese school system.

Despite complaints and criticisms from one official quarter or another, at various times and for different reasons, the Intellectual Organization was gaining ground steadily in both governmental and non-governmental fields and particularly in contacts among administrative departments concerned with intellectual matters, in consultation with scholarly and scientific societies, and in conciliation between intergovernmental and independent endeavors in education. Meanwhile it was being reinforced by the collaboration of a body of intellectual leaders throughout the world, under the presidency of Paul Valéry and including such personalities as Johan Bojer, Marie Curie, Albert Einstein, Salvador de Madariaga, Thomas Mann, Gabriela Mistral, Alfonso Reyes, T'sai Yuan-Pei, Miguel de Unamuno, and Thornton Wilder, who defended and defined the doctrine of relationship in spiritual values throughout the world. Their correspondence and discussions, published in fifteen volumes, establish a permanent record of thinking on the causes of war, on the conditions among peoples for progress toward unity, on the principles of a new humanism, and on contacts between cultures of the different regions in the world.[1]

Side by side with these enterprises went the work of the International Studies Conference. This was an autonomous body, cooperating with the Institute of Intellectual Cooperation as its secretariat and correlating a joint program for the scientific study of the international problems under consideration by more than thirty separate national committees and international agencies. Beginning in 1928 as an administrative center among a few institutions in Denmark, England, France, Germany, and the United States, it grew into an organism for related researches throughout the world. Its subjects successively were "The State and Economic Life," "Collective Security," "Peaceful Change," and "Economic Policies and the Maintenance of Peace." The last was the theme for reports at its most recent session which met in the dramatic circumstances of late August, 1939, at Bergen, Norway, and which even then and there adopted for the next period the subject of "International Organization." The delegates outlined a plan of study; this was revised and perfected in meetings at Geneva, the Hague, and Paris, during the first months of the war; and national projects were set under way. The resumption of this program presents one of the opportunities for the future.

[1] For titles of the collections, see Catalogue of the Publications of the International Institute of Intellectual Cooperation, issued by Columbia University Press.

The growing demands on the Institute of Intellectual Cooperation and the gathering burdens on the French Government which was its chief contributor had led in the years just before the war to a project for creating a broader base of autonomy and for increasing international support. The Committee on Intellectual Cooperation directed the drafting of an International Act, which was accepted by the League Council and adopted by the Assembly in September, 1938, and approved later in December of that year, at a conference in Paris of representatives from many nations, including the United States. The Act became effective on January 31, 1940, upon the deposit of the eighth ratification with the French Government. Its signatories included Albania, Argentina, Brazil, Chile, China, Colombia, Cuba, Dominican Republic, Ecuador, Egypt, France, Monaco, Netherlands, Paraguay, Peru, Poland, Portugal, Rumania, Spain, Switzerland, Uruguay, and Venezuela. Confirming ratifications through 1939 were recorded by France, Latvia, Netherlands, Norway, Poland, Portugal, Rumania, and Switzerland. In 1940 there followed four more ratifications by the Dominican Republic, Mexico, Egypt, and the Union of South Africa.

Shortly after the diplomatic conference on the International Act, the first conference of American Committees on Intellectual Cooperation met in January, 1939, at Santiago, Chile, holding sessions for which plans had been started during the general conference of national committees in 1937 at Paris; and before adjourning, the American colleagues provided for renewal of their work. The second Inter-American Conference met at Havana, Cuba, in November, 1941, the date having been advanced at the suggestion of the Cuban Government. The leading resolutions voted made proposals both to safeguard the interests of the Institute—either by transferring it to an American country or by establishing a center in an American country to serve temporarily in its place—and also to create an Inter-American Committee, under the chairmanship of Dr. Miguel Osorio de Almeida of Brazil, charged to perfect plans according to these principles.

Within a month, events in the Pacific and declarations across the Atlantic spread the war to the Americas. The Inter-American

Committee could not come together until October, 1943, when it held sessions at Washington in the buildings of the Pan-American Union and of the Carnegie Endowment for International Peace. Its recommendations then embodied a group judgment of the most pressing problems lying ahead. First, it decided to create a center at Havana, for which the Cuban Government offered quarters, and to appoint an executive committee in charge of its administration. Other than American countries interested in preserving the principles of intellectual freedom and cooperation were invited also to adhere to the center. So a way was opened for common action until the future of the institutions that were joined with the League could be determined. This action of the Committee has been confirmed by the Cuban Government through an official provision of quarters for the secretariat staff.

The Inter-American Committee further outlined projects for (1) an inquiry into the present state of intellectual cooperation and the means for it, (2) a study of the duties and rights of the intellectual in the political and social struggle, (3) special studies on freedom of expression, (4) a survey of conditions created in education and enlightenment by the occupation of populated regions, (5) development of education to the end of insuring peace, (6) investigation of economic circumstances affecting intellectual work and laws governing intellectual property, (7) assistance to intellectual workers from invaded countries in continuing their pursuits, (8) suggestion of means for improving communications, (9) measures for protecting and restoring works of art and monuments in occupied countries, (10) plans for assuring to cultural and intellectual interchange its merited place in the post-war world and for encouraging exchanges of scholars and students among universities.

It is evident that in the liquidation and rehabilitation subsequent to the war, pressing questions will require urgent treatment. For such work, the use of existing as well as emergency bodies will be advisable, both to save time and to profit as much as possible by known experience. When this has been done, however, there will come the longer period when security and welfare must continue to be assured. Events have made clear that any general international organization will need better appeal to popular sentiment and support and broader consistent education on international matters and methods than were achieved during the twenty years of League experiment between world wars. For this purpose, whether it is called "intellectual cooperation" or "cultural relations" or by another phrase, such an organization of intellectual work as was initiated and developed under the auspices of the League will be essential. It will have to be adapted and expanded to meet new situations. Particularly, as the past has indicated and current discussion has emphasized, an intellectual organization will have to face educational demands and develop effective means to meet them. Within the scope provided by its constitution, it should include a prominent place for an international education agency. It should also remedy the former neglect of the social sciences and the failure to realize the ways in which the study and teaching of them exercise an influence on cultural and political relations. Any new organization should put into operation the project already proposed to the Committee on Intellectual Cooperation for a commitee on the social sciences.

All the evidence from these experiments already made needs to be weighed by thoughtful statesmen and applied to their search for solutions of post-war troubles. But beyond the practical ends of government, the quest must go on among peoples for those reconciling truths that underly differences, for the spiritual unity of common values expressed in rich variety throughout the world.

APPENDIX

DECLARATION CONCERNING THE AIMS AND PURPOSES OF THE INTERNATIONAL LABOUR ORGANISATION SUBMITTED BY THE SPECIAL DRAFTING COMMITTEE

The General Conference of the International Labour Organization, meeting in its Twenty-sixth Session in Philadelphia, hereby adopts, this 10th day of May in the year nineteen hundred and forty-four, the present Declaration of the aims and purposes of the International Labour Organization and of the principles which should inspire the policy of its Members.

I

The Conference reaffirms the fundamental principles on which the Organisation is based and, in particular, that:

(*a*) labour is not a commodity;

(*b*) freedom of expression and of association are essential to sustained progress;

(*c*) poverty anywhere constitutes a danger to prosperity everywhere;

(*d*) the war against want requires to be carried on with unrelenting vigour within each nation, and by continuous and concerted international effort in which the representatives of workers and employers, enjoying equal status with those of Governments, join with them in free discussion and democratic decision with a view to the promotion of the common welfare.

II

Believing that experience has fully demonstrated the truth of the statement in the Preamble to the Constitution of the International Labour Organisation that lasting peace can be established only if it is based on social justice, the Conference affirms that:

(*a*) all human beings, irrespective of race, creed or sex, have the right to pursue both their material well-being and their spiritual development in conditions of freedom and dignity, of economic security and equal opportunity;

(*b*) the attainment of the conditions in which this shall be possible must constitute the central aim of national and international policy;

(*c*) all national and international policies and measures, in particular those of an economic and financial character, should be judged in this light and accepted only in so far as they may be held to promote and not to hinder the achievement of this fundamental objective;

(*d*) it is a responsibility of the International Labour Organisation to examine and consider all international economic and financial policies and measures in the light of this fundamental objective;

(*e*) in discharging the tasks entrusted to it the International Labour Organisation, having considered all relevant economic and financial factors, may include in its decisions and recommendations any provisions which it considers appropriate.

III

The Conference recognises the solemn obligation of the International Labour Organisation to further among the nations of the world programmes which will achieve:

(*a*) full employment and the raising of standards of living;

(*b*) the employment of workers in the occupations in which they can have the satisfaction of giving the fullest measure of their skill and attainments and make their greatest contribution to the common well-being;

(*c*) the provision, as a means to the attainment of this end and under adequate guarantees for all concerned, of facilities for training and the transfer of labour, including migration for employment and settlement;

(*d*) policies in regard to wages and earnings, hours and other conditions of work calculated to ensure a just share of the fruits of progress to all, and a minimum living wage to all employed and in need of such protection;

(*e*) the effective recognition of the right of collective bargaining, the co-operation of management and labour in the continuous improvement of productive efficiency, and the collaboration of workers and employers in the preparation and application of social and economic measures;

(*f*) the extension of social security measures to provide a basic income to all in need of such protection and comprehensive medical care;

(*g*) adequate protection for the life and health of workers in all occupations;

(*h*) provision for child welfare and maternity protection;

(*i*) the provision of adequate nutrition, housing and facilities for recreation and culture;

(*j*) the assurance of equality of educational and vocational opportunity.

IV

Confident that the fuller and broader utilisation of the world's productive resources necessary for the achievement of the objectives set forth in this Declaration can be secured by effective international and national action, including measures to expand production and consumption, to avoid severe economic fluctuations, to promote the economic and social advancement of the less developed regions of the world, to assure greater stability in world prices of primary products, and to promote a high and steady volume of international trade, the Conference pledges the full co-operation of the International Labour Organisation with such international bodies as may be entrusted with a share of the responsibility for this great task and for the promotion of the health, education and well-being of all peoples.

V

The Conference affirms that the principles set forth in this Declaration are fully applicable to all peoples everywhere and that, while the manner of their application must be determined with due regard to the stage of social and economic development reached by each people, their progressive application to peoples who are still dependent, as well as to those who have already achieved self-government, is a matter of concern to the whole civilised world.

TEXT OF THE PRINCETON RESOLUTIONS

A group of American citizens who have been officially associated in various capacities with nearly every branch of work of the League of Nations, meeting December 11–12 in Princeton, N. J., to consider studies which have been under way for several months to determine, first what contribution the League of Nations can best make to the postwar settlement, and secondly, what should be the attitude of the American people toward the League of Nations:

1. Welcomes the Moscow Declaration calling for a "general international organization."
2. Welcomes the subsequent Senate Resolution endorsing the Moscow Declaration as this endorsement promises to prevent a repetition of the deadlock which paralyzed United States Government action in 1919 and in subsequent years.
3. Urges the United States Government in cooperation with other governments at the first opportunity to take steps to implement the Moscow Declaration and the Senate Resolution for a general international organization.

4. Supports the action of the United States Government in initiating special United Nations Conferences on Food and Agriculture and on Relief and Rehabilitation which have resulted in the establishment of international organizations.
5. Expresses the hope that as other needs develop other conferences will follow as rapidly as possible on such specific questions as currency stabilization, aviation, shipping, etc.
6. Also welcomes the action of the United Nations Relief and Rehabilitation Council in inviting the technical organizations of the League of Nations and the International Labor Organization to send representatives to participate in the Atlantic City Conference and in all other appropriate future work and conferences, thus developing effective coordination in the work of these international agencies. The group also notes with appreciation that the Interim Commission on Food and Agriculture has invited representatives of the technical organizations of the League of Nations to participate in the work of the Interim Commission whenever appropriate.

The group urges that the United States Government give particular attention to the following considerations:

1. Full recognition and support of League agencies continuing to function during the war, including particularly those on American soil, such as the Economic and Financial Mission at Princeton and the Drug Supervisory Body in Washington.
2. Adherence to the Statute of the Permanent Court of International Justice as recommended by every President and Secretary of State since the Court's creation in 1922.

The group also urges the appropriate authorities of the League of Nations and of the United Nations to give early consideration to the necessity of coordinating the international agencies developed after the first World War with those developing during the present war for the purpose of assuring continuity and of benefiting from the experience of nearly a quarter century of international work.

The group emphasizes the necessity of developing an effective system of collective security.

In implementing these resolutions the group urges that account be taken of the following principles arising from the twenty-year experience of the League of Nations in the period between wars:

A. As regards international organization and administration

1. That the nations of the world have reached the point where a cooperative organization is not only desirable but essential for a host of activities which have reached the international stage.

2. That that organization should be universal in character and built around one central authority as representative of the broad interests of the whole community of nations.
3. That that organization may have affiliated agencies organized either (a) on a regional basis, or (b) on a subject basis.
4. That any such affiliated agencies should be fully autonomous within their particular fields but should operate within the co-operative framework of the central organization, with proper allocation of funds, and documentation between themselves and the central organization.
5. That independent or uncorrelated agencies tend to build up a separatist attitude which militates against the free cooperation which should exist between all agencies seeking peace and progress amongst nations.
6. That, on the contrary, closely coordinated agencies can often pool their experience or facilities to the greatest advantage.

B. As regards security, prevention of war, sanctions, peaceful settlement and disarmament

1. That problems of security and prevention of aggression have an urgency and compulsion which put them in a different category from other, more normal and more slow-moving international problems and thus offer the possibility of a different or even separate method of treatment.
2. That such problems depend primarily on the Great Powers and their willingness to take a positive position, and that, unless all the principal military powers agree on concerted measures, any really effective action in a major crisis is extremely difficult, if not impossible.
3. That, contrary to a wide-spread view, the smaller powers also have great importance in this basic problem, whether as areas of conflict or as support for the principle of collective security and also for specific action.
4. That the existence of a common agency of disinterested mediation can appreciably improve the chances of settlement of international disputes, as demonstrated in the Aaland Islands, Greek-Bulgar, Peru-Colombia and Paraguay-Bolivia conflicts.
5. That such an agency, again contrary to common belief, is susceptible of very quick action and can be brought into operation in a few days' time, as in the Greek-Bulgar affair.
6. That its effectiveness can be measured in very direct ratio to the degree of force known to be behind it.
7. That, in the event of aggression, it is definitely possible, and in-

deed far easier than thought, to get a large number of nations to pass a verdict of guilty on the aggressor state, as in the case of Japan and Italy.

8. That in the event of agreement of principle, it is technically possible and even not too difficult, to organize economic sanctions on a worldwide scale, as in the Italo-Ethiopian conflict.
9. That the question whether or not such agreement will be reached is again primarily a question of the Great Powers, as demonstrated negatively in the Sino-Japanese affair.
10. That, if sanctions are initiated, they must be initiated in direct relation to the probable course of military events and become effective before the military goal is achieved, as was not the case in the Italo-Ethiopian conflict.
11. That lack of an effective system of collective security is the greatest single element underlying other causes of disunity between nations, notably heavy armaments and uneconomic tariff barriers.
12. That, conversely, armaments are the result rather than the cause of political insecurity and their reduction should be sought primarily through the removal of their causes rather than on a gun-for-gun mathematical basis.
13. That once disarmament is agreed to, adequate measures of supervision and control can be set up to prevent abuse or violation of agreement.
14. That, if there is to be any hope of improving the world political situation by peaceful change recommended by the community of nations, there must be a change in the unanimity rule which made such action impossible in the 1919–1939 period.

INDEX

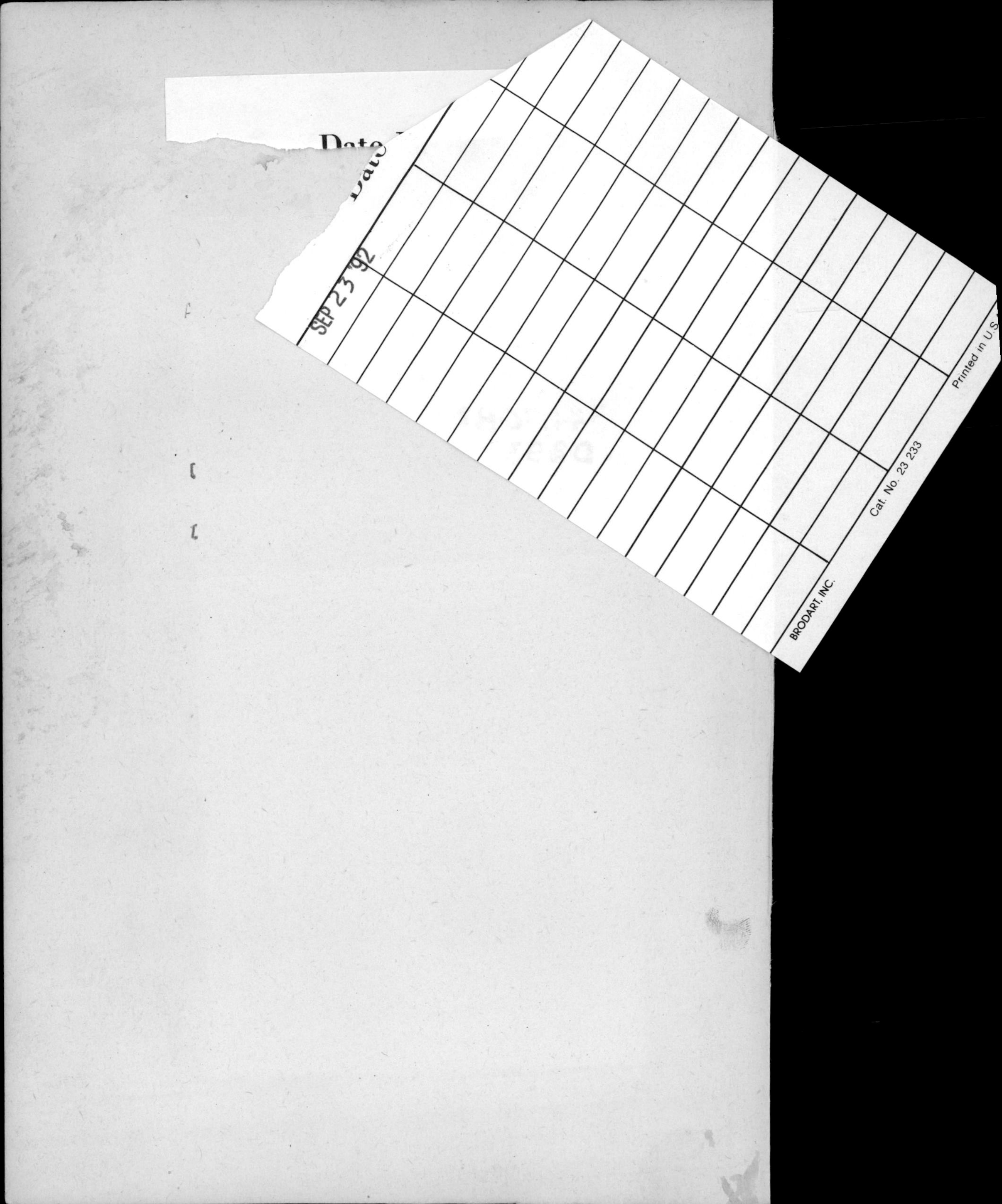
Date Due
SEP 23 '92
BRODART, INC.
Cat. No. 23 233
Printed in U.S.